SHENANDOAH

The Valley Story

Alvin Dohme

A brief and painless history of the Shenandoah Valley and the Blue Ridge—its winding rivers and streams, surrounding mountains and public parks—complete with local lore and legend, plus a handful of heroes. And a tour guide of the area with directions and road maps to points of outstanding scenic beauty, historic interest, and twentieth century recreation.

•

Illustrated

•

POTOMAC BOOKS Inc., Publishers
Washington, D. C.

All admission rates and hours listed are subject to change and should be verified.

The author will appreciate any information from readers regarding omissions or errors in this guide. Write c/o Potomac Books.

ACKNOWLEDGEMENTS

I would like to take this opportunity to thank the following people for their help and cooperation in making this book possible. They have, each in their own way, been of enormous assistance in putting together *Shenandoah — The Valley Story.* They have given me information, source material, and inspired help in assembling the text and photographs for publication. A not inconsiderable few have helped by just plain unvarnished comment and encouragement, including my long-suffering wife, Ainslee.

Lewis Allen Allen Photographic Studios, Front Royal, Virginia

Mrs. John F. Cadden, author, friend, historian, Strasburg, Inc., Strasburg, Virginia

Randy Carter, author, *Canoeing Whitewater in Virginia,* Warrenton, Virginia

Phil Flournoy, Virginia State Chamber of Commerce, Richmond, Virginia

Thomas Gibson, executive vice-president, Skyline Caverns, Inc., Front Royal, Virginia

John Goodwin, Virginia State Travel Service, Richmond.

Miss Laura Virginia Hale, Warren County historian and author, Front Royal, Virginia

Robert C. Harnsberger, vice-president — public relations, Luray Caverns Corp., Luray, Virginia

R. Taylor Hoskins, superintendent, Shenandoah National Park, Luray, Virginia

Miss Mary Ellen Massie, staff photographer, Winchester *Evening Star,* Winchester, Virginia

Mrs. Eleanor Norton, librarian, Samuels Memorial Library, Front Royal, Virginia

Harry U. Oxenham, voyageur extraordinary, Front Royal, Virginia

E. Ray Schaffner, chief naturalist, Shenandoah National Park, Luray, Virginia

A. J. Simonpietri, antiquarian, raconteur, merchant, Front Royal, Virginia

Mrs. Katherine Smith, Virginia State Library, Richmond,

Robert Sterrett, former executive director, Shenandoah Valley, Inc., Staunton, Virginia

Major Stephen Watts (deceased), and Mrs. Virginia Watts, Browntown, Virginia

BIBLIOGRAPHY

A. Aubrey Bodine, *The Face of Virginia*, Bodine & Associates, Baltimore, Md., 1967.

Randy Carter, *Canoeing White Water* River Guide Appalachian Outfitters, Oakton, Va. 1970

William Couper, *History of the Shenandoah Valley*, Lewis Historical Publishing Co., New York, 1952.

Julia Davis, *The Shenandoah*, Farrar & Rinehart, Inc., New York, 1945.

G. Allen Foster, *The Eyes and Ears of the Civil War*, Criterion Books, New York, 1963.

Laura Virginia Hale, *Warren County Supplement to Virginia History*, Front Royal, Va., 1957.

Fay Ingalls, *The Valley Road*, The World Publishing Co., New York, 1949.

Federal Writers Project, *Virginia—A Guide to the Old Dominion*, Oxford University Press, New York, 1941.

Virgil Carrington Jones, *Ranger Mosby*, University of North Carolina Press, Chapel Hill, N.C., 1944.

Harnett T. Kane, *Spies for the Blue and Gray*, Hanover House, Garden City, N.Y., 1954.

Harnett T. Kane, *The Smiling Rebel*, Doubleday & Co., Inc. Garden City, N.Y., 1955.

Samuel Kercheval, *A History of the Valley of Virginia*, W.N. Grabill, Woodstock, Va., 1902.

William Oliver Stevens, *The Shenandoah and its Byways*, Dodd, Mead & Co., New York, 1941.

Ann and Myron Sutton, *The Appalachian Trail*, J.B. Lippincott Co., Philadelphia, Pa., 1967

John Wayland, *A History of Shenandoah County, Virginia*, Shenandoah Publishing House, Strasburg, Va., 1957.

John Wayland, *The Valley Turnpike*, Winchester-Frederick County Historical Society, Winchester, Va., 1967.

John Wayland, *Twenty-five Chapters on the Shenandoah Valley*, Shenandoah Publishing House, Strasburg, Va., 1957

FOREWORD

Driving through the Shenandoah Valley on a lovely crisp spring morning, with all of the beauty of its lush green promise—new-born calves frolicking in the meadows, spring lambs gamboling in the limestone pastures, songbirds trilling their hearts out in the blossoming orchards—my thoughts go back through the years to the times when this peaceful Valley of the Shenandoah saw great turmoil in times of conflict, from frontier days through Indian wars, French wars, wars of revolution, and even wars pitting father against son, brother against brother, during Stonewall Jackson's Valley campaigns. Also, my thoughts turn to the many Americans and visitors from abroad who have never been privileged to see this superb scenic Valley. They have not witnessed the magnificent and mysterious rebirth of nature in the Blue Ridge spring, followed by the gentle verdure of summer, the haze-blue hills and fiery foliage of autumn, and the sparkling, white beauty of winter, which has now become so popular through the appeal of the Valley ski resorts.

To all of you who have never visited us here in the Valley, who have never enjoyed the springtime spectacle of the annual Apple Blossom Festival at Winchester, Arts and Crafts Week at Middletown, or the breath-taking views from atop the world-famous Skyline Drive, this is an open letter of invitation to come and see us. Journey with your family through the "Valley of the Daughter of the Stars" at your leisure, with this informative history and sightseeing guidebook in hand. Relive the frontier times described in the text. Find out how the Valley came to be, what it was, and what it is today. Discover what it has to offer in scenic beauty, historic lore, and holiday recreation. Linger with us a while, and enjoy with us our stirring heritage.

We, here in the Valley and others who are greatly interested in promoting the Shenandoah Valley, feel that Alvin Dohme has rendered a great service in writing this delightful, handy pocketbook of history and sightseeing suggestions. We sincerely hope that *SHENANDOAH—The Valley Story* will add to your pleasure in discovering our Valley.

Robert Sterrett
Former Executive Director
Shenandoah Valley, Inc.

Staunton, Virginia

CONTENTS

Shenandoah

The Valley Story

I

EARLY
EXPLORATION

The Indians had a name for it. They called the Shenandoah Valley "the Valley of the Daughter of the Stars." From the beginning their valley—and ours—was a fertile region for legend and folklore; much of it is based on actual events, and all of it is utterly captivating to the casual visitor from beyond the Blue Ridge, and the student of our past heritage who prefers his history in romantic doses.

For example, it has often been said here in the Valley that the legendary Johnny Appleseed passed this way— rather than through our neighboring states to the north—on his way west, thus giving birth to our flourishing orchards which each spring powder the countryside in its snowy mantle of fragrant blossoms. They have earned Winchester the undisputed title of "Apple Capital" of the Old Dominion, and this title is enhanced by the annual Apple Blossom Festival held in Frederick County early each May.

Similarly, there is the fascinating story of how the Old Dominion's first hot springs were discovered by a cold and lonely young Indian brave on his way to a great tribal council along the headwaters of Chesapeake Bay; or the colorful account of Mad Mary Greenlee and how she first discovered our sparkling gem-like limestone caves while hiding the fair maiden, "White Dove", from the savages. But first a few words on the early discovery and explora- tion of this lovely wilderness region to the west of the Blue Ridge.

The man who has been most frequently credited with the first official discovery and extensive exploration of the Shenandoah Valley was a wandering medical practitioner from Hamburg, Germany, John Lederer. He had been preceeded into the area as far back as 1632 by a Jesuit priest who came to convert the Indians, but the courageous missionary left no written records of his travels among the savages. Lederer, on the other hand, was a stubborn and

persevering man with an excellent command of Latin, who
left a voluminous written record of everything he heard and
saw, accompanied by crude maps of his travels. These field
notes were later translated into English and published in
London in 1673.

Lederer set forth from Williamsburg in early March of
1669, with the blessing of the royal governor of the
Virginia Colony, Sir William Berkeley, and arrived at the
crest of the Blue Ridge near Swift Run Gap in Madison
County on March 14th for his initial glimpse of the fertile
valley and its winding river. On this, his first of three forays
into the Shenandoah region, Lederer had started inland
with three Indian guides along what was later known as the
Germanna Trail (Va. Route 3) from Fredericksburg, past
Chancellorsville and the Wilderness of Civil War fame, to
the present site of Culpeper beyond the Rapidan River.
From there he headed approximately due west, past the
present site of Orange, through the Piedmont foothills, and
thence across the Conway River to the mountain pass at
Swift Run Gap. On this preliminary trip of exploration,
Lederer apparently did not tarry long on the wooded
summit of the gap; but hurried back to civilization in order
to report the inspiring discovery to his royal sponsor in
Williamsburg.

On May 20th of the following year, 1670, Lederer set
out again for the central section of the northern valley,
using approximately the same route as in his first assault
against the wilderness. This time, however, he travelled not
only in the company of an Indian guide, but also with a
small company of English adventurers from the James
River, under the command of a Major Harris. No sooner
had the party reached the eastern slopes of the Blue Ridge,
which guarded the final approach to their goal, than Major
Harris and company gave up the struggle and turned back,
weary of the long march and the rigors of the forest. Upon
parting, Major Harris presented his own musket to Lederer
and left him to go on alone with his Indian companion into
the unknown region to the west.

Lederer pressed on with his lone companion through
Swift Run Gap and out onto the broad, fertile floor of the
valley watered by the winding river. Here, during that
summer, for forty days, he wandered up and down the
length and breadth of his new domain, visiting the various
Indian villages, armed with nothing more than his note-

book, his rusty gun, and the insatiable curiosity common to all *bona fide* explorers.

Through his Indian interpreter, Lederer was told that the valley natives already knew of the white man's presence along the seacoast, calling them variously "Anglis" after the French, or "White Swan"—an allusion to the billowing clouds of canvas on their tall ships. However, Lederer was the first white man most of the valley dwellers had ever seen. As a result he was lavishly "wined and dined" at great campfire feasts wherever he went.

On one such occasion he witnessed, and duly recorded in his diary, the bloody campfire massacre of a visiting delegation of redmen who came from a distant village to smoke the peace pipe. It was on this gory occasion while making a hasty exit, that Lederer lost the musket Major Harris had left him.

At the southern end of his orbit about the Valley in the summer of 1670 the explorer ran across a strange tribe of Indians in which the women were the chiefs and warriors, while the men, rather weak and effeminate, did the domestic chores usually assigned the squaws. All of this, too, the German dutifully recorded in his notes.

Figuring that the frail chemist from Hamburg would never survive the trip, Major Harris and his band of English "explorer drop-outs" decided to cover up their own deficiencies by concocting a story for their return to Williamsburg, *viz.* that Lederer had died enroute, and that there were no such mountains, no such river, and no such valley to the west as the German had described, only endless and impenetrable forest.

Consequently, as the almost inevitable result, upon Lederer's return to the colonial capital at the end of his long and daring venture, he was greeted by the good burghers of Williamsburg with snubs of disbelief, amounting at times to downright scorn. This included his sponsor in the enterprise, Sir William Berkeley, who flatly refused even so much as to reimburse the explorer from the royal treasury, as agreed, for his labors. Lederer promptly pulled up stakes and moved farther north along Chesapeake Bay to Annapolis, Maryland. Here he sought financial help from Lord Calvert for further trips of exploration.

Under the banner of Maryland and the Calverts, John Lederer again set forth in early August of that same year, 1670, on his third and final journey into the Valley. Several

3

weeks later, after having reached the Piedmont foothills by a more northerly route from Maryland, Lederer, accompanied by an Indian guide and an Englishman named Colonel Catlet, stood astride the threshold of the northern valley at Manassas Gap and overlooked the broad expanse of the main valley from the thousand-foot heights above the present site of Front Royal. This event is commemorated by a stone marker five miles to the east, at Linden, which sets the date of the first official discovery of the northern half of the Valley by a white man as August 26, 1670—even though Lederer had already viewed the central section of the Shenandoah Valley a full year before in the early spring of 1669.

What Colonel Catlet and Lederer saw in midsummer of 1670, was very much the same breathtaking scenic view enjoyed today by the motorist entering the Valley by way of Va. 55 from Washington, D. C., via Gainesville, Haymarket, The Plains, and Marshall. Only instead of the horses, sheep, and cattle seen today, buffalo, elk, and plump roan deer dotted the lush bluegrass bottomland meadows, grazing in peace and contentment. And in place of the pall of heavy industrial fumes, the smoke of several small Indian villages rose mistily into the summer air. The brooding silence was broken only by the scream of an eagle soaring on an updraft overhead above the pass, or the caw of an alarmed crow in the distance. Almost at Lederer's and Catlet's feet flowed the South Fork of the Shenandoah River, joining, at the present site of Riverton, its twin from the far side of the dividing ramparts of the Massanuttens. The steeply wooded Massanuttens provided a strikingly dramatic backdrop which ended abruptly in the prow-like buttress of towering Signal Knob. In the hazy far distance across the rolling plain, before the explorers' gaze, there was yet another seemingly endless chain of mountains running north and south as far as the eye could see, which marked the western rim of this vast green natural bowl. It had been carved out of the solid limestone bedrock by the river and the glaciers of an ice age long past, and long ago had contained a huge inland sea teeming with strange fish whose fossils are still found in its rock formations.

These mountains were, of course, the Alleghenies, known to the early Spaniards to the south as the "Apalateans"; but what had really excited John Lederer the most, was his glimpse of the broad winding river seemingly

DISCOVERY
SHENANDOAH
VALLEY
JOHN LEDERER,
FIRST EXPLORER
TO VIEW THIS
VALLEY, SAW IT
FROM THIS POINT
AUGUST 26, 1670

flowing north until it finally disappeared through a distant cleft in the mountains. By miscalculation of some sort, Lederer was under the erroneous impression that he had at long last found the much sought-after and highly-prized water route to the Great Lakes of French Canada and the seas beyond, which led to the wealth of Marco Polo's fabled kingdom of Cathay. This misconception he shared with many another early explorer, notably, Henry Hudson, who half a century before had vanished into the ice of the upper reaches of the vast river to the north in search of a similar water route.

If Lederer was over-awed by the vision of fame and wealth, Colonel Catlet, the Englishman at his side, remained unimpressed by the heady prospect. What instantly appealed to him was the peaceful calm and contentment of the unknown region at his feet. In fact, so deeply did he fall in love with the valley below, that after a brief period of

5

probing together, Catlet and Lederer soon parted company. Catlet settled down to the life of a frontier fur trader among the Indians along the headwaters of the Rappahannock River. To be sure, Lederer's final tour of the Valley was cut short by a near-fatal spider bite which left him weak and feverish, but he hurried back to report his exciting find to his sponsor in Maryland before returning to his native Germany. It was upon Lederer's return from this final trip into the Valley that Lord Calvert's privy secretary, Sir William Talbot, began the translation into English of the German's Latin field notes.

John Lederer was followed into the central section of the Shenandoah Valley by another English Colonel, Cadwallader Jones, in 1673, the same year Lederer's travel memoirs were published in London. Like Colonel Catlet before him, Jones soon set up his trading post on the south bank of the Rappahannock River; but unlike Catlet, he did not have a town named after him. He, too, made his living by trading with the local Indians, and with several of the more enterprising tribes from further south. Jones also travelled extensively through his new wilderness domain, and then, like Lederer, wrote profusely about his findings—only this time in English rather than Latin. His memoirs were also published in England, in 1679, where they joined Lederer's in the Royal Archives. They bore out, to a remarkable extent, the findings of his Teutonic predecessor, as did those of the valley's next visitor, the Swiss Louis Michelle, or Michel, who entered the area in the summer of 1705 by a new route.

Michel travelled from Annapolis to Point of Rocks, Maryland, where he crossed the Potomac River to the Virginia shore and promptly moved northwest to the twin river gorge at Harpers Ferry, where he set up his base camp—ostensibly to prospect for minerals. However, Michel did not tarry long at Harpers Ferry. Soon, lured by the unknown wilderness, he plunged into the virgin forest, compass in hand, and penetrated at least as far south as Powell's Fort in Fort Valley, according to the maps he left behind him on his return to civilization. He recorded, in French this time—just to round out the international character of the Valley's earliest exploration—that at the present site of Winchester, Virginia, the local inhabitants had shown him huge stone sacrificial altars, sixty feet across, and burial mounds of an ancient tribe whose

warriors were over seven feet tall by actual measurement of
their remains. This fact was later verified by a squad of
Colonel George Washington's colonial militia when they
dug the foundations for Fort Loudoun during the French
and Indian War. They, too, uncovered the same grisly giant
Indian skeletons Michel describes in his memoirs. These
notes appeared in print, along with his crude maps of the
Valley, in 1707, and joined those of his predecessors,
Lederer and Jones, in the Royal Archives in London.

What all three of them, and Colonel Catlet as well, had
found was a large fertile valley set in a deep depression
between the Blue Ridge and the Alleghenies, split asunder
by the spine-like center ridge of the Massanuttens. It was
lavishly watered by the twin forks of the winding Shenandoah River, teeming with game, but only sparsely inhabited
by Indians. The villages they ran across in their varied
travels were few and far between, and for a very good
reason. The entire valley was a well-worn migratory trail
and hunting ground stopover for all of the major tribes
along the Atlantic seaboard from Canada all the way to
Georgia, used en route from their summer and winter
hunting grounds. Of what tribes there were in residence, the
Tuscaroras lived near what is now Martinsburg at the
northern gateway to the Valley. The Piscataways were
camped on the lower reaches of the Cacapon River where it
joins the Potomac. The Shawnee occupied three villages
near what is now Winchester, plus a fourth at Woodstock.

An Indian trace traversed the entire valley, running north
and south parallel to the flanking mountains. In fact, there
were two well-defined trails. One, a war party trace along
the topmost peaks of the Blue Ridge, closely approximated
the route of today's magnificent scenic Skyline Drive and
Appalachian Trail, and gave the raiding warriors an unin-
terrupted view of the surrounding country. The other was a
peace-time migratory trail leading down the center of the
valley through Fort Valley between the towering peaks of
the Massanuttens, and thence due south past Elkton to
Lexington and Natural Bridge. From there the trace led on
to the great Indian winter hunting grounds of the Carolinas
and Georgia. These trails, though usually traversed in peace,
had been the scene of several bloody and bitter inter-tribal
wars, as well as wars of close to mass tribal extinction. As
the result of their regular use of this direct north-south
migratory route to escape the snows of up-state New York

7

and Canada, the fierce and warlike tribe of Iroquois derived their name. "Iroquoia" was the original Algonquin place name for the high lush meadows, now known as "Sky Meadows", in Shenandoah National Park, which long was their favorite migratory resting place. The tribes Lederer, Jones, and Michel encountered in the Valley included, beside the Iroquois (of whom both the Tuscaroras and Cherokee were an off-shoot) and the Occoneechee and Piscataways to the north along the Maryland border: the Nahyssans, the Oenocks, the Oustbacks, Ushery, Massawomacks, and Pamunkey Indians. There were also three branches of the Algonquins—the Conoys, the Shawnee, and the Wampanoagas.

There were rumors, all up and down the newly discovered valley, of an ancient tribe of Indians called the Senedoes, who had long since been conquered and assimilated by the more warlike Iroquois. There were also tales of past bloody warfare between Sherando, chief of the Iroquois, and Opescascanough, son of Powhatan, ruler of the friendly coastal tribes. In one fierce battle Opescasanough had been slain, and Powhatan, swearing vengeance for his eldest son's death, had attacked across the mountains again and again, all to no avail. It was from this early tribe of Senedoes that the Valley probably got its name. The lovely, melodic word "Senedo" blended beautifully with the Shawnee name for the Massanutten Mountains "Cenantua", to form the haunting English appelative, Shenandoah. The legend still persists, however, that the river itself derived its name from the mighty Iroquois chief, "Sherando", who often camped along its headwaters on the South Fork.

The Monocans, a branch of the fierce and proud Delaware tribe of Mohicans to the north, occupied the middle of the main valley around Lexington and Natural Bridge. The Catawbas took up the southern section of the Valley of Virginia below Roanoke; while still farther south in the Great Smoky regions of the Carolinas, lived the proud and warlike Cherokee, who still dwell there to this day on their reservations.

It was among this primitive and confusing mixture of redmen that the Valley's first explorers wandered, jotting down everything they saw in their different languages—Latin, English, and French. They learned that in good years the Indians in the area all raised three crops of corn or

"maize", as it was then called. The Indians had also
partially domesticated the buffalo or bison and grazed them
in large herds on the lush bluegrass riverbottom meadows
which were burned over periodically to keep them clear of
underbrush. For their other staple foods, they relied largely
on their skill as trappers, hunters, and fishermen. The
forests abounded in deer, elk, bear, and smaller game; and
the shallows along the river held artfully concealed fish
traps and crude weirs.

The next attempt to penetrate the Blue Ridge came in
1716, and this effort, again somewhere in the neighborhood
of Lederer's initial assault on the wilderness at Swift Run
Gap, had a comic opera twist to it. The entire action was
under the leadership of no less an exalted dignitary than Sir
Alexander Spotswood, the Royal Governor of the Virginia
Colony, and it was duly recorded in glowing rhetoric by a

Governor Alexander Spotswood

young lieutenant in Spotswood's retinue, John Fontaine, a highly talented journalist, who was later acclaimed as a brilliant English essayist.

According to Fontaine's colorful account of the expedition, the Royal Governor gathered about him, early in May of 1716, "a retinew of servants and adventurers bolde" whose ponderous mounds of gear were in turn "pyled hyghe on gryte wagonnes" as the dashing expeditionary force from Williamsburg to the piercing accompaniment of fifes and drums headed westward. En route, along John Lederer's now well-worn Germanna Trail to the ford over the Rapidan River, there were "gryte campe feastes" beside roaring "fyres" each night, with much horse-play and general merriment among the Tidewater dandies. At long last His Excellency's small army of followers crossed the river to begin their frontal assault of the "gryte mountynes". Then all of a sudden, as they were almost in sight of their goal, the retinue began to fall apart at the seams.

In all fairness to the doughty and determined Royal Governor, this time it was disease and not mere laziness or cowardice, which brought the expedition to a halt. What sweet revenge for the little German doctor from Hamburg! For lo and behold, suddenly and as if the outbreak had been brought on by a curse in Latin, the expeditionary force was laid low with—of all things—the German Measles! Fortunately the Governor and a few others, including John Fontaine, were spared the crippling malady and fought gamely on over the crest of the Blue Ridge at Swift Run Gap. Upon descending the far slope of the mountains and after a brief look at the breathtaking view from the summit, His Excellency forded the Shenandoah River which he learnedly christened "the Euphrates". On the west bank, he buried a bottle—(an empty bottle of His Majesty's finest scotch whiskey, I trust)—containing a note penned in his own hand, claiming all of the vast territory west of the mountains as far as "the River of the Spaniards", as the Mississippi was then called, "in the name of and for King George I, of England". (This claim held good for many a day—until the end of the American Revolution, in fact— once the French had been driven out of the Ohio Territory after the French and Indian War.)

Having penetrated into the Valley, Governor Spotswood and his retinue then turned around and headed for home,

where upon their safe arrival at Williamsburg, he dubbed all
of his mounted cavalier companions in the venture
"Knights of the Golden Horseshoe". Subsequently he
presented each of them with a small gold pin fashioned in
the shape of a horseshoe, in memory of their trip west.
Several of these are still in existence today and are highly
treasured by the fortunate families who own them.

Thus ended the era of first discovery and early exploration in the Valley. It was soon to be followed by the
equally rugged age of the first pioneer settlers.

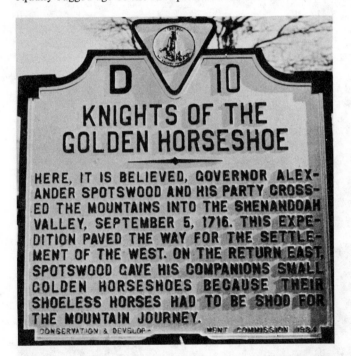

Virginia Chamber of Commerce

II

EARLY SETTLERS

Gradually over the years since its first discovery, word of this fertile valley wilderness, watered by its own broad winding river, spread through the more densely crowded coastal colonies to the east. Finally it reached the ears of a restless and ambitious German immigrant from Alsace, Hans Jost Heydt, who already was in search of *lebensraum* from what he considered to be over-crowded conditions in eastern Pennsylvania. Heydt—later known throughout the valley of the Senedoes under the anglicized version of his name, Joist Hite—first heard of John Lederer's and Louis Michel's discovery from a Dutchman named Jan van Meter, whom he met one night at a local tavern. Van Meter had spent several summers prior to 1727, trapping and trading for furs among the valley Indians, and in the course of his travels had become so enamored of the area that he had purchased a 10,000-acre northern tract from its owner by royal patent, Lord Fairfax. Over a few steins of lager, the Dutchman proceeded to describe the beauty and wonders of his new acquisition. He told of the endless fields of tall waving corn and native bluegrass, and of the plentiful buffalo, elk, and other game; of the fish in the river and the lumber in the forests, as well as of the friendly inhabitants of this productive wilderness region. In fact, so convincingly did he describe the riches of his find, that he ended up by selling the entire 10,000-acre tract to Hite at a nice fat round figure (very much like his own).

After consummating the deal with van Meter that winter, Joist Hite immediately set about rounding up the one hundred other German families required to help settle the land, as specified in the original Fairfax—van Meter sales contract. However, it was not until four years later, in 1731, that Hite was finally prepared to head south with his band of Germans to take up the option on his purchase. En route with his ox-drawn caravan through Maryland on his way to the Mecklenburg ford of the Potomac River (at what is now

13

Shepherdstown, West Virginia), he met another migratory
leader of a band of Scotch-Irish homesteaders from the
seacoast, Robert McKay. McKay, too, was headed south
towards the valley of the Senedoes in hopes of finding
available farmland on which to settle his followers. By the
time the two groups reached the Potomac ford, a partner-
ship agreement had been worked out whereby they agreed
to pool their resources in both land and money and
eventually purchase more land from Lord Fairfax. Thus was
formed by a chance meeting perhaps the first large land
development company west of the Blue Ridge.

Within the next two years (1732-34) the two partners
managed to purchase an additional 70,000 acres from Lord
Fairfax's agents, an acquisition which forced them to send
back across the mountains for more reinforcements to help
settle and till the new acres. To simplify the distribution of
the land, it was further agreed that McKay and his
Scotch–Irish would occupy the eastern half of their new
domain from Winchester south to Luray, and Joist Hite's
Germans in turn took up their homesteads in the western
half of the tract, from Winchester south to the present site
of Strasburg and beyond. About 1734, Joist Hite built
himself a home five miles south of Winchester, halfway
between Kernstown and Stephens City, beside the old
Indian trace or migratory trail which later was to become
known as "The Valley Pike"; and McKay located himself
on the west bank of the South Fork of the Shenandoah
River above the present site of Bentonville. His son, Robert
McKay, Jr., built a log house five miles north of Front
Royal at Cedarville, beside Crooked Run and the Winchester Pike. It was completed in 1734 and is said to be the
oldest house still standing in that part of the Valley. The
same year Joist Hite finished his own log cabin halfway
between Kernstown and Stephens City. In later years
Robert McKay, Jr. added a stone wing to the house at
Cedarville, as well as a saw and gristmill to grind the wheat
and corn for neighbors and to saw timbers for their new
houses and barns.

It was not until half a century later that two of Joist
Hite's grandsons erected their far more palatial homes a bit
farther south down the German side of the Valley. But
meanwhile Hite's son, John, erected charming fieldstone
"Springdale" with its tall columns, just to the north of his
father's log house (no longer standing) beside the banks of

14

Opequon Creek, in 1753. Major Isaac Hite, Jr., who served
in the Revolutionary war, began construction of historic
"Belle Grove" out of native limestone cut from nearby
quarries in 1794; and some fifty years later, another
grandson, General George Bowman, Jr., also a hero of both
wars, completed "Long Meadows" across the Valley Pike
and down the hill near the North Fork of the Shenandoah
River.

At first the Indians were friendly and helpful, trading
freely with the new arrivals. And so too, for a time, was
Lord Fairfax once he took up residence at Greenway Court

Virginia State Library

Greenway Court

near White Post in Clarke County. At the time of his arrival
from England in 1746, Lord Fairfax was the sole legal
proprietor by royal patent of some five million acres. His
grant stretched from the western edge of Alexandria,
Virginia, where he first resided, all of the way out to the
Ohio Territory; the area included almost all of the northern
Valley south of Winchester to well below Front Royal. No
sooner was he comfortably settled at Greenway Court in
1748 than he was promptly beset with a mounting rash of
squatters on his land, resulting in numerous lawsuits. By far
the most famous of these was his legal bout with Joist Hite
and Robert McKay, Sr., which went to court in Williamsburg in 1736, filed by his business agent long before the
landowner even reached the New World. So vexed did Lord

15

Fairfax become at the constant inroads on his domain, that
he decided to hire a young engineer-surveyor from the
Tidewater, George Washington, to map out his holdings so
that they could be properly staked out and recorded.

The Indians' friendliness and cooperation with the new
settlers did not last very long. Under the sudden press of
humanity pouring into the Valley, both Fairfax and the
Indians soon became restive. Lord Fairfax went to court,
but for the simple and lowly Indian, there was only one

Virginia State Library

Lord Fairfax

possible recourse—Indian "outrages" and, eventually, war.

Fairfax's lawsuit against Hite and McKay for trespass,
was one of the longest and most protracted cases ever
recorded in the annals of jurisprudence in this country, and
still is considered a textbook classic in most law school

classrooms. It lasted for fifty years—1736-1786—and by the time it had been finally settled—not by a judge on the royal bench at Williamsburg, but by a judge in the infant Republic which had been formed from the Thirteen Colonies—its plaintiff had died of a fit of apoplexy at Greenway Court, undoubtedly at least partially brought on by the incessant frustration of waiting for a final verdict. Another cause for Lord Fairfax's unhappiness was the outcome of the American Revolution, since he had always been both a staunch friend of George Washington, his teenaged surveyor turned General, and a loyal British Tory. Little wonder he succumbed before the case was closed, the court finding in favor of the two defendants, Hite and McKay!

The Indians' case was even more complex and hopeless. By 1740, people were pouring into the Valley from all sides, driving off the redmen's game and fencing in the meadows reserved to graze their buffalo. Several bands of Englishmen arrived at Happy Creek that year just east of Front Royal, by way of Manassas Gap. Some of these early settlers' family names still appear on the tax books in Warren County: Chew, Luce, Lehew, Russell, Larkin, and Millar, among others. Another band of hardy Scotch-Irish, under a Captain John Lewis, arrived at what is now Staunton. Woodstock was rapidly filling up with Joist Hite's swelling band of Germans, soon to be followed by fresh numbers of Pennsylvania Dutch under Jacob Muller; while Edinburg was in the process of receiving its initial group of the same. By 1745 Colonel Frank Thornton was leading his band of English settlers in the area just east of the Blue Ridge in Rappahannock County, which was eventually to bear his name. Colonel James Wood had come to Winchester in 1735 with still another group of Englishmen, to settle among the Germans and help build a town. So it went all up and down the Valley. Settlers, and more settlers, arrived to crowd out the buffalo, the elk, and the Indians.

In the classic reaction of all original inhabitants, since time immemorial, who were threatened with eviction or total extinction, the savages began to turn aloof and sullen. To compound the already complex situation, the new frontier farmers brought in by Hite and McKay steadfastly refused to allow the Indians to burn off the bluegrass meadows in order to clear them of underbrush for their

buffalo, as had been their custom for centuries. The
newcomers, rightly or wrongly, said it damaged their fences
and endangered their log barns and houses. So as the fateful
year 1754 drew near, the Valley slowly filled with a tense
new foreboding. Gradually there were fewer and fewer
Indians in their lean-to villages; and precious few came to
the trading posts to sell their prime pelts of fox, muskrat,
and beaver. At the same time, the incidence of Indian
outrages rose alarmingly. Then, suddenly, early in the
summer of 1754, without a word of warning, every last
Indian vanished from the entire region. It could only mean
one thing to the anxious settlers—an Indian uprising
tantamount to war.

III

INDIAN LORE AND
VALLEY LEGENDS

Both the Indian and the newly arrived white man left their indelible mark on the Valley and the Blue Ridge, and one of the most eloquent reminders of their past is a rich treasury of lore and legend. Much of it is based on fact or actual events, slightly dramatized down the centuries, but some of it is perhaps the product of pure fancy on the part of both races, white and red. Truth or fancy, all of it is fascinating to anyone caught up in the lure of this lovely and now peaceful region. But it was not always thus, for war and violence, treachery and bloodshed, hatred and mass mayhem, once swept the Valley from end to end like a pestilence. Twice, in fact, this mad plague of death and destruction descended—once from 1754 to 1763 during the Indian wars, and once again in 1861-65 during the valley campaigns of the Civil War. However, to begin with, let us start off with the pleasanter, sunnier side of the picture— the Valley's early lore and legend.

First, the fascinating story of how our now popular and justly famous limestone caves were discovered by the white man. The Skyline Caverns, the Caverns of Luray, the Endless Caverns, and many others are magnificent underground rock creations full of stalagmites and stalactites, cave flowers and rock crystals, subterranean streams and tourists.

Our story begins in far-off Ireland shortly after the turn of the 18th century, at a great feudal castle which was the ancestral home of the Laird of Clonmithgairn, and which was known as Clonmell Keep. Lord Clonmithgairn, a fiery and explosive Irishman of the blood royal, had agreed to rent his castle and its surrounding land to an Englishman of Norman descent, Captain John Lewis, who was also of a spirited and peppery disposition. Understandably, with two such headstrong principals in the bargain, it was not long before the owner of Clonmell Keep and his tenant had a falling out over the castle rents. Lord Clonmithgairn went to

19

court over the matter, and came out on the short end of the magistrate's final decision. Therefore, the temperamental son of Eire took to brooding over his wrongs and, in time, having worked himself up to fever pitch, decided to take matters into his own hands.

Bent on vengeance by the sword, he gathered a band of his followers and entered Clonmell Keep by a secret passage in the dead of night. However, John Lewis had received advance warning of the plan and was waiting, fully armed, with a band of his own men, for the sneak attack. In the ensuing midnight melee, Lord Clonmithgairn was killed. Since the laird of the castle was of royal blood and well connected in the land, the result of his death was royal banishment for the Norman, who fled to the New World with his family and his most faithful retainers. They were given sanctuary—and a very lovely sanctuary it must have been, if the present reincarnation of the Governor's palace at Williamsburg is any criterion—by the Royal Governor of the Virginia Colony, Lord Gooch and his wife. Lady Gooch had been a close girlhood friend of John Lewis' lovely Scottish wife, Lady Margaret.

While awaiting a royal pardon sought in their behalf by Lady Gooch, John Lewis met a fascinating adventurer in the person of John Peter Salling, who had just returned from about as truly astounding a venture into the western wilderness beyond the Blue Ridge as has ever been recounted in comfort and safety before a roaring fireside. It seems that while trapping for muskrat and beaver along the broad winding river of the Senedoes, Salling had been ambushed and carried off captive into the forest by a war party of raiding Ohio Choctaws. The painted warriors had led Salling, well-trussed, across the Alleghenies, all the way to the "River of the Spaniards," as the Mississippi River was then called. There they had sold him into slavery to an itinerant Spaniard who, in turn, took Salling north to the French Great Lakes in Canada as his servant and interpreter. Somewhere along the shores of the Great Lakes—at Detroit, probably, which was the chief French trading post and stronghold in that part of Canada—the French turned the tables on Salling's Spanish master, whom they imprisoned, while they set the French-speaking Englishman free.

Next, at his own request, they put Salling aboard one of their heavyladen "voyageur" freight canoes as company tally clerk and super cargo for the return trip across the lakes to Montreal. From Montreal Salling continued on south, by way of Lake Champlain and the Indian River with cargo and French crew, to the thriving Dutch settlement at the mouth of that vast river, New Amsterdam. Here he was paid by his rescuers and employers, and put aboard a southbound coasting vessel headed for the Virginia Capes and Chesapeake Bay, by no less a personage than the mayor of New Amsterdam, himself—Peter Stuyvesant. The entire round trip voyage in 1730, from the time of his capture by the Indians, until his safe arrival by ship at Williamsburg, had taken something less than three months!

Still glowing with John Peter Salling's vivid account of the fertile wilderness valley to the west, Captain John Lewis gathered his small retinue of loyal Scotch-Irish and, instead of heading home for Ireland after the royal pardon arrived, he set gamely forth for the mountain pass through the Blue Ridge at Swift Run Gap. He arrived at Middle River near the present site of Staunton, Virginia, in 1734, with a royal patent in his pocket, a gift of his recent host and benefactor, the Governor of the colony. At the outset, as the band of new arrivals struggled to build their first settlement on the banks of Middle River, the Indians were very friendly and even helped in the construction work and generously shared their game with the little colony. Soon a close friendship developed between John and Margaret Lewis' comely fair-haired daughter Alice, and Omayah, son of the local chieftain. It soon blossomed into undisguised infatuation, at least on the part of the young Indian, who asked for her hand in marriage. This posed quite a problem for Alice's parents, since they did not want to offend their new neighbors. Yet, at the same time, they were unwilling to let "White Dove", as the Indians had named Alice, marry a savage at any age, particularly not at the tender age of fourteen.

In order to get around the social problem which the proposal of marriage posed for the entire colony, the captain decided to make light of the whole matter and treat it as the impulse of a mere child. The strategem failed, and both Omayah and his proud father, Oroonah, took strong exception to John Lewis' handling of the affair. Immediately a marked chill settled over white settler-Indian relations. The head of the settlement now tried to allay this situation by planning a huge Thanksgiving harvest feast to which everyone, including Omayah and his father,

21

Oroonah, and all of the Indians in the area were invited. Omayah came, still lovelorn and sad-eyed, but not his father or any of his braves. Margaret Lewis had had a strong premonition of danger, and it was promptly borne out by ensuing events. The two young people, Omayah and White Dove, wandered off hand in hand. No sooner had they reached a stream than a blood-curdling war whoop arose from some nearby bushes, and the two young people were quickly surrounded by painted warriors and hustled off into the forest.

That was the last John or Margaret Lewis saw or heard of their daughter for a long time. Hastily the settlers erected a stockade in the center of a clearing near the stream, in preparation for further touble with the Indians. They named it Fort Staunton in honor of the Lewis' Williamsburg benefactress, Lady Rebecca Staunton, wife of Governor Gooch. Twice, while every able-bodied man in the tiny colony was out combing the surrounding country-side for clues of White Dove's whereabouts. the Indians attacked the depleted garrison. And twice the attacking warriors were driven off with severe losses under the steady and determined gunfire of the children and old people left in the fort.

After the second attack on the stronghold, a lone Indian of suspiciously stout proportions and in slovenly garb lay wounded in the meadow and moaned piteously for help. As soon as it was deemed safe, a small group sallied forth to bring in this wounded derelict, who turned out to be not an Indian at all, but Mad Mary Greenlee a half-crazed old crone, who, under suspicion of witchcraft, had fled the colony long before. While the women dressed her wounds, she babbled a strange tale of having stolen White Dove away from her captors and then having hidden her in a miraculous cave sparkling with diamonds, rubies, silver, and other precious gems. The diamonds and other jewels Mad Mary Greenlee was referring to, were, of course, the rock crystals, and other fascinating formations in the limestone caves, which glittered in the light of her candle. She begged her rescuers to loan her a horse so that she could lead them to the cave where the girl, desperately ill of a strange fever, lay hidden.

For a time, her ravings were dismissed as the dying hallucinations of a mad woman until they came to the attention of White Dove's mother. As soon as her husband

and his men returned from their fruitless search, Mrs. Lewis insisted they set forth again with the babbling old crone as their guide. They found there, in the very cave Mad Mary had described, White Dove, ill as her guardian had said, but otherwise unharmed. And thus were the first limestone caves with their stalactites and stalagmites, their cave flowers and rock crystals, discovered in Virginia by the white man in the year 1735.

Soon peace was restored around Staunton between the two warring factions, but from then on, it was a kind of uneasy peace—a sort of armed truce—until the onset of the Indian wars a decade later. However, for the romantics in the audience, I am glad to be able to report that although Omayah and White Dove never married, they remained fast friends for many years, setting a fine example for race relations for the future.

Another old Indian legend concerns the first discovery of the healing warm springs of Virginia and West Virginia by a lone Indian brave. About three hundred years ago as the redman reckoned time, a young brave was travelling east from across the mountains, bound for a great tribal council along the seacoast on the shores of Chesapeake Bay. It was late autumn and bitterly cold in the mountains of western Virginia as he passed through the Warm Springs section, which was all strange new country to the young man. He had padded steadily along the frozen rocky trails all day in his worn moccasins, and by nightfall he was extremely tired and cold; so he began looking for a suitable place to bed down for the night. All about him the earth was frozen solid and covered with a light powdery mantle of early snow. The mountains towering about him were gleaming in the twilight with an even heavier coating of snow and ice. All of the streams and ponds he passed were also skimmed with ice. Suddenly, he came upon a small clearing in the forest floor of the valley where miraculously the ground was still soft and yielding underfoot, and completely without snow. A few yards farther on he came to a small dark pond which not only was free of ice, but actually gave off a faint cloud of warm, moist air.

Everything about the place cried aloud for him to plunge in and rest his tired, aching bones. The youth dived into the steaming water without a moment's hesitation, and was soon deliciously engulfed with a feeling of renewed strength

23

and energy as he floated in the shallows of the pond. After a long revitalizing swim, he came ashore and dried himself in the remarkably warm air, ate his supper of pemmican, and soon was fast asleep. The next morning, upon arising, he not only felt marvelously refreshed, but ready for the trail east again; he set out with a renewed, springy Indian lope. Upon arriving at the council fire on the Tidewater, he told his friends of the wondrous healing warm springs he had discovered high in the mountains to the west. And from that time on, Warm Springs, and its neighbor, Hot Springs, became a regular halting place on the migratory routes of the Indians up and down the Valley.

IV

EARLY CUSTOMS
AND COMMERCE

What sort of a new world was this primitive land of the Senedoes by now? Settled, cleared, tilled, and fenced, it rang steadily to the sound of the woodman's axe, while the lowing cattle competed for the lush bottomland bluegrass with the Indian's buffalo. It was still rather sparsely settled and dangerously exposed to Indian attack, for the settlers' frontier homesteads were strung all up and down the valley floor, many weary miles across the mountains from the nearest coastal settlements. Except for Staunton, stockades and Indian forts were few and far between. The newcomers relied mostly on friendly trusting relations with the Indians for their safety. So far all had gone well as the Indians came in regularly to trade their furs for steel knives and muskets at the scattered posts. They hung about the tiny, unprotected hamlets to observe in awe and wonder their new acquaintances' strange ways and modes of living. For some time, each group remained a novelty to the other. And up until about 1750 there was still room for everybody. The forests were full of game, the rivers and streams were still unpolluted and full of fish, beaver, muskrat, and otter. Following the savages' example, the frontiersmen planted and harvested their crops of corn, and for some time the yields were plentiful.

Front Royal, then variously known as either Luce or Lehew Town, was from the very first a garrison post and important trading center where several major trade routes intersected at the confluence of the two main branches of the Shenandoah River. Supplies and manufactured goods came in over Chester and Manassas Gaps from the seacoast. They moved north through Winchester to the Potomac ford at Hancock, Maryland, and thence west to the frontier forts and settlements of western Pennsylvania and Maryland. Some headed south along the old Indian trace, soon to be known as "The Valley Pike", to the new settlements further down the valley. At the ferry crossing above what is

25

now Front Royal, where the North Fork and the South Fork of the Shenandoah meet, much of the valley produce was transshipped into flatboat river barges for the long trip down the Shenandoah to Harpers Ferry and beyond, to the seaports at Georgetown and Alexandria on the Potomac. A river port soon sprang up, and this spot quickly was christened "Helltown" because of the influx of roistering muleskinners, pack-train men, and bargemen who frequented the waterfront pubs and brothels there. Fights and bloody fisticuffs between land men and river bargemen were frequent—hence its name. And just in case anyone reading this doubts the veracity of my statement, I once found the place-name "Helltown" clearly inked at the juncture of the twin forks of the Shenandoah, on an early crude map of the area.

Winchester also flourished at the crossroads of several major trade routes and toll roads: notably the route west through the gorge at Harpers Ferry past Charles Town and Berryville to Winchester, and a second from the Potomac ford at Mecklenburg (later Shepherdstown). The Valley Pike running north along the central floor of the valley (now U.S. 11), the Berkeley Springs Pike (U.S. 522) and the Romney Road (U.S. 50 west) also channeled travellers and commerce to Frederick Town, later to be christened Winchester.

Up until the start of the Civil War, all of what is now the state of West Virginia was part of Virginia. The Virginia counties, which make up the "panhandle" West Virginia today, were the first to secede from the Confederacy and to join the Union in 1861. Of the early colonial towns in this region, Charles Town is perhaps the most charming and historic. Charles Town was settled by a mixture of English and French Huguenots, newly arrived from overseas. The French influence is still quite noticeable in and around Charles Town in the Norman turrets and New Orleans style iron grillwork on many of the houses. Colonel Charles Washington, George Washington's brother and builder of "Mordington" at Charles Town, has been officially credited with incorporating the town.

Martinsburg, West Virginia was founded by a group of settlers under Adam Stephen and named after Thomas Brian Martin, Lord Fairfax's nephew. Legend has it that a burley Charon of a ferryman operated the boat at the river-crossing at Harpers Ferry in the early days—named

Harper, of course. As we have already seen, Shepherdstown, West Virginia, was originally called Mecklenburg; so it is quite obvious there was a strong preponderance of Germans in the area during early colonial times.

Berkeley Springs, one of the earliest health spas in the country (1736), was named after Sir William Berkeley, the Royal Governor of the Virginia Colony, of which it was then a part. Hancock, Maryland, just across the Potomac River from Berkeley Springs, was named after one of the first signers of the Declaration of Independence, who became first Governor of Massachusetts, John Hancock.

Berryville, Virginia, the home of the distinguished Byrd and Randolph families, on the other hand, got its name from a more lowly level. It was named in honor of its first tavernkeeper or "publican", Benjamin Berry, who operated Berry's Tavern on the town mall at the highway crossroads. Prior to that, it was known simply as "Battletown", because of Berry's bear pit and gladiatorial ring set out on the lawn in front of the inn, which that enterprising local entrepreneur kept filled with either prizefighters or animals in the interest of increasing weekend business. There is a fascinating, authentic story in connection with Berry's tavern which will go a long way in describing the rugged customs and general spirit of those times.

One hot summer day in 1745 a young drover, or waggoneer, from Winchester, then known as Frederick Town, stopped at the end of a long hard pull from Harpers Ferry, to water his horses at the town watering trough next to Berry's Tavern. His name was Daniel Morgan, and, being hot and tired, he decided to step inside Benjamin Berry's taproom to quench his own thirst with a pint or so of ale. It was Dan Morgan's first visit to the tavern, and while putting away his fair share of refreshing cheer, he suddenly found himself being loudly accosted with a whole string of verbal abuse and insults by a huge giant, the current fighting champion of Battletown, who fancied himself cock of the walk. Now it just so happened that the drover from Winchester was no puny pushover himself, weighing in at a strapping 190 pounds in fighting trim, and thoroughly adept at every form of what passed for fisticuffs at the time, which meant mostly elbowing, groin-kicking, ear-biting, and eye-gouging between battering-ram swings of fist and shoulder. Furthermore, Morgan had a quick temper to match his muscle.

27

In a matter of seconds the fight was on. Up and down, in and out, and around about the taproom, flew the two straining contestants, much to the detriment of the decor of the taproom interior and publican Berry's best glassware and crockery. Over the counter, behind the bar, through the windows, sailed the two thrashing giants, bent on mutilation and destruction, while, with a delighted grin the proprietor looked on. Benjamin Berry was no mean scrapper himself, often filling in for an unwilling contestant at his popular weekend entertainments. One look at Dan Morgan's style and form in fighting, and the tavernkeeper knew he was gazing at a winner—and probably the new champion of Battletown.

Finally, after two hours of this bloody melee, Dan Morgan's opponent, "Bully" Davis, went sailing over the bar and out through the window for the last time, ending up head-down in the water trough. Over a fresh tankard of free ale on the house, while "Bully" Davis dragged himself off, cursing and swearing vengeance as he limped away to his mountain lair, Daniel Morgan was crowned the new champion of Berry's Tavern.

It was not until almost a full year later, that "Bully" Davis was in good enough shape to challenge the new champion for a return match, this time out on the lawn in front of Berry's tavern to a sell-out, standing-room-only crowd of eager spectators. Only, this time, "Bully" Davis was planning to bring along all three of his huge brothers, plus a rough and ready assortment of his most powerful mountaineer friends to help him revenge himself on the upstart from Frederick Town. Fortunately, some fair-minded soul—quite possibly the innkeeper himself—warned the new champion in time. When Daniel Morgan arrived at the scene of combat, before a cheering gallery of spectators, thirsting for blood as much as for Benjamin Berry's ale, he was backed up by an equal army of his own, chosen with care from the strongest members of the waggoneer contingent of Frederick Town. It is said that the fight which ensued that evening was indeed a battle royal, ending in another complete rout for "Bully" Davis and his burly crew of mountain men, amid repeated cheers for the defending champion, and a mass rush for Benjamin Berry's bar.

Years later, in the closing days of his long life at his daughter's house in Winchester, where he died, General Morgan was asked by his personal physician, where on earth he had ever gotten the badly twisted and broken toe on his right foot? The old warhorse replied with a reminiscent chuckle, "I broke it kicking 'Bully' Billy Davis at Battletown".

There were a number of other heroes-in-the-making moving about the Valley around 1750. As we have already noted, George Washington was busily engaged surveying Lord Fairfax's vast holdings in the area where he gained intimate knowledge of the terrain, which was to stand both him and his countrymen in good stead in later martial times to come. His surveying office behind his employer's "Greenway Court" near White Post in Clarke County, is still standing, although the main house at Greenway Court burned down many years ago. Washington's military—and surveying—headquarters at Winchester is also still standing and has been turned into a museum after full restoration to its original state as of 1758.

In those times, Joist Hite was still living at his log house near "Springdale", the far more pretentious fieldstone home his son erected beside Opequon Creek in 1753. His land-venture partner's son, Robert McKay, Jr., was living at his stone and log house at Cedarville, where he operated a sawmill. Other mills were springing up all over the Valley wherever there were streams of sufficient size and flow to turn the waterwheels that drove them. The first crude hillside iron furnaces, utilized the plentiful iron ore, limestone, and man-made charcoal from the forests, to turn out pig iron in big clumsy slabs. Everywhere there was field-clearing, fence-building, and construction work on farms and out-buildings. These activities drove the Indians and their game still further back into the mountains to the west, away from their ancestral hunting grounds.

The old Indian traces and game trails were rapidly replaced by primitive, badly-pitted dirt roads, carved out of field and forest by hooves and wagon wheels. The big river was beginning to fill up with flatboats and crude barges drifting downstream under the expert guidance of lusty bargemen struggling at their long steering oars and sweeps. En route to the juncture of the Shenandoah and the Potomac at Harpers Ferry, which had become quite an important center of commerce and transportation long before the coming of the railroads, the clumsy craft had a way of wiping out the Indians' weirs and fish traps, doing nothing to enamor the redmen to the barges' owners. Men

gathered in small, yarn-swapping groups at the crossroad
stores and trading posts, much as they still do today, or
quaffed their stein of beer and pints of ale at taprooms like
Benjamin Berry's.

A steady stream of manufactured goods arrived almost
daily from the seacoast; long wagon or pack trains toiled
wearily up the winding slopes of the kindlier mountain
passes. Some of this merchandise stayed in the Valley, some
moved on across the Potomac ford at Hancock to the more
distant frontier outposts opening up at Fort Cumberland,
Loyal Hanna, and Fort Bedford, then known as Raystown,
Pennsylvania. By the year 1754, the colonial frontier had
literally spilled over onto the very doorstep of the alarmed
and embittered French entrenched at the confluence of the
Allegheny and Monongahela Rivers at Fort Duquesne (later
renamed Pittsburgh to honor a champion of the American
cause in London, Sir William Pitt, Prime Minister of
England).

Thus was the stage set, slowly but irrevocably, for the
next act in the unfolding Valley drama—the French and
Indian War. For by the year 1752, the French had decided
it was high time to call a halt to this dangerous westward
advance of the English "Longknives" and their "Dutch
swine", as they scathingly dubbed Joist Hite's hardy band
of German settlers along the frontier. They had no
intention of giving up the rich new central belt of the Ohio
Territory west of the Alleghenies to the British colonials
and their allies. It was territory which they themselves had
struggled long and hard to carve out of the wilderness and
to master, and could not let go without a fight. And if that
fight meant using their Indian allies as partners, armed with
shiny new sharp steel tomahawks, scalping knives, and
rifles, and fired-up on cheap Barbados rum and blood-lust
to kill the white enemy by generous scalp bounties, instead
of invaluable and irreplaceable Frenchmen—so much the
better. Who cared? Certainly not the French King surrounded by his gay court, living it up at Versailles!

Between 1750 and 1754 there were repeated warning
forays, raids, and skirmishes along the frontier—"inci-
dents", the dandies called them from their snug haven
across the Blue Ridge at Williamsburg, along the Tidewater.
But it was not until the year 1754 that the seething
cauldron finally boiled over west of the mountains.

V

THE FRENCH
AND INDIAN WAR

When the Indians suddenly vanished from the Valley in the early summer of 1754, it came as no surprise to either Governor Dinwiddie in Williamsburg, or to George Washington, newly commissioned a major in the Virginia militia. In the late fall of 1753, Dinwiddie had sent Major Washington west into the wilderness with a small surveying party for a look around the Ohio Territory, on a mission to map out some future sites for fortifications in case of trouble. Both men had smelled trouble in the offing from the increasing irritability of the Indians and the rising tempo of their raids against the valley people.

In a wine-imbibing bout with the French garrison officers during a brief stopover at Fort Duquesne, Major Washington heard some highly disturbing news which he hurried back to report to his superior in the colonial capital along the Tidewater. At supper in the French fort, their tongues loosened by the wine and good-fellowship, Washington's hosts had started boasting that before long they would be driving the last unwanted Englishmen, or "Longknives", and their despised "Dutch swine", out of the valley for good. When asked by Washington and his colonial companions at the officers' mess table, how they planned to accomplish this feat, the French frankly declared that it was their intention to do so with the assistance of their embittered allies, the Iroquois, Algonquins, and valley Shawnee Indians who had been forced out of the territory by the Englishmen and Germans. There was little question as to what Washington's hosts had in mind—a blood-bath and reign of terror along the entire frontier, all the way from Canada to the Carolinas.

When he heard this grim news, Governor Dinwiddie decided to move fast. Coupled with the increasing urgent requests for help from the already beleaguered valley residents, Washington's information spelled out that the Royal Governor's only recourse was to bolster quickly the strength of the frontier garrisons in the Valley. However, this maneuver was easier said than done with the meager resources in manpower and money at his command. Fortunately the Indian outrages had tapered off noticeably during the late fall of 1752 and early winter of 1753; and what Indian raids occurred, had been both sporadic and poorly organized. Cold weather was the cringing settlers' best ally at the time, since the savages preferred to remain in their warm lodges in bad weather. Their sallying forth on the warpath in summer, or during occasional spells of warm autumn weather, has given rise to one of our most widely used weather phrases—"Indian summer". Today we use this term with a happy connotation, but such was not the case with the early frontier people. Spells of warm, sunny weather, between the years 1753 and 1764 could only mean one thing—Indian raids and massacres.

This, in turn, brings up another custom of that stormy period. The Indians' savage practice of scalping their fallen

Virginia State Library

George Washington during the French and Indian War

victims was a definite outgrowth of an inhuman offer of the French to their Indian allies. Scalp bounties were paid out by the French paymaster at Fort Duquesne, in either gold or the much-coveted fiery Barbados rum, to the redskins who brought in the dried and smoke-cured grim evidence of another deceased German or Englishman.

Upon Major Washington's hasty return to Williamsburg from Fort Duquesne in the early winter of 1753, Governor Dinwiddie decided to send a punitive expedition west to teach both the French and their Indian allies a badly-needed lesson in good manners. He promoted Washington to Lieutenant Colonel to head the task force. Because of the hasty nature of its assembly, which really was not the fault of its commander, there was a serious lack of organization, supply, and reserve strength, and the expedition failed miserably in its objectives. Washington soon fell back to his old stamping grounds at Winchester, where he made his headquarters for the winter and did his best to beef up his rag-tag expeditionary force of untrained militia.

Early the following year, a second, reinforced task force was dispatched to Washington at Winchester. He was living at "The Golden Buck" while he awaited the arrival of the British officer who was to be his supreme commander in the forward area. Unfortunately, the new English commander in the field turned out to be General Edward Braddock, who arrived from Boston to take command of the frontier in May of 1755. The rest is history. General Braddock ignored the pleas and warnings of Colonel Washington. First, he tarried too long amid the dubious delights of Winchester; this gave the French time to reinforce their frontier garrison. When Braddock finally decided to move against the French at Fort Duquesne, he blundered straight into a French and Indian ambush and died ignobly with many of his British Regulars along the corduroy road he had insisted be carved out of the wilderness for his artillery and supply train. The rest of his command was saved from total annihilation by George Washington's frontier militia accurately firing their Pennsylvania long-rifles from behind the cover of the trees of the surrounding forest.

It was a terrible price to pay for one man's conceit and ignorance, but the bloody lesson in frontier tactics taught the British absolutely nothing, for years to come, until long after the American Revolution. For, throughout that long

33

conflict, and others, the British Regulars were still marching into battle, ten abreast, with fixed bayonets gleaming, to the accompaniment of the stirring strains of fife and drum, never seeking cover from the enemy. Their fixed ways and downright obstinacy, based on long tradition, were to cost them dearly during the war for American independence.

Emboldened by this easy victory over a major unit of the regular British army under one of its top generals, the French and Indians now went wild; the savages literally ran amok among the more isolated and unprotected hamlets along the valley frontier as far north as Maryland and Pennsylvania. Ambush, terror, fire, havoc, and sudden death, all were always to the accompaniment of the soul-shattering cry of the war-whoop and a rain of gunfire and flaming fire-arrows. Whole towns were wiped out; families were massacred by the hundreds. Those who were not slain and scalped on the spot, were carried off to be tortured, or sold into slavery in the Indian villages of the Ohio Territory. It seemed as if the entire western frontier, from Roanoke to upper New York State, was going up in smoke and flame. Soon the rough roads leading back to the coastal settlements were clogged with fleeing homesteaders and their families, each trying to save as much of their possessions as they could pile on their groaning farm wagons. For a long terrible time from the year 1755 until 1758, when Fort Duquesne finally fell into British hands, it looked as if the French and their blood-whetted Indian allies were going to win their goal, with the redmen reclaiming every burned cabin and lost acre in the entire Valley and even eastward beyond the Blue Ridge.

It was at this crucial point in 1755, shortly after Braddock's monumental defeat, that Governor Dinwiddie determined to send George Washington, now a full colonel in the colonial militia, back to Winchester to build a fort of refuge in order to anchor the crumbling thin line of tiny Indian forts and stockades still holding out down the center of the Valley. Something had to be done, and done quickly, before the whole forward area collapsed in total panic. It was bad enough that every road was blocked with refugees fleeing eastward. But there still were a stalwart few who stood their ground against the whooping Indians and fought back, too proud and stubborn to give up their new homes and farmlands. These were the real heroes of the Valley: poor, ignorant for the most part, and untrained—but all of them, by now, experts themselves with the tomahawk, the scalping knife, and the deadly accurate Pennsylvania long-rifle. By the end of the war most of them could fight as well, ambush as well, and scalp as well, as any Indian.

In the late fall of 1755, Colonel Washington embarked on a three year program of building both a powerful fort at Winchester and an equally reliable garrison force to man it. It was no mean feat, considering the manpower he had to work with. His militiamen were all raw recruits and green conscripts drawn at random from the freemen along the Tidewater and coastal plains, buttressed by a small scouting force of valley and mountain men in buckskin and coonskin caps, who would just as soon knock an officer's teeth down his gullet, as obey an order which displeased them. They were poorly paid, poorly armed, ill-clothed and ill-equipped, and far from regally fed or housed. Military discipline—in fact, discipline of any kind—was almost unknown at Winchester.

For a long time Washington had more trouble with his own troops than he did with the French and Indians. Execution by hanging was taboo in the militia. Flogging was the only method of corporal punishment for military infraction available to the harassed commander, and Washington used it liberally. However, disciplinary action of any sort was a chancy affair; the men were inclined to simply pack up their meager belongings and go home. The desertion rate was simply appalling to a dedicated soldier like Washington, trying to forge an army out of free men and untrained rustics. Nor were things going much better, that fall and winter, in the construction of the fort at Winchester. Washington not only was unable to get sufficient food, uniforms, or proper weapons for his rabble in arms—not to mention their monthly pay—but neither could he get the big guns and materials with which to complete Fort Loudoun, as it was eventually called. Every request for supplies, or for further directives went unanswered at Williamsburg. So regularly did Washington bombard Governor Dinwiddie with urgent dispatches, that that colonial worthy, sorely beset by insurmountable problems of his own in raising men and money for the war, began tossing his field commander's messages into the fireplace, unopened.

Colonel Washington, being a man of direct action in an emergency, decided to seek help elsewhere. In mid-winter

35

of 1755-56 he set off alone on horseback for Boston, to plead his case with the Supreme Commander in Chief of the British Regulars on the entire North American continent, Lord Loudoun. After hearing Washington's tale of woe he agreed to help: first, by tightening the regulations on military disciplinary action to include death by hanging for desertion; and, second, by sending Washington his sorely needed military supplies—including heavy cannon—for the fort of Winchester. In gratitude Washington decided to name the new fortification in Lord Loudoun's honor.

Returning posthaste to his Valley command, Colonel Washington promptly set about implementing the new disciplinary decrees of his supreme commander in Boston. First, in public view, he hung several deserters, which soon took care of the desertion problem. Next, he bolstered his labor force at the fort by withdrawing some of the advance militia units stationed at Fort Cumberland, eighty miles to the west, along the very perimeter of the frontier. Then Governor Dinwiddie got into the act again by ordering that all of the frontier north and west of Winchester be abandoned to the enemy, and that all of the settlers thus exposed to attack be evacuated back behind the rising earthwork ramparts of the unfinished Fort Loudoun. They were to be brought in by force, if necessary, for their own safety. Fortunately, this last order was never carried out. Both Washington and Captain Dagworthy, the commanding officer still on duty at Fort Cumberland, resolutely backed up the enraged homesteaders in the forward area, who stoutly refused to leave their homes and barns at the mercy of the Indians.

At this point, to further compound Colonel Washington's mounting headaches, a new British field commander arrived to replace Braddock as head of the Winchester task force. General Sir John Forbes soon proved to be as mulish as his predecessor; he was equally obsessed with Braddock's passion for wagon trains, artillery, and road-building through the wilderness. In fact, so intense was Forbes' obsession for corduroy log roads that his superior in Boston, Lord Loudoun, was obliged to recall him at the continued insistence of Washington, his staff, and Governor Dinwiddie; but it was not before Forbes had squandered the whole winter of 1755-56 on his pet project. When the first spring thaws arrived, setting the Indians across the mountains swarming like a hive of angry bees, the fort at

Winchester was still far from finished. The big guns which had been so laboriously dragged by sledge all the way from the seacoast, still lay rusting and useless on the parade ground, instead of properly set in the gun embrasures along the parapets of Fort Loudoun.

Meanwhile the French, with their screaming hordes of blood and rum-crazed Indians now out of hand, had descended en masse at the very gates of Fort Cumberland. Having failed in their initial goal of surprise, they prepared to lay siege to the stockade which had been strongly reinforced by a retreating flood of angry refugees, many of whom were by then expert in handling the Pennsylvania long-rifle. However, siege was a method of warfare unsuited to the Indian temperament. By the time Washington arrived at Fort Cumberland with his relief column he found the savage redmen were eager to go howling though the wilderness in search of easier and swifter prey. Lifting more scalps as they went, they spread a new wave of terror along the settlements scattered up and down the unprotected frontier. Captain Dagworthy and his besieged garrison were saved with scarcely a shot being fired, and the discouraged French melted into the forest, headed back to their winter lair at Fort Duquesne. But for a long time afterward, the entire western frontier was ablaze with Indian attacks and sudden skirmishes in isolated hamlets and against unprotected farms.

The new troops Governor Dinwiddie had forwarded to bolster Winchester soon turned out to be even worse than the first batch of raw recruits of the year before. And to increase Dinwiddie's woes, no sooner had the Fort Cumberland siege been lifted, than Washington was struck down by a severe attack of dysentery and had to be evacuated to his estate at Mount Vernon for rest and recuperation.

The only thing that saved the entire frontier from going up in flames that summer and fall was the fact that the French commanders at Fort Duquesne had been badly misinformed as to the exact status of Fort Loudoun. They were deceived by all of the 12-pounders being dragged through the forest the winter before, and thought that the fortification had been armed and completed, ready to repel any attack made on it. So, for the rest of 1756, and well into the summer of 1757, the French laid low in their stronghold to the west, biding their time—while their Indian allies squandered their strength and powder along the unprotected perimeter of the frontier, doing no real tactical harm to the enemy—instead of attacking Winchester, which would have fallen easily to their assault.

By early 1758, British bungling during this God-given pause in serious fighting, plus the generally deteriorating state of affairs along the entire frontier, accomplished what all of Washington's repeated pleas for help had failed to do. At long last the Virginia Assembly and House of Burgesses at Williamsburg was stung to action, led by a close friend and admirer of Washington, John Robinson, who was speaker of the house. In a remarkably short period of time, sufficient money, material, and manpower were found to forward an additional 2,000 well-equipped troops to the frontier. At the same time, Lord Loudoun, having replaced Sir John Forbes with General Stanwix as supreme commander at Winchester, gave his new staff officer the green light to go ahead with an aggressive offensive campaign against the French at Fort Duquesne.

Then began the third act in the comedy of errors in road construction. Only eighty miles west of Winchester, at Fort Cumberland, the spearhead of the creeping column bogged down in the wilderness under a fierce fusillade of enemy sniper fire and some equally fierce debate about their construction details among the British staff officers on the scene. Some of them wanted to go first north, then west; others first west, then north; and a few die-hards even wanted to approach Fort Duquesne in misleading concentric circles. And so it went until General Washington was well enough to rejoin his troops at Raystown—now Bedford, Pennsylvania. By September 1, 1758, some forty-five miles of new road had been added in the general direction of the French stronghold on the Allegheny River. Then suddenly all work stopped as word came in by scout that the fort ahead was manned by a mere 800 Frenchmen who would quickly surrender at the first show of strength. To hurry matters along, Major Grant was sent ahead through the forest with his Royal Highlanders to take the fort without waiting for the cumbersome artillery mired down on the log road.

Much to the Major's surprise and General Stanwix's chagrin, Grant was soundly defeated in front of the ramparts of Fort Duquesne, and his celebrated Royal Highlanders driven off with considerable loss of life and

equipment. Among those taken prisoner by the French that
day was a young colonial scout named Andrew Lewis,
whose father was the founder of Staunton, Virginia, and
whose sister was the fair-haired maiden the Indians had
christened "White Dove". Upon news of the disaster,
Washington moved his militia and scouts to an advance
position at Loyal Hanna, to cover the Highlanders' retreat
and the English left flank in case of counter-attack.
Whereupon, suddenly and unexpectedly, Sir John Forbes
entered the picture again as General Stanwix's right-hand
man and chief military adviser, much to Washington's
disgust. Forbes suggested a fourth new road be begun, to
take the French stronghold by the flank, and work was
started on it promptly, before the first severe winter snows
set in. November 20, 1758, found Washington just thirty
miles short of the fork of the two mighty rivers where Fort
Duquesne sat on a high bank commanding every approach
from the east and south. His men were cold, hungry, bitter,
and exhausted from their labors.

However, on that day, a miracle happened. Scouts raced
back from the woods towards the toiling road gangs, yelling
at the top of their lungs that Fort Duquesne was in flames
and the enemy, and a whole host of painted warriors in
overloaded canoes, were fleeing downriver into the vast
Ohio Territory.

Actually Forbes and Stanwix had been right, in their
own stubborn way. The French, too, played by the
formalized rules of continental warfare. They considered
themselves to be out-flanked by the network of roads
creeping up on Fort Duquesne. There was nothing left for
them to do, in their book, but burn their fort and retire
westward. They departed without another shot being fired,
thereby surrendering the entire eastern section of the Ohio
Territory to the advancing British and American colonials.

As the ruins of Fort Duquesne went up in smoke that
chilly November day in 1758, the new Royal Governor at
Williamsburg, Lord Fauquier, was aware that truce negotia-
tions were underway in France to end the conflict. The
treaty was not signed until 1763. Long before that, the last
hostile Indian had vanished from the Valley and peace had
returned to the Blue Ridge. In 1764, a French Colonel
Bouquet arrived at Winchester, under a flag of truce, to
arrange for the final release of some ninety Virginians still
held captive against their will by the Indians to the west.

Among them, little White Dove's brother, Andrew.

Already fresh storm clouds were gathering on the Valley horizon. But, before we get into Lord Dunmore's War and the first rumblings of the long struggle for independence, let us pause long enough for a fascinating insider's look at a few events in the Valley during the ten years of the French and Indian War, and learn of a handful of heroes.

VI

INDIAN FORTS AND INDIAN DOINGS, PLUS A HANDFUL OF HEROES

Fortunately for the frontier people, in spite of the best efforts of the French commanders at Fort Duquesne to organize their primitive allies into an effective fighting force, the Indians were far too impatient and mercurial by nature to keep up a steady running battle against the English and Germans at any one place or time. As we have already seen, they preferred to stay in their snug, if smelly, lodges during bad weather, sallying forth on the warpath only in spells of good weather. Even then they only attacked in small units—Indian style—using elements of surprise and terror. Perhaps "fortunately" is not the kindest word to use in this context, since the Indians' savage tactics were hell on earth to the poor reeling settlers who stubbornly remained to defend their homes and possessions, in preference to retreating to safety eastward. But the Indians' unwillingness to fight the war, in the way their French leaders wanted, did prevent the commanders at Fort Duquesne from any success in clearing the Valley of the hated "Dutch swine" and "Longknives". The French seldom had an army to fight with, since their Indian allies were forever slipping away into the forests, bent on civilian rather than military destruction.

These raids gave rise to the series of frontier Indian forts which soon sprang up throughout the Valley, set roughly fifteen miles apart to serve as temporary refuge for the inhabitants in the neighborhood in case of attack. A few of these old Indian forts are still standing in the Valley: the Frontier Fort at the edge of Strasburg; Fort Bowman, northeast of the same community; Stephens Fort near Lebanon Church, north of Strasburg; and the Indian fort a few miles west of Luray beside the South Fork of the Shenandoah River. Other ruins still exist, but these four are by far the best preserved examples. The squared-log or stone walls—often surrounded by a pole stockade to insure double strength—of even the smallest fortification, usually

41

Robert M. Wick
Fort Stephens — Old Indian Fort at Lebanon Church, Va.

provided sufficient safety for the settlers inside, since the Indian attacks, dependent on initial surprise, seldom lasted more than a day or two. A few personalized accounts of these raids, between the years 1754 and 1764, are on record and should serve to illustrate the sufferings of the victims.

One of the first severe Indian attacks at the very outset of hostilities in 1754, came at Mills Gap, on the Berkeley Springs road, directly under the loom of North Mountain above Winchester. Twenty whooping Indian braves raced out of the forest to attack Patrick Kelly as he did his spring plowing. After dispatching him and lifting his scalp, they then crept silently up and murdered his wife as she was milking in the barn. Then they surrounded the house and killed all the Kelly children but one, who managed to escape the tomahawk and run off to spread the alarm. As the grim news spread, all of Patrick Kelly's neighbors raced at top speed for the nearest Indian stockade, John Evans' fort on the Martinsburg road. Some made it; some did not.

Tom Evans, brother of the builder of the fort, barely made it; fighting a single-handed, rear-guard delaying action, he covered the flight of his family. Polly Martin was not so lucky. She delayed her initial departure to gather up a few precious belongings, then turned back again towards what she thought was the smoke of her neighbor's chimney, to warn them. She arrived just in time to see the victorious ring of painted warriors in a war dance, circling the burning house. She was quickly overpowered, taken prisoner, and dragged off to an Indian village far to the west across the Alleghenies. For several days after the initial attack on Mills Gap, the people remained barricaded and under arms at Evans' fort, but on the third day, thinking the attackers had surely gone, a party of men set out from the fort to give the Kellys and the other victims decent burial. While the men were absent, the Indians attacked again, certain that they would quickly be able to overcome the women and children left in the stockade. It was John Evans' brave and resourceful wife who saved the day for the seemingly helpless occupants.

Grabbing a loaded musket from the pile of stacked arms, she began handing them to the old men and older boys in the terrified crowd, while outside, the fort rang with the war whoops of the savages. Next she picked up a military drum lying beside the stacked firearms, and handed it to the eldest boy present, Joey Hackney, and told him to beat it for dear life and to imitate as best he could the warlike ruffle known as the "call to arms". With the boy banging away at top speed with the drumsticks, and Mrs. Evans barking off random military commands in a gruff voice, all hands began to discharge their weapons through the gun ports in the general direction of the attacking savages. Although not a single Indian was hit, the ruse worked like a charm. By the third volley the redskins had had enough. Convinced by their eyes and ears that they must have miscounted noses among the able-bodied defenders who had left the fort, the Indians soon withdrew. When spurred on by the sound of gunfire, the men came hurrying back to the stockade. They must have heard plenty from the triumphant defenders of the fort, or I miss my guess!

Along the Opequon River farther south and nearer Winchester, things soon grew even grimmer that summer of 1754. The Indians burned Fort Opequon to the ground after massacring the entire garrison and other inmates sheltered there, with the exception of a few of the younger women and older children whom they took prisoner, among them the Cohoon family. Mrs. Cohoon, heavy with child, could not keep up with the others in the retreating party, including the children of some near neighbors, George and Isabella Stockton. The Indian braves soon put an end to her miseries with a single blow of a war club. Stumbling across his wife's body, Mr. Cohoon fell across her with a terrible cry and went out of his head in grief. The raiding Shawnee, having a superstition of great dread and respect for the insane, let Mr. Cohoon go home with his children; but the two Stockton youngsters they kept.

They herded the children, tightly bound with thongs, ever further westward across the mountains in the direction of the Ohio River. The war party seldom stopped to rest or eat; and when they occasionally did so, young George Stockton did his best to forage for food—wild berries and water—for his exhausted sister, cupping his bleeding hands to pick them in spite of his thong bindings. Only once, on the entire journey back to their village across the Ohio River, did the Indians pause long enough to kill a buffalo and devour the meat. For nearly three years, young George Stockton lived as a slave in a Shawnee village before finally managing to escape and return home on foot to the Valley.

Little Polly Martin, sole surviving child of Tom Evans' neighbors over on North Mountain, lived as a slave child in the same village; and she, too, eventually managed to escape and make her lonely way back through the hundreds of miles of mountain and valley wilderness to her home in the northern part of the Shenandoah Valley. But young George Stockton's sister, Isabella, had the most remarkable adventures of them all. Sold into slavery by her Indian captor, Chief Black Wolf of the Shawnee, she was treated very badly by her second master, a French fur trader with an evil reputation, even among the Indians. When she was thirteen years old he took her north with him to Canada, where she met another Frenchman with the odd name of Plata, who quickly fell in love with her. And now comes the amazing part of this true story of her adventures

44

in the wilderness at the hands of the French and Indians.

Plata was so deeply in love with Isabella that he bought her from her first French master, then set her free and, at the same time, humbly asked her hand in marriage. This in itself is not so strange, considering that her brother's written account of their experiences in the west states that his sister was a very pretty girl even as a small child. What is really remarkable in the light of all that she had already been through at the hands of her captors and masters, was her reply to Plata's proposal of wedlock. She firmly insisted on travelling all of the way back home to the Shenandoah Valley from the Great Lakes to obtain her father's consent to the marriage! What is more, like most pretty young women, she had her way in the matter, too. The two of them headed back towards Winchester to seek the parental blessing, her mother having died in childbirth before Isabella's capture. I sincerely wish I could follow this fascinating tale of filial piety and devotion with a happy ending, but such is not the true account. One look at the Popish Frenchman and the senior Stockton said a loud and final "No!" to his daughter's tearful entreaties. The two lovers decided to elope, and in righteous wrath, stole two of her father's horses for the return trip to Canada. Enraged, Stockton sent Isabella's two half-brothers in pursuit of the couple, with orders to bring back his missing horses. They did better than that, for the two Virginia ruffians not only retrieved the horses, but also killed Plata in cold blood.

The shock of this third tragedy in her life temporarily deranged Isabella Stockton's mind. But in time she recovered and married a fine upstanding young Irishman named McClary and raised a large family, this time with her father's blessing, out in the vicinity of what is now Morgantown, West Virginia. No wonder our early American heritage got off to a flying start with people of the Stockton's and Martin's fortitude settling the land. And now here are, briefly chronicled, a few more excerpts from authenticated Indian War anecdotes of the valley region.

Colonel James Patton of Battletown was an ocean voyager, veteran of twenty Atlantic crossings prior to his retirement from the sea in 1755. He was busily engaged at writing his memoirs—as so many old soldiers and sailors seem to do down the centuries—scribbling away at his writing desk in the parlor, when he was suddenly transfixed by an Indian arrow winging in through the open window.

Mr. Wolfe, of Frederick Town, was more fortunate. He owned an "Indian dog" whom he swore could smell a redskin a good country mile off and warn his lucky master. And just to be on the safe side, in case his master did not get the message in time, it was said that this remarkable canine was in the habit, when getting on the scent of a skulking "varmint", of rearing up on his hind legs, placing his front paws on his master's shoulders, and propelling Wolfe backwards out of harm's way until the emergency was over. One account of Mr. Wolfe's Indian dog even goes so far as to state that, while backing his master out of danger, the sage animal shook his shaggy head from side to side in mute warning!

The Sheets and Taylor families of Narrow Passage unfortunately did not own such a talented creature and had a dangerously close call with the savages. Both families were caught in ambush on their way by wagon to the safety of the Indian fort at North Fork, and both heads of households were killed instantly in the first exchange of shots between madly careening farmwagons and circling savages. But when the triumphantly whooping Indians rushed the fleeing women and children, Mrs. Sheets took such effective aim with a handy wood axe, while her partner, Mrs. Taylor, did the same with her horse-whip, that the raiding Iroquois took off into the bush with howls of anguish; several of them were nursing ugly whip welts and bleeding stumps where, just a moment before, there had been fiercely groping fingers. Except for the two men who had received the opening surprise gun blast from the enemy, the entire Taylor and Sheets families made it safely to the stockade.

Our final episode in the private trials and tribulations of the Valley settlers, during these gruesome years of death by fire and pillage, deals in a slightly lighter vein, with a lady who was not as warlike by nature as Mesdames Sheets and Taylor. Mrs. Horner was waylaid on her way to the woodshed, and struck down in cold blood by the savages, while her companion in the house—a Mrs. Smith—was carried off captive by the redmen. She returned to civilization three years later and presented her astonished husband, who had been away at the time of her capture, with a brand new half-breed son. I am happy to be able to report that Mr. Smith was of a very understanding and Christian nature and not only forgave his wife, but eventually—once he had fully recovered from the shock—also legally adopted the half-breed into the family.

It is an interesting footnote to the history of the era, to note in passing that many of the prisoners during this violent period along the frontier, especially the younger white women, readily fell into the crude ways of life among the Indian lodges, and never bothered to return home. Three of the Painter girls, carried off in a raid on Woodstock in 1757, married young Indian braves. In that one raid alone, forty-five prisoners were taken by the Indians. It was not until 1766 that the Indian terror subsided completely, some of the last victims in the Valley being a Mennonite preacher named Hans Roth, and most of his family. Hans Roth was gunned down in the doorway of his cabin along the South Fork of the Shenandoah River, while earnestly trying to "reason" with the war party of redskins. His wife and two sons were tomahawked inside the house before it was set on fire. Only two daughters were able to hide in a thick field of hemp behind the burning cabin, watching in horror the wanton slaughter. The last recorded Indian "outrage" took place just south of Woodstock in 1766. After that the Valley was finally free of the red menace, and has remained so ever since.

There were other martyrs—and a number of recognized heroes—during those twelve years of the Valley's initial blood-bath. One local hero was Captain John Ashby of Front Royal, a member of the Second Virginia Rifles, serving as the advance scouting screen for General Braddock during his ill-fated advance from Winchester towards Fort Duquesne. When disaster struck, Major Washington told Ashby to carry the news of the defeat to Governor Dinwiddie at Williamsburg. He was instructed to move fast and to circle the victorious French and their Indian allies now in the midst of an orgy of scalping. So well did Ashby carry out his orders that afterwards Washington was moved to report: "His ride from the field to the capital and back was done with such remarkable dispatch that he was back at his post in Frederick Town almost before I was aware he had departed". Ashby also carried himself with great distinction during the brief flare-up shortly after the French and Indian War known as Lord Dunmore's War, about which we will hear more later. As a reward for his bravery during the battle of Pleasant Point in the Ohio Territory during that conflict, the Virginia House of Burgesses in

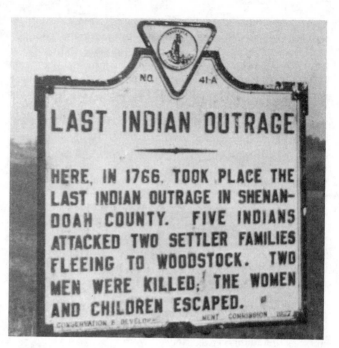

LAST INDIAN OUTRAGE

HERE, IN 1766, TOOK PLACE THE
LAST INDIAN OUTRAGE IN SHENAN-
DOAH COUNTY. FIVE INDIANS
ATTACKED TWO SETTLER FAMILIES
FLEEING TO WOODSTOCK. TWO
MEN WERE KILLED; THE WOMEN
AND CHILDREN ESCAPED.

Williamsburg presented the Front Royal officer with a fine
inlaid watch and, in recognition of his exceptional services,
an additional grant of 2,000 acres of land in that same Ohio
Territory. At that date the Ohio Territory was considered
to be part of the Virginia Colony (it was not incorporated
into the sovereign state of Kentucky until some time after
the American Revolution).

But, beyond question, the greatest and most fabulous
hero of them all during these tense and often terrible times,
with the possible exception of Colonel Washington, was
that veritable Paul Bunyan of a waggoneer-turned-soldier,
Daniel Morgan, who was then a captain in the Virginia
militia at the personal request of Washington. Morgan had
arrived at Frederick Town from New Jersey at the tender
age of six—if anything about a giant-killer who had laid
"Bully" Billy Davis low twice in a row at Berry's Tavern,
could be termed "tender". He had had his first taste of
formal battle as a waggoneer in the supply train of General
Braddock on that fateful trek towards Fort Duquesne. It
was at approximately this same time that he got his first
taste of British arrogance and brutality, in the form of

military "discipline", while hauling supplies for the British Regulars to a forward base at Fort Chiswell, Pennsylvania. He and a young lieutenant, stationed at the fort, were downing a few flagons of ale side by side in the fort's taproom, when Dan Morgan, who already had a snootful, grew too noisy and obstreperous. Ordered to quiet down by the young lieutenant, Morgan flatly refused to do so, replying, instead, with a whole string of oaths and abuse. Whereupon the line officer took out his sword and with the flat of his blade rapped the unruly waggoneer across the backside. This was too much for the alcoholically-inspired frontiersman. Picking up the impeccably attired Britisher by the scruff of his neck and his uniform coat-tails, Morgan playfully tossed the officer out the window. Within twenty-four hours Morgan found himself sentenced to five hundred lashes in front of the assembled post garrison, a sentence which apparently was carried out by the fort blacksmith wielding the cat-o'nine-tails. General Morgan carried the scars of this brutal punishment with him to the grave—both on his mutilated back, and in his heart, which from that day on was filled with a hatred of all things British.

Dr. William Hill was Daniel Morgan's personal physician in later years at Winchester, and attended the dying old hero in his last illness. Once, noting the mass of healed scar tissue on his patient's back as he lay on his side in bed, the doctor was moved to ask Morgan where he had received such terrible wounds. They scarcely resembled the scars usually received in battle. The old warrior is said to have replied: "That was the doing of old King George. Once long ago he promised me five hundred lashes, but the man laying them on miscounted, so old George still owes me one. But now I think he'll not likely collect his due—eh, William?"

A year later, in 1757, Dan Morgan received his second grievous wound, this time in battle. They were the only two serious injuries he was to suffer in a long and active career as waggoneer and soldier. At a place in Pennsylvania named Hanging Rock, he and two companions on horseback rode straight into an Indian ambush while carrying urgent military dispatches back to George Washington's military headquarters in Winchester. Both of his companions were killed in the first volley from beside the trail. Morgan was hit by a musket ball in the back of the neck; the bullet grazed along his right shoulder blade, and then was deflected upward and out of his body through his right jaw and cheek, carrying away all of his teeth and much of his jawbone on that side of his face. Covered with blood and in severe shock, Morgan somehow managed to remain upright in his saddle, clutching his horse's mane in both hands to steady himself. He drove his heels into the excited animal's flanks, urging him forward through the startled ring of dancing, war-whooping savages, to safety. He arrived at Winchester, more dead than alive, to hand over the urgent request for reinforcements for the beleaguered garrison at Hanging Rock. It was a full six months before he completely recovered from this major wound.

Upon his complete recovery, Morgan was commissioned a captain in the Virginia militia by Colonel Washington. He then promptly set about recruiting and training his own unit of crack militia sharpshooters, for use in the Indian conflict, later to be known as "Morgan's Virginia Rifles". At a later date, during the American Revolution they won for themselves and their commander wide national acclaim at the battles of Cowpens and Saratoga.

The outstanding hero of them all, however, during the tense times of the Indian Wars, was Morgan's supreme commander in that war, as well as in the Revolution— General George Washington. The pressures upon Washington, who was still a young man at the time, as head of the rag-tag, untried Virginia militia throughout the war, were enormous. His intimate knowledge of the valley terrain and the wilderness as far west as Fort Duquesne, largely gleaned from his stints as Lord Fairfax's chief surveyor and Governor Dinwiddie's head scout into the French-held territory to the west, was of little help in his almost hopeless task of molding a fighting force out of the green militiamen Dinwiddie sent him. Nor was his task made any lighter by the continual icy superiority and bungling of the British officers placed in command over him. The Virginia House of Burgesses and the Royal Governor at the colonial capital repeatedly compounded his problems either by completely ignoring his urgent requests for more and better-equipped troops or, when he did get them, failing to come up with the supplies and pay needed to keep them in fighting trim. That he managed to accomplish the miracles he did, under the circumstances, was not only a great tribute to his stubborn will and ingenuity, but also a happy indication of the great qualities of organization and leadership he was to display in behalf of his country in the years ahead.

And now, to wind up this chapter on a happy note, one final anecdote involving the two principal heroes mentioned above. Although Captain Morgan's wound healed cleanly enough—leaving him only with a badly scarred cheek and no teeth on the right side of what remained of his jaw—by the time he had risen to full general after his brilliant victory against Burgoyne at Saratoga, the toothless right side of his face had become somewhat of a social liability. To put it quite frankly, he could not chew on that side of his mouth, and the repeated mealtime acrobatics in mastication which the loss involved soon became a steady irritant to his commander in chief during that bleak and unhappy winter of enforced idleness at Valley Forge. Finally, George Washington could stand the noise and gymnastics no longer. Whereupon he, already possessing a set of steel and silver false teeth, fashioned for him by a silversmith in Boston, ordered a set made for his second in command. When the two great American heroes finally went to their separate resting places at the end of their long and illustrious careers, each did so wearing a set of false teeth custom-made for him by another hero of the American Revolution—Paul Revere.

Daniel Morgan

VII

THE AMERICAN REVOLUTION

The gruelling and prolonged experiences of the French and Indian War left their marks on the Valley people in more ways than one. The British bumbling and indifference throughout the long struggle, as well as their high and mighty attitude of aloof superiority, thoroughly disillusioned the settlers as to English invincibility and leadership. Even before the fighting was over, Governor Dinwiddie had been forced to imprison, on charges of sedition, at least one opponent of British rule and inefficiency at Williamsburg. Another outspoken critic of English stupidity was jailed at Staunton for calling both His Most Imperial British Majesty and the Royal Governor of the Virginia Colony, "blockheads", in the town square. A third had labelled the British Regulars and their Hessian mercenaries "Lobster Backs". And he further called them, after the wilderness campaign against the French, "a bunch of toy tin soldiers who couldn't shoot a sparrow" and "not worth a farthing in a fight". Throughout the thirteen colonies, complaints were being openly voiced about taxation without representation and the high-handed methods of the British press gangs, on land and sea, who literally kidnapped free men for service in the Royal Navy and elsewhere. Thus began the first rumblings of discontent which were to lead to the war for independence.

In the Virginia Colony this discontent first boiled over against the unpopular successor to Governor Fauquier, the Earl of Dunmore. Without so much as a by-your-leave from the populace, he twice summarily dissolved the Virginia Assembly at Williamsburg. These actions, coupled with his unpopular "Lord Dunmore's War" against the Indians in the Ohio Territory, brought on Lord Dunmore's hasty recall to England in the summer of 1775, for reassignment as Governor of the Bahama Islands. But by the end of his brief tenure, (1772-1775) the damage had already been done both in Williamsburg, and along the western frontier.

53

British popularity and prestige reached a new low in the colonies; in fact, after an abortive attempt of the burghers of Williamsburg to seize the powder magazine and royal arsenal in the colonial capital, the Royal Governor was obliged to hole up in his palace, surrounded by a ring of British Redcoats with fixed bayonets and powder charges in their muskets.

He had begun his unpopular reign by twice dissolving the Assembly, first in 1772, then again at the height of his "war" in 1774. Lord Dunmore's War was being fought to drive the Indians out of the Ohio Territory so that the unpaid militia veterans of the French and Indian War could take up the government land grants they had received in lieu of their long-overdue pay. Then right in the middle of the war, Lord Dunmore called it off without a word of explanation, sending the militia home, and himself retiring to embattled Williamsburg.

A number of prominent Valley men and veteran Indian fighters were involved in this second brief war against the redmen, including Captain John Ashby of Front Royal, little White Dove's brother, Major Andrew Lewis of Staunton, and Colonel Angus McDonald of "Glengary", Winchester. It was in the middle of all of Lord Dunmore's mounting troubles that, in the fall of 1773, a drover from Winchester named Jacob Baumgartner, and his son, returned from a freight run to Boston with a strange tale. The two Virginia waggoneers had witnessed the dumping of an entire cargo of valuable tea into Boston Harbor by a band of brightly painted English-speaking "Indians". As far back as 1765, Patrick Henry, then a member of the Virginia House of Burgesses, had risen at a meeting of that august body in Richmond to deliver his first inflammatory speech against the Stamp Act, shouting to the rafters at the close of his seditious outburst, "If this be treason, then make the most of it!". In 1775 he followed up his original public blast against unreasonable taxation with his celebrated and stirring lines delivered in the First Presbyterian Church in the same city—"Give me liberty or give me death! Death to all tyrants!"

Rebellion shifted again to Boston, a city already deeply aroused by the wanton killing of three unarmed civilians on Boston Common in what later was to become popularly known as "The Boston Massacre." In April of 1775, Paul Revere made his famous ride through the countryside, and soon the war was on, sparked by the pitched battle between the "Lobster Backs" and the minutemen at Lexington and Concord. Soon after the Battle of Bunker (or Breed's) Hill, Virginians were in the forefront of the action. George Washington quickly answered the call to arms, as did his fellow Indian fighter from the Valley, Daniel Morgan, now a major in the colonial militia. He and his crack Virginia Rifles stood in the front ranks drawn up on Harvard campus at Cambridge, Massachusetts, on August 7, 1775, as Washington was administered the oath of Supreme Commander of the Continental Army.

Now came the time when all of the stern experience and training of the Valley blood-bath of 1753-1764 in the Indian wars paid off to the benefit of the infant Republic fighting for its freedom. It was this very reserve pool of Indian-fighting, sharp-eyed veterans from the Carolinas, Maryland, Virginia, Pennsylvania, and New York State, that produced the hard core of the fighting strength of the Continental Armies. Buckskin-legginged, coonskin-capped experts with the tomahawk, long-rifle, and axe were ready and waiting for action, and they were deadly marksmen, experienced in the ways of the wilderness, and wise to every use of tree and cover.

Among the many Valley men who carried themselves with great courage throughout the war, to name a random few, were: Colonel Thomas Allen of Limeton, who at the end of hostilities received a handsome silver sword from the Virginia Assembly for his service; Colonel Charles Thruston of Milldale, known as "the fighting parson"; Major Isaac Hite, Jr. of "Belle Grove"; and his cousin, General George Bowman of nearby "Long Meadows". There were also John Buck, George and Jeremiah Matthews, William Jennings, John Harden, Baylis Earle, John North, John Ray, Marcus Calmes, Jacob Stickley, and Abraham and Jeremiah McKay, all of Warren County. Other officers and men from the Valley who served with distinction during the American Revolution were: Major Robert Wood of "Glen Burnie", son of the founder of Winchester; innkeeper Peter Lauck of the Red Lion Inn; Colonel William Washington of Warrenton; Colonel Lewis Washington, along with the two brothers of George Washington—Charles and Sam, all from Charles Town. Nathaniel Burwell of Millwood, builder of magnificent Carter Hall, also covered himself with glory, as did General Horatio Gates—along with Daniel Morgan.

55

Then there was the Reverend Peter Muhlenberg of Woodstock, who led his German Lutheran parishioners out of his church after a rousing sermon ending with a call to arms from the pulpit. Andrew Lewis of Staunton was then a Brigadier General in the Continental Army, a rank he had won throughout three major wars. But not all of the Valley's great figures and landowners were loyal heroes. Thomas, Lord Fairfax, of Winchester, was an outspoken Tory, and promptly retreated to his country seat at Greenway Court near White Post, to wait out the war.

Experienced leadership in battle and military manpower were not the only Valley contributions for the fighting front. The primitive smelters dug into the limestone hillsides of the Shenandoah Valley were one of the four principal sources of pig iron for the forges in Maryland and Pennsylvania. Besides pig iron, the Valley also produced grain and flour, leather and meat, fruit, vegetables, and lumber for the cause of freedom. But everything was not entirely wine and roses as far as the Valley's contribution to the war went. To be sure, Gates and Morgan won a glorious victory at Saratoga, thereby foiling the British General Burgoyne's masterful attempt at cutting the Thirteen Colonies in half. Then, at a later date, January 17, 1781, Morgan won a second spectacular victory, at Cowpens with the help of "The Swamp Fox", Colonel Francis Marion, over the hated Lord Bannister Tarleton, known as the scourge of the Carolinas.

At Charleston, South Carolina, General Charles Lee of Charles Town drove the British—and their vaunted fleet— from the very sea gates of that key port. However, he eventually fell into utter disgrace and was court-martialed and cashiered out of the army after his miserable showing at Valley Forge and Monmouth Courthouse.

Charles Lee had enjoyed a very checkered, and, at times, dubious career in both the Polish and British armies abroad before coming to America. He was an extremely cocky and vain man and his ego greatly expanded with his success at Charleston. Thereafter Lee began plotting with a group of congressmen in the First Continental Congress, who were dissatisfied with General Washington's military performance at the time, to replace the supreme commander in the field. Fortunately, General Lee's capture by the British soon put an end to his political maneuvering.

However, he was paroled in time to take part in the

Battle of Monmouth Courthouse, during which his miserable leadership and cowardice came close to robbing the Continentals of their victory, and earned his court-martial and dismissal in disgrace from the army. At the crucial moment of the battle, when Washington already had the British Regulars and their Hessian henchmen retreating in great disorder towards the seacoast, Lee, mistaking their rout for a counter-attack against his flank column, ordered his men to retreat in the face of the enemy trying to fight their way out of the pocket the Continentals had formed around them.

It was at the height of this tense moment, shortly after George Washington had been informed of the impending disaster, that perhaps one of the most intimate and colorful word pictures of General Washington in battle was drawn for posterity by either friend or foe. Washington was well-known for his quick temper at times, and on that day he swore. And how he swore, dashing up and down the length of Lee's retreating column on horseback, trying desperately to rally his men—often with the aid of the flat of his naked sword! Years later, when asked about the incident, one of his generals replied with great feeling:"Yes, sir, he swore once that I know of. At Monmouth Court House on a day that would have made any man swear. He swore that day until the very leaves shook on the trees; charmingly, delightfully. Never have I enjoyed such swearing before or since. Sir, on that memorable day he swore like an angel from heaven."

From the other side of the coin comes this dramatic word portrait of the American supreme commander in action. An English subaltern reportedly wrote in his diary after the battle:

"I and Will Harker crouched under a summacke bushe that day, our eyes bleary, and choking in the smoke of battle, when suddenly out of the gunsmoke there appeared a tall figure on horseback, so dashing and gallant as he strove to rally his men, that I perforce lowered my musket without firing a shot at pointblank range. So, for some reason, did Will. The man was in such a towering rage and hurry, galloping up and down the line on his great white horse, oblivious to everything but turning the tide of war, that I could not bring myself to shoot him down."

To close this chapter on the American Revolution and its effect on the Valley and its people—as well as vice-

versa—I present this last anecdote as at least one explanation as to how Fort Valley got its name.

During that gloomy and grim winter at Valley Forge,
George Washington was pondering whether to retreat with
the remnants of his half-starved, ragged army to some
impregnable natural stronghold far to the west and south,
or whether to advance to surprise attack on the now
over-confident British bivouacked in New Jersey. A favorite
haunt came to General Washington's mind from his younger
days under Lord Fairfax. South of Winchester there was
a long, narrow valley, guarded by steep mountains on
either side, watered by a good stream down its center, with
high gorges at either end which could readily be barricaded
and fortified. Promptly, Washington sent his fellow Vir-
ginian, Dan Morgan, with a company of engineers, to survey
the area and, if feasible, to construct a log road to its
northern gateway to accommodate his artillery and supply
wagons if need be.

All we know today is that the road was built, for its
remains—and those of several gun emplacements atop the
peaks at the Elizabeth Furnace entrance to Fort Valley—
still are discernible. Upon completion of the project,
Morgan returned to Valley Forge, only to discover that his
superior had finally made up his mind to attack the British
in New Jersey, rather than retreat into Virginia. As history
has long since proven, this decision turned out to be a
blessing for the future of the infant Republic.

POSTREVOLUTIONARY GROWTH

In the wake of the struggle for independence, commerce boomed in the Valley during the early 1800's. The principal exports from the area were lumber, pig iron, hemp, grain, wool, leathergoods, flour, and tanbark from the sumac trees with which to cure hides. Lime and limestone were also valuable valley exports, along with pork products from the corn-fattened swine and beef. Waterground flour and corn-meal were turned out at a host of streamside mills—one of the largest of these stood at the foot of Belair Hill in Front Royal. Other large mills were at Buckton on the Strasburg road, Wakeman's Mill on Passage Creek near Waterlick, and Bowman's Mill on Cedar Creek north of Strasburg. The big Timberlake Mill in Clarke County gave its name to Milldale, as did Burwell's Mill to nearby Millwood. In fact there were two mills at Milldale, the second located at Mt. Zion. All of these, as well as the humming mills along the Opequon river around Frederick Town, were driven by flumes diverting the waters of the millstreams onto the blades of the huge waterwheels, which in turn drove the heavy stone grinding wheels through a complicated series of wooden gears and sprockets. One such mill, with all of its wooden works still intact, can be seen at Kline's Mill, three miles east of Middletown.

There were a number of fords across the shallows of the Shenandoah River, the most popular one at Front Royal being Kendrick's Ford at the foot of Kendrick Lane. Ferries were also very much in demand for the increasing flow of commerce, especially McKay's Ferry over the South Fork of the Shenandoah River at the Page-Warren County line, and bustling Chester Ferry at Riverton, which carried horse-men, foot passengers, and freight wagons north from Front Royal towards Winchester; it went into public operation on October 19, 1736, under the management of—you guessed it—a Mr. Chester. In issuing him his permit to operate the ferry, the town fathers officially licensed him (still in the courthouse records):

> *"to keep a publicke ferrie and charge the price of threepence per crossing for each man; plus an additional threepence for his horse if he rode one."*

Castleman's Ferry, east of Berryville, was also in great public demand, as was Mr. Harper's Ferry at the river port of the same name at the junction of the Shenandoah and Potomac Rivers. George Washington was very much interested in the navigation potential of both rivers, and as early as 1798, the Virginia Assembly granted a charter to the Shenandoah Company to operate a fleet of flatboat barges on the river. By 1820 the drovers and river bargemen were faced by a new kind of competition in heavy transportation—the canal companies. By the late 1820's the James River Canal Company was in business, moving heavy barges through some fifty locks between Lynchburg and Richmond. Shortly thereafter, the first stretches of the Chesapeake and Potomac Canal—later to be enlarged into the Chesapeake and Ohio Canal all the way to Cumberland, Maryland—were completed and open to traffic. The Shenandoah River remained commercially navigable until around 1880, when the water level finally became too low for safe or efficient barge operation except during the spring rains and flood seasons. By then, the railroads had taken over most of the heavy freight traffic in the Valley and beyond the Blue Ridge.

The freight wagons, too, were growing larger. The first to appear were the clumsy prototypes of the "Knoxville Wagons", which, in turn, gave way to the famous Conestoga Wagons (which played such a major role in the winning of the west, as "covered wagons"). The bigger Knoxville models were drawn by teams of as many as eight or ten horses, with doubled teams for the steep mountain grades through the passes. For more cozy travel there were private carriages and coaches similar to the one Thomas Jefferson loaned James and Dolley Madison for their long and dusty trip from Philadelphia to their wedding at George Washington's nephew's home near Charles Town, "Harewood", (built in 1771 by the first President's brother, Colonel Samuel Washington). By then, the first regularly scheduled mail stages were cruising the Valley floor and there was even a crude variety of pony express for fast mail service throughout the region. And, of course, for the man who could not afford a horse, there was always "shank's mare", or foot travel.

Men like Thomas Jefferson, James Madison, George Washington, Major Isaac Hite, Jr., and James Monroe seemed to be constantly on the move about the Valley, sometimes on business, sometimes on pleasure trips. Distinguished visitors from far and near flocked to the fashionable health spas of the area "to take the waters", coming from as far afield as Alexandria, Washington, Baltimore, and Philadelphia to enjoy the mineral waters at Bath (later named Berkeley Springs), Hot Springs, and Warm Springs. Among the most foreign and distinguished of them all were the three Bourbon brothers, Louis Philippe, Duc d'Orleans, later king of France (1830-1848), the Duc de Montpensier, and the youngest in exile of the royal line, the diminutive Duc de Beaujolais. The first part of their extensive travels into the frontier, from their home base in exile of Philadelphia, took them to Mount Vernon, where their gracious host mapped out their route to the western frontier and Indian outposts in Kentucky and Tennessee. The first leg of their journey took them through Leesburg to Winchester, and thence down the old Indian Trace, or Valley Pike, to Cumberland Gap beyond frontier Bristol. En route, the

Virginia State Library

Loudoun Street, Winchester — 1845

three royal brothers visited the President's nephew, George Steptoe Washington, at "Harewood", the mineral baths at "Bath" beyond, and a Mr. Philip Bush, German proprietor

61

of "The Golden Buck" in Winchester, who was well known for his democratic ways and hot temper. Upon requesting their evening meal served in their rooms because of a brief indisposition of one of the three dukes travelling incognito, the host flew into a rage at the mere temerity of the request, and ordered them to leave immediately if they would not take their supper in the public dining room among "their equals, if not their betters". Whereupon the three royal youths were obliged to move on to Strasburg to seek less militantly democratic lodgings.

Toll roads were springing up all over the Valley, and two such roads met at Double Tollgate, halfway between Front Royal and Winchester, and gave that tiny hamlet its name. It is interesting to note that one of these two toll roads continued in operation until 1922. Tolls were also collected in the form of town taxes in transit. Such a municipal town tollhouse still stands at the center of Shepherdstown, West Virginia—once known as Mecklenburg, Virginia. It is now the combined Odd Fellows Hall and town library. While on the subject of the origin of town names, let us pursue this fascinating item further as it concerns the Valley.

We have already learned that Berryville got its original name from Benjamin Berry's popular free-for-alls on the lawn of his crossroads tavern. White Post, near Double Tollgate and Berryville, in Clarke County, got its name from the tall wooden highway marker set up at the community's only crossroads by George Washington back in 1750, on orders from his nearby employer at Greenway Court, Lord Fairfax. Warren County, founded in 1836, was named in honor of Joseph Warren, Massachusetts patriot who was the first American to lose his life in the Battle of Bunker Hill at the start of the American Revolution. There is a school of thought which says that Warrenton was also named in his honor, but this latter statement remains open to question. Nearby Cedarville however was obviously named for its trees.

Front Royal was first named "Helltown" in honor of the riotous living of the packmen, rivermen, and waggoneers in the local pubs and wenching parlors while either awaiting transportation across the river on Mr. Chester's ferry, or the transhipping of their goods into the river barges. Later it was changed to either Luce or Lehew Town in honor of the tavern where much of this horseplay occured.

How it eventually got the name Front Royal is a matter of legend and considerable conjecture. One account has it

that during the latter part of the eighteenth century, before
the American Revolution, a British garrison of Redcoats
was stationed at Front Royal to protect the teeming trade
routes from the French and Indians. The "royal oak" stood
at one end of the town common where the Red coats
drilled, its stump now located under the front steps of the
Stokes Clothing Store on East Main Street. One day, in
drilling his British Regulars, the drill master barked the
order, in accents both loud and probably cockney: "Front
the royal oak!"

Winchester, first named Frederick Town in honor of a
prince of the House of Orange, was renamed in 1752,
largely as the result of its designation at about that date as
the official seat of the northern Virginia diocese of the
Church of England; its name stemmed from the capital
cathedral city of the same name in far off Hampshire.
Staunton was named for Lady Rebecca Staunton, benefactress of the town founder, John Lewis. Strasburg took its
name from the capital city in Alsace, whence came many of
its first settlers back in 1734. Middleburg in Loudoun
County got its name for obvious geographical reasons, with
its location on the postroad halfway between Alexandria
and Winchester. The same goes for Middletown, approximately halfway between Strasburg and Winchester. Strasburg, incidentally, was long famous for its fine earthenware
pottery, fashioned from the native clay by Joist Hite's
German settlers. Middletown, on the other hand, was
known during the first half of the nineteenth century, for
its fine clocks and precision navigational and surveying instruments, manufactured by George Danner and his family.
Charles Town was named in honor of its founder, George
Washington's brother, Colonel Charles Washington, who
donated the land on which the community was built and
himself built lovely "Happy Retreat" there (later renamed
"Mordington").

Berkeley Springs long was known simply as "Bath",
probably in remembrance of the English spa of the same
name, but the name was eventually changed to its present
form in honor of John Lederer's first skeptical sponsor in
the discovery of the Valley, the royal governor, Sir William
Berkeley. Fauquier County was named for another colonial
governor, Lord Fauquier; Fairfax County for the area's
number one landlord; and Loudoun County for George
Washington's superior officer in Boston during the French

and Indian War, the Earl of Loudoun. Warrenton was named for its founder, Warren Greene; Leesburg for Thomas Lee father of General Francis Lightfoot Lee; and so it goes all up and down the Valley and the Blue Ridge.

In the human category, the "drovers", who served as the early traders, packmen, merchants, bankers, and waggoneers of the region, received their names not merely because they drove the produce and freight to market by pack horse or wagon, but also because they literally drove the frontier farmer's livestock to market for him, often tied behind their wagons. And they collected the homesteader's cash receipts for him and delivered same on their next trip to their client's area, thus serving as middlemen or bankers.

As far back as the winter of 1785, a tinkerer-inventor by the name of James Rumsey—"Crazy James Rumsey" they called him at Shepherdstown—was tinkering on a strange contraption at that community east of Charles Town. For three years, to the amusement of his fellow townspeople, he cussed and banged away at his "flying teakettle". On a raw December day, in 1787, on a curve of the Potomac River nearby, Rumsey launched the first successful steamboat in history—some twenty-five years before Robert Fulton navigated his more sophisticated "Claremont" down the Hudson River. Rumsey's boat, unlike Fulton's, was not driven by paddle sidewheels, but propelled by what probably was the world's first water jet, a mode of small pleasure-boat propulsion very much in vogue today.

Model of Rumsey's Steamboat

On the day of Rumsey's first trial run with his insane invention, the entire neighborhood turned out, lining the cliffs above the river, to laugh and jeer. Their jeers soon turned to cheers, however, as Rumsey's "flying teakettle", leaking steam from every crudely soldered joint of its copper boiler, gained momentum and began steaming up-stream against the river current at a rousing four miles an hour!

Among the spectators lining the cliff edge was no less a dignitary than General Horatio Gates, who had come to see the fun from his home, nearby "Traveller's Rest", at Kearneysville. Upon seeing Rumsey start upstream against the current, the victorious hero of the battle of Saratoga is said to have tossed his stovepipe hat high in the air and cheered like a youngster with the best of them, shouting—"My God! She moves!". She not only moved up-stream then, against the current under her wheezing jet pro-pulsion, but did so again, often and successfully, once a proper boiler had been installed in her open engine room. Benjamin Franklin—no mean "tinkerer" himself—soon headed the "Rumseyan Society", as the inventor's holding company on the patent was called. The Society sponsored Rumsey's trip to England to demonstrate a more advanced model, "The Columbian Maid", on the Thames River to a group of scientists, engineers, and spectators including James Watt and Sir Benjamin Rush, later the inventor of the first reciprocal steam engine.

Although the trial runs of "The Columbian Maid" were a bitter disappointment and brought financial ruin and, even-tually, premature death to her inventor, Rumsey was invited to lecture before a select audience of the members of the Royal Society of Mechanical Arts. It was during this lecture that suddenly he died of a stroke. He was the first American officially buried with full Parliamentary sanction in West-minster Abbey, where he still reposes. Belatedly and post-humously, in 1893, he was awarded a special gold medal by the American Congress; and it was followed some years later by a monument in a riverside park of his home town, Shepherdstown, West Virginia.

In another part of the Valley—the year 1838, and the location Augusta County—another inventor was busy at work on a strange contraption, this time landbased: a horse-drawn rig. It was not until two years later, in 1840 at Middletown, that Cyrus McCormick first successfully dem-

65

onstrated his revolutionary horsedrawn mechanical reaper. Although originally a Yankee import from Connecticut, another successful inventor-turned-industrial-tycoon of the same period was James Gibbs, who along with his partner, Robert Cox, began turning out the world's first efficient portable home sewing machines at a factory near Raphine, Virginia.

Another valley man was born at Timberville, the grandson of a charter member of Dan Morgan's crack Virginia Rifles, and moved west at an early age. He became Governor of Kentucky and then a founder of the state of Texas. His name was Sam Houston. Ephraim McDowell, a graduate of the University of Edinburg in Scotland and a native of Rockbridge County, performed what is said to have been the first successful abdominal surgery in modern medicine by removing a benign tumor from a very frightened young woman out in Kentucky in 1809. But long before even this early date people had begun to move about the Valley and its environs with ever-increasing ease.

Major Isaac Hite, Jr. of Middletown attended William & Mary College down at Williamsburg and received both a degree, and one of the first Phi Beta Kappa keys ever awarded in this country. George Washington travelled back and forth between his home at Mount Vernon, and Winchester, Philadelphia, New York, Annapolis, and Boston as if he were driving a modern sports car. Thomas Jefferson did likewise. At one time or another all of them visited such health spas as Berkeley Springs, where there were nightly cards and dancing during the season, and at Warm Springs, somewhat further to the south. One carefully itemized bill for a night's lodging incurred by Thomas Jefferson on a visit to the inn at Warm Springs, contains the following revealing items:

Madeira wine ....7 pence
Two cooked quail ....6 pence
Claret, little ....6 pence
All other wines .... 4 shillings
Strong beer..7 pence
West Indies rum pr. gil ....1 shilling 4 pence
Continental ditto .... 3 shillings 4 pence
Whiskey pr. gil.. 2 shillings
Double Distilled ditto .... 4 shillings
Pasture for a horse one night ....6 pence
Stableage with hay & fodder pr. night ....9 pence

Lodging with clean sheets pr. night...................... 6 shillings
Breakfast ....1 shilling
Dinner ....1 shilling 3 pence
Supper..1 shilling
Oates & corn pr. gallon.............................1 shilling 6 pence
Punch pr. quan. .... 2 shillings 6 pence
Toddy pr. quan...1 shilling 3 pence
A cold supper ....1 shilling 9 pence

Jefferson's other two favorite spots in the Valley, which he frequently visited from either Washington or his home near Charlottesville, were Natural Bridge and the hanging rock at Harpers Ferry.

Between the years 1817 and 1825, his term of office as President of the United States, James Monroe spent a great deal of his time at his lovely brick home, "Oak Hill", south of Leesburg. It was built for him by the same architectual genius who produced the Capitol and the White House in nearby Washington—James Hoban. Farther south in the Valley, the Carters, the Randolphs, and the Burwells were lavishly entertaining an endless succession of distinguished guests. Their magnificent valley and Piedmont estates were surrounded by formal gardens, woods, and rich croplands, and set among limestone or clay fields liberally dotted with grazing sheep, cattle, and some of the finest thoroughbred horseflesh in the country.

John Brown

IX

CIVIL WAR
IN THE VALLEY

In the year 1859, a strange and sinister figure with his three sons slipped quietly into the Valley through its northern gate at Harpers Ferry. His name was John Brown—alias Isaac Smith, Shubal Morgan, or Osawatomie Brown—a man with a criminal record and a price on his head as a murderer, placed there by no less a personage than the President of the United States, Abraham Lincoln. This was done long before Brown and his three sons, plus some fanatic followers, went into hiding at a remote farmhouse in nearby Knoxville, Maryland. Like Braddock's defeat in the wilderness at the hands of the French and Indians, John Brown's raid on the federal arsenal at Harpers Ferry is in every schoolboy's history book; but few of the textbooks go on to say that in reality Osawatomie Brown was a madman, the leader of a weird fanatic religious sect, and a compulsive killer with at least two cases of wanton mass murder on his hands—one in Kansas, one in Canada.

Although a self-proclaimed abolitionist and "preacher", there was insanity in John Brown's family. Both his mother and grandmother, as well as three uncles back home in Torrington, Connecticut, had died in insane asylums. Actually, although accused of madness by the sworn testimony of seventeen different witnesses at his trial in Jefferson County Courthouse, Charles Town, in the wake of his useless raid on the federal arsenal, Brown was in reality only a sinister kind of symbol. He was a symbol of the general sickness already, by 1859, gripping much of the North American continent, brought on by a long period of peace and prosperity, and too much time to complain and grumble. Instead of revealing his true colors, the religious fanatic and self-styled abolitionist, with the blazing eyes and chin whiskers, was forever immortalized in the opening lines of the stirring Battle Hymn of the Republic, soon the marching song of the Union forces during the Civil War:

"John Brown's body lies a'mouldering in the grave".

What few Americans know is that in addition to his two acts of fanatical homicide, he kidnapped at gunpoint one of George Washington's descendants, Colonel Lewis Washington of Charles Town, from his home, after accepting the colonel's hospitality; and beat him unmercifully at Harpers Ferry. John Brown was hung on December 2, 1859, at Charles Town, not only as a maniac and a trouble-maker, but also as a murderer. Prior to his capture, it required the combined talents of Colonels J.E.B. Stuart and Robert E. Lee, both then officers in the United States Army, to overpower Brown and his renegades, and to drive them from their barricades inside a fire engine house.

Although John Brown's raid shook the entire nation that summer of 1859 as a prelude to the Civil War, the war itself did not come until almost a year later with the firing on Fort Sumter in Charleston Harbor. Much of the long and tragic war took place in the Valley, highlighted by Stonewall Jackson's brilliant, lightning campaigns against the Union commanders, Banks, Sheridan, and Shields. Books, treatises, histories, and novels literally by the thousands have already been written on this painful subject. Therefore, it is our intention, in this brief story, to spare you further lengthy repetitions and to concentrate instead on two extremely romantic and colorful local figures in that long conflict. Both of them were little known to the general public, but both were extremely active throughout the entire war in the area: Major John Singleton Mosby, better known as "The Grey Ghost of the Confederacy", who was a veritable Robin Hood in grey; and Belle Boyd, the highly controversial female Confederate spy from Martinsburg and Front Royal, who was reputedly such a help to Stonewall Jackson.

Although John Singleton Mosby was born in Powhatan County, forty miles west of Richmond, Virginia, it is only with his dashing and meteoric career as a cavalry officer in the Confederate army—all of it concentrated either in the northern valley area or just to the east in the Blue Ridge Piedmont—that we are concerned in this thumbnail sketch. Throughout the Civil War the cavalry served as the scouts—the eyes and ears—of the field commanders. Colonel Jeb Stuart served in this key capacity for Robert E. Lee. The most famous of his probings on horseback was his celebrated "ride around McClelland" in front of the defenses of Richmond. Colonel Turner Ashby of Markham

and Front Royal, served in like capacity for Stonewall
Jackson in the Valley. Working closely with Turner Ashby,
and taking over his scout and probing assignment after that
gallant calvaryman's death in 1862, was Major John Mosby,
known to both armies as "The Grey Ghost". He was a
constant thorn in the flesh of the Union commanders
maneuvering from their field headquarters at Fairfax
Courthouse and, upon occasion, Manassas, Virginia.

Mosby's specialties were lightning-quick raids and
phantom flank attacks, many of them deep behind the
enemy lines, while Jackson marched up and down the main
valley in a classic series of maneuvers which not only
constantly kept the Union Army off balance and very much
occupied, but which also still appear in many military
textbooks as classic examples of military strategy and
maneuver. Mosby was also a steady and ample provider of
food and military material for Jackson's flying columns; he
brought in sorely-needed provisions, cattle, horses, medicines, and ammunition, as well as cash, for the slowly
strangling southern cause. His cavalry unit, which the
Federal general staff bitterly referred to as "gorilla
fighters", were in fact a band of highly-trained, casually-

uniformed horsemen
officially listed on the
Confederate payrolls as
"Mosby's Rangers", al-
though Mosby affec-
tionately dubbed them
"The Tam O'Shanter
Boys". When captured
by the Union forces, as
happened on several oc-
casions—notably at War-
renton, Middleburg,
and Riverton near Front
Royal—they were given
short shrift by their

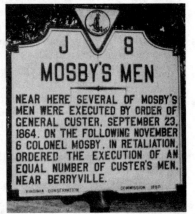

captors, and quickly strung up to the nearest tree without
benefit of trial. Six Rangers were thus summarily executed
at Riverton, and four more at Middleburg; but the Grey
Ghost himself seemed to lead a charmed life. He was never
captured, and only once seriously wounded—at a house near
Rector's Crossroads just before the end of the war. By then he

had been promoted to Lieutenant Colonel by General Robert E. Lee for his daring exploits.

Perhaps Mosby's most remarkable single exploit of the entire war, and a good one with which to commence this brief account of his adventures, started just to the west of Aldie in Loudoun County, at a place called Dover, on the evening of March 8, 1863. In spite of numerous dashing portraits to the contrary, Major Mosby never wore a sword into combat, preferring two sets of trusty Colt revolvers, one brace tucked in his waist-band, the other strapped in twin holsters on his saddle. He did, however, upon occasion, affect a cavalry cape, and always wore a plummed, broad-brimmed hat on horseback. On this particular night, which was raw, black as the inside of his hat, and rainy—ideal weather for a raid behind enemy lines—his flowing cavalry cape must have felt especially welcome.

At all events, assembling according to plan at Dover in the steadily pouring rain, all twenty-nine men in Mosby's hand-picked unit for the raid set off on a pre-arranged course eastward through Aldie Gap, and, three miles from Chantilly, turned off the main road onto an obscure path known best by their guide for the night, John Underwood. It was Mosby's plan to cut through the triangle formed by the intersection of the Little River Turnpike, the Warrenton-Centreville highway, and Frying Pan Road, thus avoiding the Union pickets by passing through a thick grove of alders in the darkness. The men dismounted here and led their mounts single file through the wet bushes, their hands firmly clamped over their horse's quivering nostrils to prevent any whinnying back and forth between the mounts on the opposing sides, which would promptly have given them away. Part of the Ranger unit got lost and was forced to turn back into the foothills, but the balance, once safely past the Federal pickets guarding the lightly-held highways, quickly remounted and set off at a brisk canter, their accoutrements brazenly rattling and clinking in imitation of the enemy patrols they had just circumvented, down the Warrenton-Centreville road. From time to time they paused long enough in the pitch-black night to climb key telegraph poles and cut the wires. To every passing challenge in the rainy darkness, either Mosby or their guide replied jauntily, "New York Fifth Cavalry on patrol"—a Federal unit known to be active in the area.

It was 2 o'clock in the morning when they reached their

destination at Fairfax Courthouse, which was General
Stoughton's headquarters, as well as that of Mosby's cavalry
arch-rival in the sector, Colonel Percy Wyndham. Upon
reaching their goal and finding all the Union headquarters'
troops sound asleep in their quarters, including several of
the sentries who were intent on keeping out of the cold
rain, Mosby divided up his small force, sending one group
to round up the horses in Wyndham's command, and the
other to do likewise at General Stoughton's. Then they
were to rout all of the officers out of bed and take them
prisoner. At the time Mosby had no thought of kidnapping
in mind, but a sleepy-eyed sentry who, upon capture,
identified himself as one of the guards on duty at the
headquarters of General Edwin Stoughton, soon gave the
Grey Ghost an added inspiration. It was but the work of a
moment to force the terrified sentry to point out the
general's personal sleeping quarters in the home of a Dr.
Gunnell, down the street. In no time at all Mosby was
knocking at the door and, in reply to a sleepy "Who's
there?" from inside, smartly replied in a crisp military
manner, "Fifth New York Cavalry with a dispatch for
General Stoughton".

When the door opened, a speechless young Lieutenant
Prentiss of Stoughton's staff found himself staring down
the glinting barrel of Mosby's revolver.

"Lead me to the general's room", ordered the Grey
Ghost icily.

General Stoughton was lying in bed under the covers,
very much asleep. Pulling away the groggy Vermonter's
covers and finding that this, alone, failed to rouse him,
Mosby now did the one unpardonable thing no one ever is
supposed to do to a Brigadier General. He slapped the
general sharply on his exposed behind. The startled general
officer sat up to look straight down the barrel of a gun as
the figure bending over him asked, "General, did you ever
hear of Mosby?".

"Yes, have you caught him?" eagerly asked the still
drowsy General.

"He has caught you!" replied the Grey Ghost in
triumph.

Giving both the general and his staff little time to dress
for their long damp ride west through their own lines,
Mosby and his Rangers soon had the whole captive column,
including a rich haul of Colonel Wyndham's best mounts

and men, trotting under escort, carefully bound and gagged, back towards Warrenton. When the bedraggled group reached Confederate headquarters at Culpeper, Mosby turned Stoughton and his staff over for transfer to prison camp and eventual exchange for an equally important batch of Confederate officers languishing in the Federal prisoner-of-war compounds.

Probably the best known of Mosby's raids was his "Greenback Raid" against a Federal train on the B & O line near Kearneysville, which happened to be carrying some $175,000 in army payroll destined for the Union supply depot at Martinsburg. Derailing a train was a familiar trick of Mosby's, but the plunder was a delightful surprise to the

This picture is a copy of one taken in Richmond in January 1863. The uniform is the one I wore on March 8th 1863 on the night of General Stoughton's capture

Jn.S. Mosby

southern treasury. When he was informed of this exploit of Mosby's, Abraham Lincoln is said to have exclaimed at the White House with a wry, admiring grin, "Not only do my generals seem unable to win any battles for me; but now it also seems they no longer are able to collect their own pay!".

Other daring raids against large Federal supply trains took place at Point of Rocks, Maryland, and on the main road from Berryville to Winchester. During the latter, Mosby's Rangers managed to either make off with or destroy over 250 loaded supply wagons, 200 head of cattle, 600 horses and mules, plus some 200 Federal prisoners, but missed a second army payroll intended for General Sheridan at Cedar Creek, lying in a metal box by the roadside. On hearing of this triumph, General Lee was prompted to say in Richmond, "Thank God for Major Mosby! I only wish I had a hundred like him!" He then promoted him to Lieutenant Colonel.

On another occasion Mosby penetrated the Union lines all the way to the port of Alexandria, Virginia, in sight of the Capitol, disguised as an old man driving his farm cart to market. For an entire day he cruised the area unnoticed, gathering vital information for himself and Stonewall Jackson concerning the Union rearguard strength and the extent and location of their supply depots. So galling did the Grey Ghost's constant forays eventually become to the Federal high command that he was in large part responsible for the embittering "scorched earth" campaign upon which Generals Grant and Sheridan finally embarked—in order "to smoke out this viper's nest once and for good in the valley". Wrote Sheridan to General Halleck, his immediate superior in the region, "I will soon commence work on Mosby. Heretofore I have made no serious attempt to break him, as it would require ten of my men to every one of his slippery phantoms to bring him to heel. Now I intend to turn to the torch and smoke him out".

Sheridan did even better than that. On August 17, 1864, having failed in his attempt to beat the Valley people into submission with fire and torch, he hired a professional gunman "bounty killer" from the far west, named Richard Blazer, to run the Grey Ghost to earth. Issuing, with Grant's approval, 100 of the precious Spencer repeating rifles to Blazer's paid posse, Sheridan turned the hired civilian assassin band loose in the Blue Ridge foothills—all to no avail. It took Mosby and his mounted Rangers only one week to ambush and round up the imported western killers. Soon the 100 Spencer repeating rifles were barking savagely back at Sheridan's main column pillaging the valley, much to that Union officer's bitterness and chagrin. Colonel Mosby lived to a ripe old age, dying at 81, in Washington, D.C., a successful and respected lawyer. However, we know from the record that he had at least one more narrow escape before the tragic war came to a close in 1865.

In the process of "firing" the farms around Harpers Ferry in early December of 1864, in hopes of flushing out their quarry or his sympathizers and helpers, a Union cavalry patrol was searching through the smoking ruins of a farmhouse along the bank of the Shenandoah River. One cavalryman's mount suddenly broke through the smoldering wreckage of what seemed to be a crude trapdoor leading underground. The trapdoor led down some rickety steps to an underground passage tunneled through the dripping limestone rock. At its far end the passage opened out into a large natural limestone cave set in a cleft of rock beside the river. There was a narrow passage large enough to accommodate a dismounted rider and his horse at the far end, leading out to the sandy riverbank. But most interesting of all, the cave had only recently been evacuated, obviously having been occupied by a large troop of cavalry. Crude cribs and stalls lined the walls, and there were fresh horse-droppings in the trampled straw on the cavern floor. Still-smoldering cookfires occupied the center of the cave plus the litter and refuse of a large detachment of armed men. Had the Union patrol stumbled on one of Mosby's Ranger's recently-evacuated secret hideouts? So it would seem from the fresh tracks along the deserted riverbank, which was thoroughly screened from view by the tall overhanging cliffs of the Shenandoah River. And so, with this stirring picture of a truly narrow squeak in warfare, we will close the first half of this brief chapter of the Civil War in the Valley. The Grey Ghost had done it again!

Belle Boyd, the female Confederate spy, or "army courier" as they were called, was born in Martinsburg, West Virginia, of a well-to-do merchant family. She was an accomplished horsewoman and attended a fashionable seminary for young ladies in Baltimore before moving on to a social debut in Washington. On July 4th, 1861, at the age

Belle Boyd

of seventeen, she shot and killed a drunken Union soldier
trying to invade the Boyd home after partaking of too
much whiskey in celebration of Independence Day. She was
quickly cleared of a murder charge by the area Provost
Marshal of the Federal troops occupying the town, because
of her youth, good connections, and great beauty. As a
Southern sympathizer, she remained, however—quite understandably as things turned out—on the Provost Marshal's list
of spy and informer suspects until the end of the war.

Shortly after her release on a plea of self-defense, she escaped from Martinsburg to Winchester, but not before she stole a generous supply of invaluable drugs and medicines from the Federal supply depot, which she took with her, hidden under some straw in a farm wagon.

During a brief spell in Manassas in the company of her mother, Belle was formally enrolled in the ranks of the Southern corps of women spy couriers headed by the famous lady spy from Washington, D.C., Mrs. Rose O'Neal. Mistress Boyd then moved on to Front Royal to live with relatives and to be closer to the Valley commander for whom she was to work—General Stonewall Jackson. For a year or more, while staying with the Stewarts in Front Royal, she was secretly engaged in carrying coded messages hidden on her person or in her neatly coiffured dark hair, between Generals Beauregard, out on the Piedmont plains facing the Federal Army, and Jackson. She also made occasional, even longer and more dangerous trips between a lonely farmhouse strategically located along the Virginia shore of the Potomac River above Leesburg and Jackson's constantly shifting headquarters in the Valley.

In the spring of 1862 at Front Royal, came the dedicated spy's dream opportunity of a lifetime. Upon returning from a visit to Winchester to her cottage beside the Fishback Hotel on Main Street, Front Royal, Belle found the town's leading hostelry, which only recently had been turned into Union military headquarters, ablaze with lights. At the door of the hotel she ran into General Shields, the Federal commander of the Front Royal garrison. On the off chance of picking up some passes through the Federal lines for future use in her dangerous calling, she asked Shields for two safe conduct passes through his lines to Richmond, for herself and her ailing mother. That worthy, who, like many of his kind, frequently talked too much and to the wrong people, is said to have garrulously replied:

"We dare not entrust two such fine ladies to the tender mercies of General Jackson, Mistress Boyd. Now if you and your mother care to remain with us a few more days, the coast should be clear all of the way to the very gates of Richmond and you will be able to proceed to your destination under the protection of my marching troops. And now, my dear, if you will be good enough to excuse me, my staff is eagerly awaiting me inside for a very important conference."

After a safe interval had elapsed, Belle Boyd followed the Union commander, quite unobserved, into the Fishback Hotel, using a back servants' entrance to gain admittance to an unoccupied room on the second floor that had a closet with a knothole in the rough pine floor directly over General Shield's conference room. She bolted the door behind her, kneeled in the closet, cramped and motionless, and listened through the knothole to the conference below. Until early morning, Belle was busy memorizing every detail of information concerning Banks' and Shields' forthcoming plans to carry south to her own commander, Stonewall Jackson.

After encoding the message later that night, dressed in a soldier's cape and forage cap she had taken from a dead trooper, she saddled up her favorite mount, "Fleeter", in the hotel stables, and, silently slipping from the stable yard, took off like the wind across the town in the direction of Jackson's headquarters at Harrisonburg, further down the Valley. At each Federal picket point she passed en route in the dark, she replied to the sentry's challenge by producing one of many military safe conduct passes signed by the Provost Marshal. These she had collected from the bodies of a number of severely-wounded Confederate soldiers who had been paroled from further fighting and had subsequently died on their way home to their families. In the no-man's land between the two encamped armies, somewhere in the vicinity of Bentonville, she drew up her foam-flecked mount in front of a darkened and apparently deserted farmhouse and, dismounting, hurried over to rap in a pre-arranged code on the front door. A minute later the door opened and her contact with Stonewall Jackson, Colonel Turner Ashby, the cavalry commander, greeted her warmly. Belle gave him the message, and was back in her bed asleep before dawn.

When Jackson heard of the Banks and Shields plan to withdraw a good part of their forces from the Valley in order to reinforce McClelland and McDowell in front of Richmond, it did not take that astute field commander long to make up his mind about his next move against the Union Army of the Potomac. On May 23, 1862, he launched a surprise attack against the unprepared Shields at Front Royal, throwing in his entire army in a determined effort to

79

prevent the Union Army from leaving the Valley to bolster the attack against Lee's defending troops at Richmond. That same morning, before Jackson's flying grey columns had launched their surprise attack, Belle Boyd had slipped out once again from her cottage in Front Royal, this time in her best feminine finery. She dashed past the astonished Union pickets in broad daylight, running madly across the fields, and led Jackson into town to the attack over a little-used back road buried along the wooded slopes of the Blue Ridge (today known as the Browntown Road). Belle later received a note which read: "I thank you, for myself and for the army, for the immense service that you have rendered your country today. I am your friend.—T. J. Jackson, C.S.A."

With the element of surprise so much in his favor, the outcome of the Battle of Front Royal was never really in doubt, as Jackson swept into the city with his rebel-yelling columns. There was one determined rearguard stand of the Union forces under Colonel Kenly at Cedarville, after which the Federal troops understandably broke again and ran, this time all the way to the outskirts of Winchester at Kernstown. General Banks at Strasburg had been completely outflanked, and was also forced to hastily withdraw north to regroup for another stand at the Battle of Kernstown. Actually the rout of the Union forces did not actually halt, except for this abortive attempt to stop Jackson at Kernstown, until the Federal columns reached the wooded heights overlooking Harpers Ferry, where they dug in for a last ditch defense that turned the tide. The panic that followed the arrival of this grim news in Washington and Baltimore eventually forced McClelland to withdraw a substantial number of his best troops from in front of Richmond in order to properly defend the Capital. According to military historians, the war was prolonged by several painful years.

One of the most remarkable things about each of our two northern Valley heroes is the fact that in spite of their extremely dangerous assignments, both died of old age, comfortably in their beds—Belle Boyd in Wisconsin and the Grey Ghost in Washington, D.C. He was later buried at Warrenton, his favorite secret base throughout the Civil War.

VIII

RECONSTRUCTION

In the summer of 1834, the first passenger train steamed into Harpers Ferry from Baltimore, carrying 100 soot-smeared people. It had taken them six hours to cover the 82 miles of track, which comes out at the dizzying average speed of 13½ mph, including cows, whistle stops, and breakdowns. A year later a branch line of the B & O was in operation between Harpers Ferry and Winchester. This achievement called for a major celebration in Winchester, complete with bands, speeches, and parades, while a pair of cannon boomed a salute in the background. When the B & O mainline finally reached Martinsburg the following year, the elite Lafayette Guards gave a grand ball and some local wags hung a farm wagon, minus the horse, from the top of the town's tallest church steeple, signifying the death knell of the lumbering Knoxville wagon and old Dobbin. In 1854 the Virginia Central Railroad—now part of the C & O system—crossed the Blue Ridge into Staunton. That same year the first Iron Horse panted into Front Royal, arriving by way of the Manassas Gap Railroad, through Gainesville, Thoroughfare, and The Plains. It was soon followed by the Shenandoah Valley Railroad, now part of the Southern system.

The Civil War first proved the great value of the railroads. Front Royal was not only an important rail center, but also a major supply depot for the Union Army, with its railroad bridge replacing the old freight wagon routes across Morgan and McCoy's Fords, as well as the weary colonial ferry originally operated by Mr. Chester.

In 1866 five "Yankees" showed up at Linden, just to the east of Front Royal, armed with wagon loads of picks and shovels. They came in search of the plentiful copper ore which had first been unearthed by the Federal army engineers' digging fortifications in the Valley. One of the largest mining operations resulting from their ore prospecting was carried on by the Warren Mining Company at Happy Creek, which at one time shipped out as much as 100 tons of crude ore per day from their Larkin Lake property, sending the ore by rail to the big smelting and rolling mills in Pennsylvania.

At the same time, other old and new industries started up again in the area. With the abundance of tanbark from the native oak trees and the chemical derivative "quercitron", extracted from the plentiful mountain sumac,—both of them used in the curing and tanning of leather—the leather industry soon was flourishing again throughout the Valley. Ladies' kid gloves and shoe leather were among the chief manufactured products exported from the region. Much of it moved by canal boat and river barge, while the rest went by train, horse or Knoxville wagon.

Farm produce travelled almost exclusively by farm wagon to the Tidewater markets of Alexandria, Washington, and Richmond, moving east, through Manassas and Aldie Gap, and south, to the former Confederate capital, by way of Chester and Brown's Gap Turnpike. The Valley men urging their straining teams over the passes were accustomed to encourage their horses forward up the steeper grades with cries of "Cohee!", which gave rise to an old and long-familiar nickname for all Valley residents—"Cohees". The Valley people, in turn, dubbed their rivals, across the mountains on the Piedmont plain, either "Piedmonters" or "Tuckahoes", the local idiomatic name for any tuberous vegetable like the lowly but nourishing potato. There was considerable rivalry between the two factions, with periodic epidemics of broken heads on both sides, particularly when, like Dan Morgan and "Bully" Davis before them, they met at roadside taverns serving beer and ale.

There are two versions of the grave-snatching affair which took place at the very end of the Civil War, in 1865, at Winchester. They concern the mortal remains of that stalwart old warhorse, General Daniel Morgan. Upon his death at the age of 66 in the year 1802, he was duly buried with fitting pomp and ceremony as one of Winchester's outstanding heroes, in the old Presbyterian churchyard, and there he remained in peace until the late summer or early fall of '65. Rumors began flying around Winchester that a band of grave-robbers from either New Jersey, where Morgan had been born, or Cowpens, where he had his

greatest victory, had formed and were on their way to steal
the General's mortal remains for proper reburial in their
bailiwick.

A group of public-minded citizens of Winchester
promptly set to work, digging up Morgan's remains and
transferring them in the middle of the night to Mt. Hebron
Cemetery, where they now lie. One version has it that on
news of the transfer, the New Jerseyites lost their nerve and
never arrived in Winchester to attempt their grave-robbing.
Another version, and my personal favorite, says that the
body-snatching delegation hailed from Cowpens and, in
spite of the shift in location of General Morgan's bones,
they arrived anyway. Furthermore, they were met by a
defending posse of Winchester volunteers armed with clubs,
pole axes, staves, and axe handles. There was a pitched
battle that night in Mt. Hebron Cemetery, which, though
silent and secret, was said to be a magnificent thing to
witness, resulting in numerous broken heads and the
pell-mell retreat of the South Carolina rednecks.

It was not until many years later that General Morgan's
beloved and ever-faithful "Dutch Mess" was transferred to
lie in a defensive circle around the grave of their Revolutionary War leader; and that a fitting, and very moving,
marker was placed over the old Winchester veteran's
remains in memory of his service both to his country and to
Winchester. The six members of General Morgan's Dutch
Mess, all of whom were dedicated and fighting local
Winchester Germans of Joist Hite ancestry, included Peter
Lauck, the colonial proprietor of the Red Lion Inn which
still stands today on the corner of Cork and Loudoun
Streets.

A molasses and sugar cane factory went up at Happy
Creek in Warren County, shortly after the close of the Civil
War. At about the same time newer and larger apple grading
and packing sheds were appearing in Winchester and in
Berryville. Bell & Hoster turned out cigars "for the carriage
trade" in Front Royal. J. F. Forsythe & Co. became the
largest stove manufacturers in the Valley. Samuel Carson, a
bustling immigrant fresh from Ireland, founded the Carson
Lime Works at Riverton in 1868. Quercitron was produced
by George and Samuel Macatee, and shipped in huge
reinforced demi-johns to tanneries the world over. King &
Bowman made ladies' fine kid gloves. The Cover Brothers
tannery at Browntown cured hides for the New England

leather industry, as did King & Shotwell, along with a Luray tannery still in operation. Middletown continued to turn out fine clocks, and Strasburg, pottery. One surprising industry, now long gone, was the Belmont Vineyards, which, in its peak years, produced some 30,000 gallons of fine wine, plus an additional 10,000 gallons of first-rate Catawba brandy.

Sawmills, lumber yards, and gristmills also flourished, turning out fine waterground flour and corn meal wherever they had been left standing in the wake of Sheridan's whirlwind scorched earth campaign through the Valley. Hemp was a big money crop, as were sheep and wool. The bumper corn crops, together with the endless procession of private and commercial smoke-houses, turned out hams and country bacon which soon became famous throughout the country. The fruit orchards annually filled the bins of the grading houses in Winchester, Berryville, and Martinsburg, to overflowing. The pockets of the growers were lined with ready cash, even as the faces of the orchardmen were lined with careworn creases over the danger of frosts and the fluctuation of the market. The lush limestone bluegrass belt of the northern Valley and the neighboring Piedmont soon became synonymous with fine thoroughbred horseflesh and beef cattle. The big Remount Station of the United States Cavalry at Chester Gap, overlooking Front Royal, did not come into existence until after the turn of the century. By then Virginia was already internationally noted for its thoroughbreds in the hunting field, the show ring, and on the racetrack.

In the last quarter of the 19th century, the great depression struck, wiping out many businessmen overnight. By the early 1890's much of the economic slack of this temporary setback had been taken up by a new kind of local industry, born of increased leisure time and improved transportation. Tourism began slowly at first, with a mere trickle of summer boarders. They were soon followed by a steadily increasing influx of cottagers and weekend campers, seeking a little fresh air and *lebensraum* in the country. By 1900, the flow of summer visitors into the Valley from Richmond, Baltimore, and Washington led to a brief land boom, giving birth to such wildcat enterprises in investment and finance as The Front Royal Land Improvement Company, which sold lots and capital stock in a wild rash of speculation for a few years. Summer hotels and

resort spas appeared almost overnight at such locations as
Orkney Springs and Capon Springs among others. One of the most fashionable for a brief time was at Burner's Springs in the Fort Valley—now Seven Fountains—of which not a trace remains today. Guests were met at the nearest railroad station by the hotel carriages, buckboards, and tally-hos. The hotels, themselves, were "gingerbread Victorian" in design; they were huge wooden firetraps graced with long airy porches for the rocking chair fleet, and the inevitable croquet court on the front lawn.

Virginia State Library

Orkney Springs Hotel

There had been a kind of strictly unofficial summer White House under three successive late 19th-century Presidents—Hayes, Garfield, and Arthur—at a small island in the middle of the Shenandoah River above Harpers Ferry, called "Shannondale", of which also no trace remains today; the Blue Ridge summer White House honors have been long since taken over by Camp David in nearby

Maryland. Shortly after the turn of the century, a group of dedicated hikers and naturalists began blazing the Old Dominion section of the now famous Appalachian Trail through the mountain-top wilderness of the Blue Ridge. Starting at Snicker's Gap, south of Harpers Ferry, the Trail pretty much follows the old Indian war trace atop the mountains, as does its close neighbor, the Skyline Drive. Much to the hiking pioneers' surprise, they found the area a solemn tomb, sadly bereft of all songbirds and wildlife. One noted American naturalist in the early days sadly reported that in an entire month-long trek from Maine to Georgia, on the newly-opened portion of the Trail, he had never sighted nor heard the song of one.sparrow. They had all long since gone into the cookpots of the starving, backward, and isolated mountain men.

Another early wayfarer on the Trail wrote later in his memoirs of a trip that, having become temporarily lost on the peaks, he descended into a narrow valley gorge where he had seen the smoke of a mountaineer's cabin. On approaching the man, as close as he dared—the mountain people were notorious for their shyness and quick trigger fingers in those days—he called out for directions to the nearest town below. The man, who was hoeing a row of stunted corn, motioned for the stranger to come closer, whereupon the traveller yelled:

"How do I get down there? Isn't there a path of some kind?"

"Don't rightly know, son," came the gruff reply up the hill. "I was born down hyar, ye know!"

Early in the 20th century, a young man appeared in the Luray area of the Valley who was to change its face. George Freeman Pollock had inherited a large tract of birdless and barren mountain land atop the Blue Ridge overlooking Luray at old Stony Man Mountain. He proceeded, with great energy, imagination, and dispatch, to turn it into a veritable wilderness paradise known as "Skyland". Before long, Presidents of the United States and large corporations, senators and businessmen, sportsmen, and lovers of the great outdoors were flocking to Pollock's doorstep.

Some doorstep! To reach Skyland in the early days, you were met at the train in Luray by an old farm wagon. On reaching an isolated farmhouse under the loom of Old Stony, you transferred to a heavier wagon drawn by six stout horses. Then the climb began; or you went afoot, if you liked mountain climbing. Old hands at the trip reported that it was rough going, both up and down Thornton Gap in those days; but every bruise was well worthwhile, once you were safely ensconced in a tent or cabin at Skyland. There was horseback riding, jousting and other games, hiking, and walks with famous visiting naturalists by day. At night there were big campfire gatherings under the twinkling stars, with all the trimmings, including live snakes and Indians, horror tales, and displays of marksmanship by the chaps-clad host at unannounced intervals, "just to keep everybody on their toes", according to Pollock.

As the years wore on, the fame and popularity of Pollock's Skyland grew—"Pollock's dream" they called it. He dreamed of a huge national park, to rival Yosemite and Yellowstone, far to the west, with perhaps even a roadway through the clouds. A national park would be once again full of birds and game, wildflowers and tall trees, with superb panoramic views of the Valley and plains below. George Freeman Pollock was materially aided in seeing his dream brought to reality for all of us, by several close friends and enthusiastic frequent visitors to his Skyland. His friends were men of vision and integrity—as well as power—like President Herbert Hoover, who often fished the trout streams at Jeremy's Run and along the rapids of the Rapidan and Thornton Rivers, and senators from Virginia like Harry F. Byrd and William Carson. President Franklin Delano Roosevelt cut the ribbon and took off on the first wild ride "through the clouds" with his official party in the summer of 1936, after the completion of the first section of the Skyline Drive and Shenandoah National Park by the Civilian Conservation Corps. The first section of the Drive took some six years to build, and the last section was not completed until after the end of World War II, in 1948.

Today you can drive the same route that President Roosevelt followed back there on opening day in 1936, only much farther—all 105 miles of the magnificent Skyline Drive to Rock Fish Gap where it joins the Blue Ridge Parkway, leading southwest to the Great Smokies. Furthermore, you can do so in complete safety and comfort, behind stout stone guardrails with frequent strategically placed turnouts and overlooks for breathtaking panoramic views across the Piedmont foothills or the lovely Shenandoah Valley.

There are two natural history and geological museums featuring continuous illustrated lectures by trained Park Rangers—one near the Front Royal northern entrance at Dickey Ridge, the other at Big Meadows. Picnic grounds and rustic service stations with every public facility are spaced at intervals along the entire Drive. There are

Virginia Dept. of Conservation
and Economic Development

Skyline Drive

camping grounds, cabins for rent by the week, and overnight accomodations at Skyland, Big Meadows, and Lewis Mountain. Snackbars and restaurants are open at Thornton Gap, Elkwallow, Skyland, Big Meadows, Lewis Mountain, Swift Run Gap, and Loft Mountain.

There are trout streams for fishing at Jeremy's Run and Thornton Gap. Bear, fox, weasel, quail, grouse, and deer, along with bobcats and other wild game in profusion, are lurking in the depths of the woods along the game trails; and the wildflowers are profuse in season.

In fall, the foliage seen from high above draws visitors by the hundreds of thousands to revel in the mad riot of autumn colors spread like a divinely-inspired patchwork quilt on all sides. Although, some of the visitors from the big eastern cities come as much for the smell of autumn leaves and woodsmoke in the air, I suspect—and the sense of peace and quiet. In spring, the dogwood, redbud, and mountain laurel take over, covering the slopes in another feast of brilliant color.

Close to 2½ million people visited Shenandoah National Park in 1970 with an additional 12½ million visiting the adjoining Blue Ridge Parkway, bringing the total count to 15 million, or the largest annual attendance of any national park area in the country. Each year the tally grows. But in spite of the big weekend and holiday crowds Shenandoah National Park is so large and well-planned that even at the height of the autumn coloring, you seldom have the feeling of its being overcrowded.

Over the years a number of national forests have been added in the area, and they are carefully kept in their natural, unspoiled state for public use and enjoyment. In Virginia, the largest is George Washington National Forest, which begins in the north at the magnificent entrance gorge to Fort Valley and Elizabeth Furnace at Waterlick, and winds up 100 miles to the southwest at Lexington and Hot Springs. Next in size comes Jefferson National Forest, along the eastern rim of the main Valley of Virginia, which begins in the north at Sherando (named after the Iroquois chief) and Rock Fish Gap, and runs from there, southwest, all the way to the Tennessee border at Bristol, covering almost the entire length of the Virginia section of the Blue Ridge Parkway. Monongahela National Forest lies to the west of the Valley in West Virginia. Among them, these three forests and the Shenandoah National Park cover an area as large as the State of Maryland. In all of these carefully preserved public domains, as in many other sections of the Valley, the majority of ponds, lakes, and streams are stocked annually with game fish. There are hiking and horseback trails, picnic and camping grounds; and most of the larger creeks and all of the rivers are safely navigable by either canoe or kayak.

Much of the slack of the local economy in the wake of the folding land boom of the 1890's in the Valley fortunately had been taken up by the arrival of the first vanguard of wealthy industrialists and captains of commerce from the north. They bought up the run-down farms and estates of the old impoverished landed gentry and restored them to their former glory—and frequently more—as their summer homes and seats of sporting pleasure in the hunt field and paddock, the show barn and pure-bred cattle ring. In some cases this monetary blood transfusion, revitalizing the area with increased employment and capital outlay, was accomplished by a combination of marriage and tax deductions. The end result has been the gain of the area in all respects. New blood, new capital investment, and some of the loveliest country estate horse and cattle centers in the entire United States, besides full employment for the local natives. These horse and cattle breeding centers are concentrated around such carefully preserved and charming capitals of relaxation and country pleasure as Middleburg, Upperville, Leesburg, The Plains, and Warrenton in Loudoun and Fauquier counties. There are more of the same, simpler, perhaps, but even more exclusive, to be found farther west in the rock-ribbed hills of Rappahannock County. Here the pure-bred bull and thoroughbred horse are king, closely followed by the registered English Southdown ram, surrounded by gamboling flocks of his wooly progeny in springtime.

The hunt meets of such select equestrian gatherings in pursuit of the fox—or fox scent, as is the case in "drag hunts"—as the Rappahannock, the Blue Ridge, the Orange County, and the Piedmont Hounds, is deadly serious business to its members in fall and early winter. So is the choice of bloodlines for the mounts the huntsmen ride, the cattle in their barns, and the thoroughbreds they send to the race tracks at nearby Charles Town, Pimlico, Bowie, and Laurel. Not all of the Valley is given over to the sport of kings and agriculture, however. With the influx of northern capital and capitalists in this century, has come its inevitable counterpart—industrialization. So far, it is situated in well-defined and remote pockets. Industry is drawn here by the untapped labor market, special tax inducements, and the plentiful supply of water from the Shenandoah River and its tributaries.

The American Viscose plant of the FMC Corporation employs over 2,000 people in the world's largest rayon plant at Front Royal. In and surrounding Winchester in a loose industrial cordon, are O'Sullivan Rubber, Rubbermaid, American Brake Shoes, Henkel-Harris Furniture and Capital Records. Doubleday & Company has a modern printing plant at Berryville, not far from the Byrd Orchard packing plant and headquarters. Badger Powhatan is located in Charles Town, Merck & Company south of Elkton, and General Electric is at Waynesboro. American Safety Razor and Westinghouse have large plants near Staunton, Walker and Dunham Bush at Harrisonburg, and DuPont between

Reconstruction that city and Waynesboro. There are a number of smaller plants, scattered up and down the sector, turning out everything from hosiery and clothing to molded fiber boats. United States Steel has several "captive" limestone quarries in the Middletown – Strasburg area.

But by and large, this is still an agrarian land. The fields and forests, streams and silos, red barns and white ones, are made rich by the Valley's dramatic and colorful past history, and are dominated for eternity by the worn ancient haze-blue hills which once held back an inland sea and the lazy, winding river of the Senedoes meandering down its center.

* * * * *

So now, if you will turn to the Tour Guide section of this book, you can begin selecting your target for today—or tomorrow. And what a fascinating array of prime targets! Old inns and taverns, Indian forts and burial mounds, iron furnaces and creaking waterwheels all await your pleasure. You can visit George Washington's surveying headquarters at White Post (1748), his military headquarters at Winchester (1754-63), or the old Robert McKay house at Cedarville (1734), built when our first President was only two years old. You can drive past any of his brothers' or cousins' homes outside Charles Town: Harewood, Mordington, Blakeley, or Claymont Court. You can visit "lawyer's row" behind the old Shenandoah County courthouse (1791-92) in Woodstock.

You can stand on the high bank of the Potomac River at Shepherdstown, West Virginia overlooking the bend in the river where in 1787, Crazy James Rumsey successfully navigated his "flying teakettle", long before Fulton had dreamed up his paddle-wheel steamer, the "Claremont". Then drive on through charming Sharpsburg to Antietam Battlefield National Park—"Bloody Antietam", they called it back in 1862.

From here on it is up to you; but whatever you do, remember to keep your eyes open wherever you go! For who knows, you may drive right past the Grey Ghost at the head of a column of his galloping band of Rangers. Or you may pass the ghost of John Lederer, notebook in hand, and clutching his ancient musket. Surely, if you look closely and hard enough, you will see an "Indian tree" or two, bent down in a crooked "S" to mark the hunting trail of the long-vanished first residents of the Valley. They were made by tying a young sapling to the ground with a leather thong, about halfway up its shaft, until the tip end began to grow straight up towards the sun again. Then the Indian braves cut the thong and released the tree. I know where there is one. It is right beside the road leading into the Elizabeth Furnace Gorge on the Fort Valley Road south of Waterlick, and it looks like this:

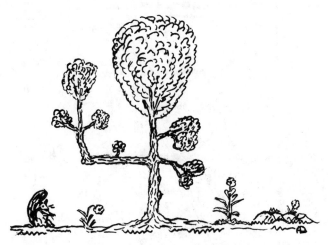

Indian Tree – Fort Valley, Virginia

94

TOUR GUIDE

On the accompanying tour maps in this section, all roads in the U.S. highway network are so marked, all Interstate and dual-lane highways are indicated in double lines, and all state roads are marked either "Va.", "W. Va.", or "Md." Note that no mileages are given on any of these maps. They are not drawn to exact scale, but, used in conjunction with the highway markers and your regular travel maps, are clear and dependable.

All of the roads shown or suggested in this guide section are absolutely safe and are either hard-surfaced or of well maintained gravel construction. As in most states, there are roadside rest and picnic areas along the main highways. There are also state historical markers at important points, plus numerous Civil War battle maps along the roadsides. For additional convenience and clarity in our tour and sightseeing directions, we have selected Winchester and Front Royal as our two focal points. Winchester and Front Royal, 18 miles apart, are connected by scenic U.S. 522, which has particularly breath-taking views on a clear day. Every tour starts and ends at the nearer of the two communities, both of which are excellently equipped with tourist and vacation facilities. Please note, however, that if you are coming to the Valley from the Baltimore-Washington area, you may find it more convenient to take some of the tours in reverse order.

This limited and highly-selective Tour Guide is not intended as either a gourmet guide to good dining in the Valley or a guide for the best overnight lodging. There are plenty of booklets and brochures available from travel bureaus, chambers of commerce, service stations, and the state travel information centers. The comfortable and helpful Virginia state travel information centers are located at the rest area on I-66 at Bull Run; on U.S. 250 near Charlottesville; and I-81 at the Virginia-West Virgnia border north of Winchester. Shenandoah Valley Travel Assn. has an

95

information office on U.S. 11 just north of the Staunton city
limits. If special or more detailed information is needed,
contact Shenandoah Valley Travel Assn. at 1900 N.
Coalter, Staunton, Virginia 24401. Tel. 855-5145.

1. BERKELEY SPRINGS AREA

This section of the northern Valley served as the chief
gateway to the west in colonial times, much as the
Cumberland Gap did in southwest Virginia. Should you
happen to be entering the Valley along this route (I-70 and
U.S. 522 from the Breezewood exit of the Pennsylvania
Turnpike), there are several points of interest along your
run from Hancock, Maryland, to Winchester, Virginia.

The old Potomac River ford at **Hancock** has long since
been replaced by a highway bridge, but once you touch
West Virginia soil on the south bank of the Potomac you
are at the northern entrance to the Shenandoah Valley and
the even more extensive Valley of Virginia. The first slopes
of the Allegheny Mountains, with the Cacapon River
winding at their feet, will lie to your right as you head
south into the Valley. And then, as you approach Winchester and cross the Virginia state line, you will get your
first glimpse of the Blue Ridge, far ahead, winding down
from Maryland at Harpers Ferry to form the eastern
ramparts of the Shenandoah Valley.

Six miles south of Hancock on U.S. 522 — at **Berkeley
Springs**, W. Va.—you will come to one of the oldest
hot-spring spas still in existence on the North American
continent (1736). Known as "Bath" in early colonial times
it was a fashionable gathering place for the more sophisticated and venturesome of the east-coast dandies. George
Washington and his two brothers from nearby Charles
Town often went there, as did the Marquis de Lafayette,
Thomas Jefferson, and Louis Philippe, later King of France,
and his two brothers during their three-year American
period of exile. There were card games and dancing nightly
at the casino—now long gone. Families of wealth from as
far away as Baltimore and Philadelphia came here both for
recreation and "to take the waters".

George Washington, as a surveyor for Lord Fairfax, first
visited "Ye Fam'd Warm Springs" in 1748. Twenty years
later, remembering the beneficial and salutary effects of the
mineral springs, he brought his family "to try the effect of

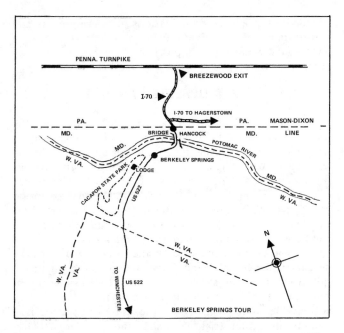

Berkeley Springs
Area
Tour No. 1

the waters". After Bath was established as a town in 1776, Washington, General Horatio Gates, and other Revolutionary Army officers purchased land there. The lot owned by George Washington, where he built a house, a kitchen and stables, is diagonally across from the present-day post office at S. Mercer and Fairfax Streets (about two blocks up from Washington Street).

Ten miles farther south on U.S. 522, **Cacapon State Park** will be on your right, marked by a rustic stone entrance gate and sign. A short drive through lovely woods brings you to **Cacapon Lodge**, its complex of family vacation cabins, the ranger quarters, and riding stables. There are attractive rooms, good food, and evening programs the year round at the air-conditioned Lodge, but there is no card gaming as there was at Bath in the old days. If you plan to stay there, advance reservations are advisable during the season. In the park grounds swimming, fishing, boating, hiking, riding, tennis, and sunning on a soft, sandy beach lake-front are also to be enjoyed.

The drive to **Winchester** from Cacapon Lodge over a wide well-paved road, U.S. 522, is hilly, and scenic. At Winchester, there is a generous offering of history plus

97

excellent overnight accommodations to fit every purse, and
a wide range of restaurants. Plan to spend several days in
and around Winchester, if possible. With history at every
turn, you won't regret it.

2. WINCHESTER AREA

A tour of **Winchester** is a trip into history and the
past—a very pleasant look into our early heritage and the
frontier struggles during the trying period of the French
and Indian War. The all-wise and perceptive civic adminis-
trations down through the years have carefully preserved
everything of historic significance with the sole exception
of George Washington's strategic frontier rampart, Fort
Loudoun, which long ago was swallowed up by the streets
and houses of a rapidly-expanding community.

The end result of this wisdom and forbearance down the
decades is a delightful and often picturesque community,
full of charming old streets and homes. It is a small city of
excellent shops, comfortable accommodations and every
conceivable modern facility for the visitor and the tourist—
plus teeming industrial, financial, and agrarian activity.
Perhaps it is best known nationally for its annual Apple
Blossom Festival held early each May, which crowds the
town with out-of-state guests and onlookers. All of this
present-day hustle and bustle is set against a delightful
background of old, tree-lined streets with fascinating
names. Heaving brick sidewalks and yawning gutters are fit
to challenge the stability and sobriety of the hardiest
sightseer. The streets have names to conjure the fancy:
Cork, Amherst, Boscawen, and Piccadilly; Kent, Cameron,
Washington, Braddock, and Loudoun; Pallmall, Leicester,
Cecil, and Wolfe; Monmouth, Paper Mill Road, and Featherbed Lane. There is even an Indian Alley! All of them sing of
Winchester's largely English origin.

About 1750, Colonel James Wood, the city's founder,
built lovely **Glen Burnie** at the western edge of Winchester
and his son, Robert, added the striking south wing onto the
original house in 1794.

Officially founded in 1744 by Colonel Wood and his
band of English settlers, there were already a few German
residents who had been brought in by Joist Hite in 1732
near a Shawnee Indian village. The combined talents of
these two ethnically industrious groups helped to make

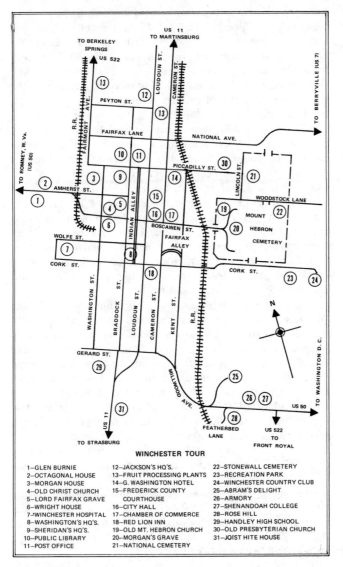

TO BERKELEY
SPRINGS

US 11
TO MARTINSBURG

US 522

TO BERRYVILLE (US 7)

PEYTON ST.

FAIRFAX LANE

NATIONAL AVE.

TO ROMNEY, W. Va.
(US 50)

R.R. FAIRMONT AVE.

LOUDOUN ST.

CAMERON ST.

PICCADILLY ST.

LINCOLN ST.

AMHERST ST.

WOODSTOCK LANE

INDIAN ALLEY

BOSCAWEN ST.

FAIRFAX
ALLEY

MOUNT
HEBRON
CEMETERY

WOLFE ST.

CORK ST.

CORK ST.

WASHINGTON ST.

BRADDOCK ST.

LOUDOUN ST.

CAMERON ST.

KENT ST.

R.R.

N

GERARD ST.

GOODWILL AVE.

TO WASHINGTON D. C.

US 11

TO STRASBURG

FEATHERBED
LANE

US 50

US 522
TO
FRONT ROYAL

WINCHESTER TOUR

1—GLEN BURNIE
2—OCTAGONAL HOUSE
3—MORGAN HOUSE
4—OLD CHRIST CHURCH
5—LORD FAIRFAX GRAVE
6—WRIGHT HOUSE
7—WINCHESTER HOSPITAL
8—WASHINGTON'S HQ'S.
9—SHERIDAN'S HQ'S.
10—PUBLIC LIBRARY
11—POST OFFICE

12—JACKSON'S HQ'S.
13—FRUIT PROCESSING PLANTS
14—G. WASHINGTON HOTEL
15—FREDERICK COUNTY
    COURTHOUSE
16—CITY HALL
17—CHAMBER OF COMMERCE
18—RED LION INN
19—OLD MT. HEBRON CHURCH
20—MORGAN'S GRAVE
21—NATIONAL CEMETERY

22—STONEWALL CEMETERY
23—RECREATION PARK
24—WINCHESTER COUNTRY CLUB
25—ABRAM'S DELIGHT
26—ARMORY
27—SHENANDOAH COLLEGE
28—ROSE HILL
29—HANDLEY HIGH SCHOOL
30—OLD PRESBYTERIAN CHURCH
31—JOIST HITE HOUSE

Frederick Town, as it was then known, quickly grow and
prosper at the hub of a number of major trade routes. The
Harpers Ferry-Berryville Pike (now U.S. 340) entered from
the east, the Germanna Trail (U.S. 522) and the Valley Pike
(U.S. 11) from the southeast and southwest, and the

99

southern branch of the Cumberland Trail (U.S. 522 north) from the northwest. The English were excellent planners and organizers, while the skills of the Germans as master craftsmen are illustrated by many of the lovely brick and limestone houses. They were especially adept at fine woodcarving and moulded plaster-wood, creating the magnificent sculptured ceilings throughout the Valley area, including those at **Saratoga** near Boyce, and many others.

It was from Winchester that General Braddock started off on his ill-fated expedition through the wilderness against the French. Winchester was George Washington's military base and headquarters during the French and Indian War and, before that, his surveying headquarters for the region while he was in the employ of Lord Fairfax. Washington, with the help of the British supreme commander for all of the colonies, Lord Loudoun, built an impregnable frontier fort in Winchester and named it to honor his superior officer. Not a trace of it remains today, but **Washington's Headquarters**, on the corner of Cork and Braddock Streets, is still standing.

Daniel Morgan, born in New Jersey, but a native of the Winchester area from age sixteen and later a national hero for his victories at Saratoga and Cowpens, served as a waggoneer in Braddock's ambushed column that fateful day in 1755. Morgan was promoted to militia captain by George Washington and served under him faithfully throughout two wars at the head of his celebrated Morgan's Virginia Rifles, many of whom came from the Winchester area. Finally laid to rest in 1802 in the **old Presbyterian Church** graveyard, Morgan's remains were later removed secretly in the dead of night for reburial in the **Mt. Hebron Cemetery** in 1865. It was a safety precaution because there had been rumors of a midnight raid to steal his coffin by some union soldiers from New Jersey. It was some time later before Daniel Morgan's celebrated "Dutch Mess", six of his most faithful Winchestrian bodyguards, including Peter Lauck, the proprieter of the old **Red Lion Tavern**, were buried around him.

General Morgan was not the only famous resident of Winchester to be exhumed and then reburied in a new and more impressive location. Lord Fairfax, the fifth Baron Cameron, largest land proprieter by royal patent in the entire Virginia Colony (extending over five million acres, from Alexandria, Virginia to as far west as the Ohio River), was first removed from his family plot at his country home, Greenway Court, near White Post in Clarke County, for reburial in the Frederick County Parish Church at the corner of Loudoun and Boscawen Streets. When that property was sold and the church torn down in 1828, forty-six years after his death, he was again reburied—this time in the present location beside Christ Episcopal Church at the corner of Washington and Boscawen Streets. There is an old and persistent rumor to the effect that when the original workers were at Greenway Court to dig up Lord Fairfax's grave, there were no headstones marking which was his grave and which were those of his retainers (he never married). The story persists to this day that the exhuming detail, forced to pick at random, dug up not the remains of the master, but those of his faithful old slave, Plutarch.

General Horatio Gates, another hero of the Saratoga battle, lived out his declining years at his country seat, Traveller's Rest, at nearby Kearneysville, now in West Virginia, as did the notorious General Charles Lee, who finally drank himself to death at his country home near Charles Town, after his public disgrace in the wake of cowardice in battle and political conniving at Monmouth Courthouse,

During the Civil War, Winchester changed hands 71 times as the result of its importance to both Confederate and Union forces throughout the war. "Stonewall" Jackson's Headquarters while he occupied the city is now a public museum on North Braddock Street. General Sheridan's Headquarters is located a few blocks away. The National Cemetery on Monument Avenue contains the Union dead fallen either in attack on, or defense of, Winchester during the war. Across from it is Stonewall Cemetery where 3,000 Confederate soldiers are buried.

Winchester is a bustling town, seat of Frederick county, with a county courthouse on Loudoun Street. Every visitor should see its lovely courtrooms and clerk's office which have been recently restored. On Saturdays, like Cinderella's pumpkin coach, Winchester suddenly turns into a busy farm community. Its streets are crowded with country people come to town to shop and pass the time of day. Weekdays, "Frederick Town" is its old self again, except during the Apple Blossom Festival in early May when, for a week, the whole place goes slighty mad.

On top of that, Winchester is quite a well-known banking, industrial, and shopping center. It has many fine stores and antique shops as well as an excellent hospital with many doctors and fine surgeons to staff it. In addition to being known as "The Apple Capital", Winchester has numerous other industries. Fortunately, most of the plants are beyond the city limits. O'Sullivan Rubber, Abex (auto brake lining), F. G. Shattuck Co. (Schrafft's), Capitol Records, and National Fruit Products are among the more prominent industries. The apple warehouses and packing plants are at the north end of town and there is a thriving livestock market just to the west, on U.S. 50. Visitors may be taken on tours of some of these industrial plants. For details contact the Winchester-Frederick County Chamber of Commerce at 29 South Cameron Street. Telephone: (703) 662-4118.

An alphabetical list of places of interest in the area follows:

Abram's Delight (1754): This fine old limestone home, residence of Abraham Hollingsworth, is the oldest house in Winchester. It is maintained and furnished by the Winchester-Frederick County Historical Society. Nearby is a replica of an early Winchester loghouse. Located off Millwood Pike (U.S.-522 South), opposite the Rebel Restaurant and behind the Winchester Armory. Open to the public year round for an admission fee.

Apple and Fruit Processing Plants: North Cameron Street and Fairmont Avenue.

Christ Episcopal Church: Built in 1825, diocese of the Episcopal Church, northern district. Corner of Washington and Boscawen Streets. In the church yard is the **Tomb of Lord Fairfax**.

Daniel Morgan House (1794): This white stucco house on West Amherst Street was the home of Betsy Heard, General Morgan's daughter. Morgan died here in 1802.

Daniel Morgan Grave: **Mt. Hebron Cemetery** stands at the foot of East Boscawen Street. Daniel Morgan's grave, surrounded by his celebrated German "Dutch Mess", lies roughly in the left fore-center of the cemetery opposite the ruins of the old stone Lutheran Church.

Frederick County Courthouse (1840): The charming main courtroom of the early Federal period and its adjoining juvenile court on the ground floor are open to the public at all times except during closed courtroom proceedings. Of particular interest are the brass doorlocks, the fine chandeliers and the replicas of the original spindle

Ruins of Lutheran Church

benches along the walls. It was restored in 1968 and is very much worth a visit. The Courthouse is on Loudoun Street near Boscawen Street, and there is public parking off the street (metered) a half-block north on Cameron Street.

General Sheridan's Headquarters: Now an Elks' Lodge, it is located at the corner of Piccadilly and Braddock Streets, diagonally opposite the Winchester post office. This house was occupied in 1864-65 by Union General Philip Sheridan, the scourge of the Valley.

George Washington's Office Museum: At the corner of Cork and Braddock Streets was George Washington's office while he was in the employ of Lord Fairfax as a surveyor (1748). Later it served as his military headquarters during the French and Indian War and while he was building Fort Loudoun to protect the valley frontier (1756-58). Open to the public daily for an admission fee. Children under twelve are admitted free.

Glen Burnie (1750): Completed in 1794 by Robert Wood, son of the town's founder, Colonel James Wood, and only recently fully restored and refurnished with museum pieces, this handsome home and complex of brick outbuildings and formal gardens is one of the showplaces of the entire valley. Unfortunately, it is not as yet open to the general public except on special occasions. Mr. Julian W. Glass, Jr., the last decendant of Colonel James Wood, is the present owner. You can drive past it and obtain a view of the house and its lovely setting beside a willow-lined stream. Glen Burnie is reached by driving west on Amherst Street (U.S. 50). It is on your left just past the A&P shopping center.

Hite Homestead, "Springdale" (1753): The present stone dwelling was built by Colonel John Hite, son of Joist Hite, first settler in the Valley. The original Joist Hite cabin foundations have been preserved in the barnyard area behind the house. The house is 4½ miles south of Winchester on U.S. 11, past Kernstown and just before Opequon Creek. It is on your left and there is an historical marker alongside it.

Lord Fairfax Grave: The tomb marker stands beside **Christ Episcopal Church** in the small brick courtyard between the church and the vestry building. Corner of Washington and Boscawen Streets.

National Cemetery: On National Avenue (Va. 7) four blocks east of the George Washington Hotel. **Stonewall Cemetery** is opposite. In these two cemeteries nearly 7,500 Union and Confederate soldiers are buried.

Octagonal House: On Amherst Street (U.S. 50 west) opposite the A&P shopping center, the house stands in a grove of trees on a hillside. It is an example of a rather rare type of house which is usually confined to the seacoast and to seaports.

Old Stone Presbyterian Church (1788): On East Piccadilly Street, recently restored, and open to the public. General Daniel Morgan, a member of this church, was buried here in 1802. At the end of the Civil War his remains were removed to Mt. Hebron Cemetery.

Red Lion Tavern: At the southeast corner of Cork and Loudoun Streets stands an old stone building with a tablet on its outer wall proclaiming it as innkeeper Peter Lauck's original Red Lion Tavern (built about 1753). It was frequented by George Washington, Daniel Morgan and others in colonial times.

Rose Hill (1789): The finely-proportioned limestone colonial home on Featherbed Lane behind the Rebel Restaurant is privately-owned and was long in the Barr and Ball families of Winchester. Turn off Millwood Avenue (U.S. 50-522 South and East) onto Featherbed Lane. Rose Hill stands at the first bend in the lane, set back from the roadway.

Shenandoah College and Music Conservatory: This modern and modest college campus was begun in 1958, when Shenandoah College moved to Winchester from Dayton, Virginia. It is south of the Winchester Armory, just off Millwood Avenue (U.S. 50-522).

"Stonewall" Jackson's Headquarters and Civil War Museum: Located at 415 North Braddock Street, two blocks north of the Winchester post office, this building was used by the Confederate commander as his official headquarters from November, 1861 to March 1862 when he left Winchester to begin his famous valley campaign. Open daily for an admission fee.

Indian Alley: This reminder of the earliest frontier days is a place of no great beauty. Today, it is scarcely more than a commercial alleyway for delivery trucks and local drivers "in the know". Nevertheless, the site of this unobtrusive back alley, running up the center of town from Cork Street north to Piccadilly, was once the burial ground of a long-vanished race of giant Indians, reported to have been seven feet tall. Their skeletons were uncovered by a squad of Colonel Washington's militiamen while they were digging the foundations of Fort Loudoun during the French and Indian War. Louis Michel, the Swiss explorer, was first told of the ancient redmen by the Indians around the Winchester area, back in 1707. In his travel dairy, he wrote down what he saw and heard, as did the first explorer of the Shenandoah Valley, John Lederer, who wrote in detail of the local Indians and their customs during his sojourn with them in the northern valley—of which Winchester is today the focal point. So now, from Lederer's first walking tour of the Valley, to modern delivery vans in Indian Alley, we have come full circle.

3. BERRYVILLE—BOYCE AREA

This sedate and charming area of the northern valley lies mostly in Clarke County, with Berryville as its county seat. Clarke County has the distinction of being the ancestral family seat of both the illustrious Byrd and Randolph families which, between them, have contributed so much to the history and culture of the Old Dominion, as well as the nation. Among their combined early founders we find such well-known names as John Randolph, a signer of the Declaration of Independence, Edmund Randolph, an early governor of the state who later became the first Attorney General of the United States and then Secretary of State, and Nathaniel Burwell, a man of stature throughout the Thirteen Colonies, who, in 1790-92, built magnificent Carter Hall at nearby Millwood. More recently numbered among the distinguished descendants of the Byrd dynasty are such outstanding national figures as Admiral Richard E. Byrd, discoverer of the South Pole, his brother, Senator Harry F. Byrd, whose home stands at the west end of Berryville beside Va. 7, and who established the extensive **Byrd Orchards**, one of the largest apple-producers in the country, and General "Wild Bill" Donovan, who, after commanding the Rainbow Division in World War I, led the highly effective cloak and dagger organization, the OSS in World War II.

Berryville, once known as Battletown, is a delightful rural community of considerable, although unostentatious, wealth and is surrounded by many fine homes and estates of the early colonial landed gentry. These estates, unlike their counterparts in Loudoun and Fauquier counties, are still largely owned by the descendants of the original builders. Among the largest and best known of these, historically, is **Audley Farm**, now a top thoroughbred horse-breeding farm. It was the home of George Washington's adopted step-daughter, Nellie Custis, after the death of her husband, Major Lawrence Lewis, in 1839.

106

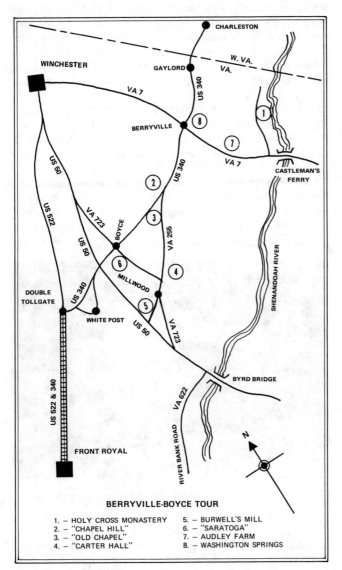

CHARLESTON

WINCHESTER

GAYLORD

W. VA.
VA.

VA 7

US 340

1

BERRYVILLE

8

7

VA 7

CASTLEMAN'S
FERRY

US 50

2

US 340

US 522

VA 723

3

BOYCE

VA 255

US 50

6

4

MILLWOOD

DOUBLE
TOLLGATE

US 340

5

WHITE POST

US 50

VA 723

US 522 & 340

BYRD BRIDGE

SHENANDOAH RIVER

N

VA 622

FRONT ROYAL

RIVER BANK ROAD

BERRYVILLE-BOYCE TOUR

1. — HOLY CROSS MONASTERY	5. — BURWELL'S MILL
2. — "CHAPEL HILL"	6. — "SARATOGA"
3. — "OLD CHAPEL"	7. — AUDLEY FARM
4. — "CARTER HALL"	8. — WASHINGTON SPRINGS

Another outstanding estate from both aesthetic and historical viewpoints is magnificent **Carter Hall**. Both its builder, Nathaniel Burwell, and Edmund Randolph lived there. Stonewall Jackson used Carter Hall as his military

107

headquarters briefly in October, 1862, during his campaign against Generals Banks and Shields who were temporarily entrenched at Winchester. Carter Hall was named for Nathaniel Burwell's maternal great-grandfather, the fabulously wealthy landowner, King Carter, who lived and ruled, literally, like a "king" on the James River below Williamsburg. Carter Hall is considered to be one of the finest examples of a Federal manor house in the grand style. Set in the standard "park" of English origin, it is privately-owned and not open to the public. However, it can be seen from the road while driving by on Va. 255 at the eastern edge of Millwood.

Another privately-owned estate of great charm and beauty, **Chapel Hill,** the old Byrd family homestead, is now occupied by General Donovan's widow. It is located across U.S. 340, slightly north of the Byrd-Randolph family chapel and cemetery, **Old Chapel.** Old Chapel is by far the

Old Chapel

most important and charming mecca in the entire area. Open the year round for a mere gratuity to the local grounds keeper, it is beside the highway, 3 miles south of Berryville and on your left where Va. 255 branches off just beyond the entrance of Chapel Hill. Old Chapel, built of native limestone in the late 18th century, has a quiet, peaceful charm of its own as it nestles beside the graveyard under the tall, brooding trees. Old Chapel would delight the most meticulous visitor, even if the tiny private cemetery did not contain some of the greatest names in our early colonial and federal history. See it by all means.

The limestone home of General Daniel Morgan, Revolutionary and French and Indian War hero, **Saratoga**, is a half mile south of Boyce on Va. 723. Though smaller and far less pretentious than either Chapel Hill or Carter Hall, it is another fine example of late colonial design and construction. Unfortunately, these three handsome houses are open to the public only on special occasions. Completed in 1782, the house is named for the battle of Saratoga in upper New York State and was constructed by Hessian prisoners of war taken by General Morgan. Saratoga is especially noted for its magnificent dry-stone masonry and lovely interior panelling, as well as the graceful designs of its molded plaster "Hessian" ceilings. The Winchester general spent his declining years here until the start of his last illness, at which time he moved to his daughter's home in Winchester where he died in 1802.

General Daniel Morgan built the **Burwell-Morgan Mill** at Millwood in 1782 for Colonel Nathaniel Burwell of Carter Hall. The Mill is being restored by the Clarke County Historical Association and can be seen at the foot of the town hill at Millwood, beside U.S. 255 and Va. 723, almost directly opposite the tiny hamlet's post office.

George Washington's surveying office at **Washington Springs**, just northeast of Berryville off the Charles Town road (U.S. 340), is no longer standing. The site is near **Soldier's Rest** where Morgan convalesced between wars, but is difficult to find. (Washington's two principal surveying headquarters, however, were at White Post and Winchester and both are still in existence.)

The Berryville-Boyce area is largely devoted to sheep, horse, and cattle farms and, surrounding Berryville on all sides, are the huge apple and peach orchards of the Byrd family. Some of the farms are operated as strictly commerical agricultural enterprises. Others are in the "hobby" category of the more wealthy landed gentry. Here, as in Fauquier and Loudoun counties, the registered pure-bred bull and blooded horse are king and riding to hounds is a deeply-cherished pastime. The Blue Ridge Hunt meets regularly in season at Carter Hall and other large estates. Members of the local equestrian community are regular competitors at the Warrenton, Upperville, and Middleburg horse shows and race meets.

The Hunt meets at Carter Hall

In Berryville itself, on North Church Street, are the delightful county courthouse and **Grace Episcopal Church** where Benjamin Berry, the town's founder, is buried. Near the main intersection of town (U.S. 340 and Va. 7) is **Battletown Inn** which has long been known for its fine cuisine and charming colonial decor. **Doubleday & Company** has its modern, automated printing plant in Berryville and the **Byrd Orchard** plant next door is a year-round business, with the planting, pruning, and spraying which goes on between harvesting, grading, and packing seasons.

To the east of Berryville on Va. 7 (Harry Flood Byrd Highway), 4 miles beyond Audley Farm, is **Castleman's Ferry** on the banks of the Shenandoah River. Although replaced by a highway bridge today, Castleman's Ferry carried a steady stream of commerce across the broad, flowing river from the Piedmont into the northern valley. It was also the scene of several spirited cavalry engagements during the Civil War because of its strategic location along the supply route of the Union forces.

Just before you reach the highway bridge at Castleman's Ferry, a left turn at the small sign "Monastery" onto a hard-surfaced secondary road will take you approximately one mile to the entrance of **Holy Cross Monastery** and its gift shop. The Monastery is famous for its fine breads and other table delicacies which draw people to its gates every year.

110

Leave Winchester by heading east on Piccadilly Street
past the George Washington Hotel. Then go east on
National and Berryville Avenues, the beginning of Va. 7.
Follow Va. 7 for 11 miles to Berryville. At the first traffic
light at the main intersection, continue straight ahead, east
on Va. 7 through Berryville past Audley Farm to the
Shenandoah River Bridge at Castleman's Ferry (6 miles).
Turn left at the sign "Monastery" just before reaching the
bridge. Another mile will bring you to the **Holy Cross
Monastery** gateway on the right-hand side of the road.

After visiting the Monastery, return to Va. 7 and turn
right. Go back to the main traffic light in Berryville, and ,
unless you plan to dine at the **Battletown Inn** just beyond
the traffic light on Va. 7, turn left onto U.S. 340 South,
towards **Boyce** and Double Tollgate. Drive south on U.S.
340 about 3 miles, passing the entrance to **Chapel Hill** and
turn left onto Va. 255. **Old Chapel** is on your right. After
visiting Old Chapel, continue on Va. 255 for the 3 miles
past **Carter Hall** at Millwood. Turn a sharp left at the
bottom of the hill below Carter Hall from Va. 255 onto Va.
723 to see **Burwell-Morgan Mill.** Head west on Va. 723 for

Phil Flournoy

Saratoga

111

Daniel Morgan's **Saratoga**, and the little town of **Boyce** a quarter of a mile beyond. Saratoga is on your left on Va. 723. The house is not visible from the road, but, by turning left at the sign and driving between the two narrow stone gateposts and down the dirt lane for a quarter of a mile, you will be able to view Saratoga, which is privately-owned and can be seen on the inside only with the permission of the owners.

On reaching the main intersection of Va. 723 and U.S. 340 at Boyce, just beyond the railroad tracks, continue west on Va. 723 for 5 miles until it joins U.S. 50. Follow U.S. 50 the additional 3 miles back to Winchester.

If it is a nice day and you have the time to extend your sightseeing day tour by an hour or so, an additional tour of **Charles Town**, West Virginia, can be incorporated into your outing by turning at the main traffic light in Berryville onto U.S. 340 north to Charles Town (13 miles). After a tour of Charles Town, as outlined in the next section of this Tour Guide, reverse your course to Berryville on U.S. 340 and continue south to pick up the Berryville-Boyce tour again at Old Chapel.

4. CHARLES TOWN—HARPERS FERRY AREA

The principal charm of **Charles Town**, West Virginia, besides its interesting older houses of Norman French architecture, is not only the rolling nature of the surrounding countryside, but also four Washington homes in the area. Three of these houses were built by George Washington's brothers and one by a cousin. Perhaps the most formally imposing of these, although a relatively small house, is the townhouse of Washington's brother, Colonel Charles Washington, the founder of the town after whom it is said to have been named. **Mordington** stands at the south end of Charles Town, just off Va. 9, on Mordington Avenue. Begun in 1783 and originally named "Happy Retreat", this charming white brick residence played host to many a famous name in its heyday, including Charles' brother, George, as well as Thomas Jefferson, Benjamin Franklin, the Marquis de Lafayette, and many others. The delightful country house of Washington's other brother, Colonel Samuel Washington, is 3 miles to the west on Va. 51. Built in 1771 of native fieldstone, **Harewood** also played host to many of those illustrous names, and James

112

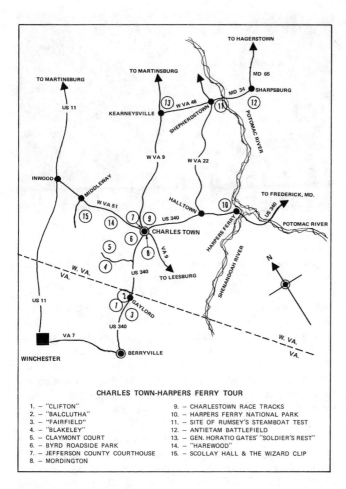

TO HAGERSTOWN

TO MARTINSBURG

MD 65

TO MARTINSBURG

MD 34 SHARPSBURG

TO MARTINSBURG

US 11

13 W VA 48

KEARNEYSVILLE

SHEPHERDSTOWN 11

12

POTOMAC RIVER

W VA 9

W VA 22

INWOOD

MIDDLEWAY

TO FREDERICK, MD.

W VA 51

HALLTOWN

10

POTOMAC RIVER

15

14

7 9 US 340

CHARLES TOWN

US 340

HARPERS FERRY

SHENANDOAH RIVER

6

5

VA 9

4

8

US 340

TO LEESBURG

W. VA.
VA.

N

US 11

2

GAYLORD

1

3

US 340

VA 7

WINCHESTER

BERRYVILLE

W. VA.
VA.

CHARLES TOWN-HARPERS FERRY TOUR

1. — "CLIFTON"	9. — CHARLESTOWN RACE TRACKS
2. — "BALCLUTHA"	10. — HARPERS FERRY NATIONAL PARK
3. — "FAIRFIELD"	11. — SITE OF RUMSEY'S STEAMBOAT TEST
4. — "BLAKELEY"	12. — ANTIETAM BATTLEFIELD
5. — CLAYMONT COURT	13. — GEN. HORATIO GATES' "SOLDIER'S REST"
6. — BYRD ROADSIDE PARK	14. — "HAREWOOD"
7. — JEFFERSON COUNTY COURTHOUSE	15. — SCOLLAY HALL & THE WIZARD CLIP
8. — MORDINGTON	

and Dolly Madison's wedding took place within its portals in 1794.

Bushrod Washington's **Claymont Court** and charming **Blakeley** lie to the southwest of town, 1 mile off U.S. 340, to your right as you head south from Charles Town for the Virginia state line and Berryville. All four of these Washington family homes are clearly visible from your car along the roads listed in the tour guide of the area, and all four of them are well worth seeing (even if they had not been the homes of the Washington family).

In Charles Town proper, the **Jefferson County Court-**

113

Mordington, home of Col. Charles Washington

house is located at the town's main intersection. It was here
that John Brown's trial was held in December of 1859,
when he was condemned to death by hanging. The twin
race tracks lie to the east of Charles Town, along U.S. 340
as you head for Harpers Ferry. The **Charles Town Race
Course**, nearest the highway, has been in operation for
many years and both it and **Shenandoah Downs** draw huge
crowds of horse-lovers annually. The two tracks operate
almost continuously year around, but the raffish element
they have brought to Charles Town has not sat too well
with the older, more conservative element among its
citizens.

Delightful, sleepy, unspoiled **Shepherdstown**, formerly
called Mecklenburg by its largely German inhabitants, should
be a "must" on your tour of the area. It was across the
Potomac River ford here that much of the traffic and
commerce from the northeast costal states first arrived in
the Valley. The Valley's first two fully-accredited settlers,
Hans Joist Hite and Robert McKay, entered the Valley
here. At a later date (1787), the river bend, where the
highway bridge leading into Maryland and **Antietam National Battlefield Site** now stands, was the scene of the first
thrilling test run of James Rumsey's "Flying Teakettle",
perhaps the first successful steam-propelled vessel in the
world.

Today, Shepherdstown is the home of Shepherd College
and a true delight to the eye, with its quaint streets,

old-fashioned shops and ice cream parlors, and fine old houses. Especially noteworthy is the early 19th century old **tollhouse**, long since converted for a wide variety of civic uses: Women's Club, Town Library, and, at one time, Odd Fellows Hall. Another outstanding relic of past and present

civic pride, beside the neat campus of Shepherd College, is the **Rumsey Memorial** located in a park at the east side of town, overlooking the same placid curve in the Potomac River where his "Flying Teakettle" inched upstream against the current, spewing steam in all directions. The two sets of stone piers below the park are all that remain of the old highway and railroad bridge destroyed in the Civil War in the wake of the Battle of Antietam. One of the loveliest and most intimate rural jaunts through unspoiled farmland to be found in the area is the drive from **Halltown** to **Shepherdstown** on W. Va. 23.

Harpers Ferry is best described as a 19th century "Federal" style hilltown, laboriously nailed down to the slopes of the Blue Ridge, overlooking the magnificent twin gorges at the confluence of the Potomac and Shenandoah Rivers. At first a key ferry point into the Valley from the seacoast, as well as the gateway through which the Swiss explorer, Louis Michel, entered the Valley in 1705, it soon became a canal port and then a railroad town. In the mid-19th century, it was a major supply depot and arsenal

115

for the United States Army where its rifling lathes were turned by the waters of both rivers. Until the coming of "Osawatomie" Brown and his fanatical band in 1859, its principal hazard had been the repeated floods which, from time to time, ravaged the lower sections of the community. Brown and his followers soon changed all that, substituting fire and the sword for rampaging rivers.

Virginia State Library

U.S. Armory, Harpers Ferry – 1858

Until the coming of the railroads, Harpers Ferry was an important canal town on the Chesapeake and Ohio Canal system. Today, with the passing of canals and the railroads, it is a scenic backwater, a kind of precipitous "nostalgia-ville", beautifully restored and maintained by the Park Service as **Harpers Ferry National Historical Park**, with **John Brown's Fort** and several museums at its center.

A peaceful setting of a far different type awaits the visitor at **The Wizarde Clippe**, the colonial section of the tiny hamlet of **Middleway**, West Virginia, to the west of Charles Town. Originally settled in 1732 by a Mr. John Smith of Cambridge, Massachusetts, on a direct land grant from Governor William Gooch of Virginia, Middleway was first known as Smithfield, until a town in the Old Dominion further to the south became too well-known for its hams and a conflict of interest developed at the post office.

At one time, before being rechristened "Middleway", Smithfield was called Wizarde Clippe, and there is quite a fascinating story connected with this old nomenclature.

116

The legend of Wizard Clippe begins with the arrival, on a wild and stormy night, of a stranger on horseback at the little town of Smithfield. It was around the turn of the 18th century that this wet and bedraggled stormbound stranger knocked on Elder Livingstone's door, seeking shelter. Later on, after he had been admitted and given a spare room for the night, and his horse had been snugly bedded down in the Livingstone stables, it developed that the visitor was not only on the point of death from exposure and some strange disease, but also was a devout Catholic who needed "shriving" before his death. The nearest priest was 8 miles away through the stormy night in Charles Town, and Smithfield was a strictly English Protestant town.

Among the most bigoted Church of England men in the community was the dying man's host, Elder Livingstone, who firmly refused to have a Popish priest in his house on any pretext. The stranger died, unshriven, with a strange curse on his lips. Since nobody knew who the dead stranger was or where he came from, he was given decent burial in the town's Protestant graveyard—still without benefit of priest. Soon after, strange things began to happen in the Livingstone house and a whole series of terrible, devastating storms struck Smithfield. Bolts of lightning levelled Elder Livingstone's barn, along with those of several of his neighbors, and what was even worse, at the height of the mysterious midnight tempests, all sorts of terrifying things occurred in Elder Livingstone's house. Furniture flew through the air, invisible bells rang, dishes, plucked from the kitchen cupboard by unseen hands, were scattered about the premises and, weirdest of all, unseen scissors clipped strange demonish halfmoon designs on every bit of cloth material he owned, including his clothing and the saddle-blankets in the stable! Badly shaken and duly sobered by these manifestations, Livingstone finally agreed to call in the Catholic priest from nearby Charles Town to say a prayer at the stranger's grave. The village churchyard was proclaimed holy ground in order to put the demons to rest.

Overnight the storms and other scary goings-on came to an end. In grateful recognition, Elder Livingstone deeded forty acres of his best farmland along Opequon Creek to the Catholic Church. In due course, a chapel was built on this land, which to this day is known as "The Priest's Place."

This plot of holy ground was, until just recently, the scene of an annual pilgrimage by the townspeople of Middleway for a memorial service to honor the mysterious stranger and to celebrate the anniversary of the final lifting of his terrible curse.

Scollay Hall, built in 1789, was named in the honor of a Harvard College surgeon who, in 1790, joined his former classmate, John Smith, to practice medicine in the area. It is located just off the village common and today serves good, substantial country meals in its dining room with the usual country trimmings. All you have to do is to go inside Scollay Hall and sit down in the faded light of its ancient blue-tinted windows, while you listen to its current mistress tell the yarn of "Ye Wizarde Clippe", and you will soon find out why the little by-road town of Middleway was once called Wizarde Clippe in honor of a galloping, clipping ghost. The names in the Scollay Hall guest book may surprise you. The guests who have come to dinner, only to fall victim to the charm of the place and its strange true tale of long ago, come from every section of this continent—and quite a few from overseas. Remember, Charles Town is only 50 miles from Washington.

SUGGESTED TOUR: 95 Miles — 4 Hours, Round Trip from Winchester. (Add Extra Hour for Antietam)

Leave Winchester on Va. 7 for **Berryville**; turn left off Va. 7 at the main traffic light in Berryville, onto U.S. 340 north for the West Virginia state line and Charles Town. There are three rather striking manor houses at **Gaylord** near the West Virginia state line. Two of them, **Clifton** and **Balclutha,** lie to your left on adjoining hilltops. The third, **Fairfield** appears first to your right with its horseboarding Redpath Stables.

Approximately 5½ miles after crossing the state line into West Virginia, you will see a road to your left, marked **Claymont Court.** A newer sign indicates Spring Valley Hunt and Country Club. Turn off U.S. 340 onto this road and drive 1½ miles to Claymont Court, Bushrod Washington's home. Opposite Claymont Court, on your left, is lovely **Blakeley Farm,** another Washington home. Reverse your route and return to U.S. 340. As you turn left, you will see another large grove of the **Byrd Orchards.** There is a charming picnic grove and rest area donated for public enjoyment by the late Senator Harry F. Byrd about a half mile farther down the road.

Continue one mile on U.S. 340 to **Charles Town**. At the third traffic light on U.S. 340 in Charles Town stands the **Jefferson County Courthouse**, where John Brown was tried and sentenced to death for both his armed insurrection against the U.S. government and his previous killings in Canada and Kansas. The sentence was carried out in a field beside George Street, and a plaque marks the site of the gallows where he was publicly hanged A right turn at this intersection in front of the Courthouse onto George Street, (W. Va. 9 South) takes you past this grim reminder.

A quarter of a mile further on, Mordington Avenue branches off George Street to the right and takes you one block to **Mordington**. It was first named **"Happy Retreat"** by its builder and lifetime owner, Colonel Charles Washington, who was George Washington's brother and founder of the town which bears his name.

For the 6-mile drive to **Harpers Ferry**, turn back to the main traffic light in front of the Courthouse. Here, turn right again, onto U.S. 340 North. As you leave town, note the two race tracks to your left, the **Charles Town Race Course** and **Shenandoah Downs**. The first Charles Town track began operation back in 1783.

Approaching Harpers Ferry watch for a sign to your left and the road leading one mile to **Harpers Ferry Caverns**. Just before you reach the Shenandoah River bridge, turn left off U.S. 340 at the **Harpers Ferry National Historical Park** sign. A half-mile drive will bring you to the park headquarters and **John Brown's Fort**. Although it is quite steep and hilly, a leisurely ten-minute drive, or a more extended walk, around the restored park section of the town will prove worthwhile. There are several gift shops and museums and a fine view of the twin river gorges can be obtained at either Jefferson Rock or the new plot of national park ground above Bolivar, at the west end of town.

Upon leaving Harpers Ferry, turn right, off U.S. 340 West at Halltown, just before you cross the railroad tracks in front of the Halltown Paper Board Company, onto W. Va. 23, where the arrow points toward **Shepherdstown**. An 8-mile drive through rolling farmland will bring you to a delightfully sleepy and unspoiled community on the banks

119

of the Potomac River where "Crazy" James Rumsey tested his "Flying Teakettle" in December of 1787. Follow W.Va. 23 into town to Main Street. Turn right, and then left on Rumsey Street and follow signs to the Rumsey Monument and riverside park. Go back to Main Street. On your left at the corner of S. King Street and Main is the old **tollhouse.** Continue on Main Street to W. Va. 48 and turn right. Pass the **Shepherd College** campus on your right just before the Rumsey Bridge over the Potomac River.

If you care to add the hour or so needed to tour Sharpsburg, Maryland and **Antietam National Battlefield Site,** continue over the bridge (W. Va. 48 becomes Md. 34) about 4 miles through Sharpsburg to Md. 65 and turn left about one mile to the Visitor's Center. There is a 20-minute slide lecture at the Center and also maps for an 8-mile self-guiding automobile tour of the entire battlefield.

After reversing your route to the Rumsey Bridge at Shepherdstown, continue straight ahead on W. Va. 48 past the traffic light to **Kearneysville** (5 miles). At the intersection of W. Va. 48 and W. Va. 9, turn left onto W. Va. 9 for the 8 miles back to Charles Town. At Charles Town, turn right beside the courthouse at the main traffic light, to W. Va. 51 west for a short 3-mile ride to Colonel Samuel Washington's lovely fieldstone home. **Harewood** will lie on your left at the rise of a crest on the road marked by an appropriate state historical marker informing the visitor that it was the scene of James and Dolley Madison's wedding and was built in 1771. Another 5 miles west, just past the Midway Inn, turn left to **Middleway. Scollay Hall** and **The Wizard Clip Gift Shop** are about a half mile down the road. After your visit to Scollay Hall, return to W. Va. 51, turn left, and go 5 miles to its intersection with U.S. 11 at Inwood. Here turn left onto U.S. 11 (the Valley Pike) or 1-81 for the 14-mile return trip to **Winchester.**

5. LEESBURG AREA

Although this lovely area is at the very eastern perimeter of the Blue Bridge Piedmont foothills, we have included it here because it is closely tied to Valley history, especially during the Civil War. Colonel John Singleton Mosby, the Grey Ghost, roamed and raided here. Mistress Belle Boyd, the lady spy from Martinsburg and Front Royal, used a nearby farm along the Potomac riverfront as her head-

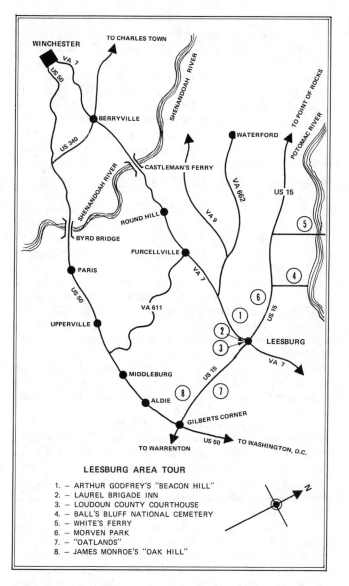

TO CHARLES TOWN

WINCHESTER

VA 7

US 50

SHENANDOAH RIVER

BERRYVILLE

US 340

WATERFORD

TO POINT OF ROCKS

POTOMAC RIVER

CASTLEMAN'S FERRY

VA 662

US 15

SHENANDOAH RIVER

VA 9

ROUND HILL

BYRD BRIDGE

PURCELLVILLE

⑤

④

PARIS

VA 7

⑥

US 50

VA 611

①

US 15

UPPERVILLE

②

③

LEESBURG

VA 7

MIDDLEBURG

US 15

⑧

⑦

ALDIE

GILBERTS CORNER

TO WARRENTON

US 50

TO WASHINGTON, D.C.

N

LEESBURG AREA TOUR

1. — ARTHUR GODFREY'S "BEACON HILL"
2. — LAUREL BRIGADE INN
3. — LOUDOUN COUNTY COURTHOUSE
4. — BALL'S BLUFF NATIONAL CEMETERY
5. — WHITE'S FERRY
6. — MORVEN PARK
7. — "OATLANDS"
8. — JAMES MONROE'S "OAK HILL"

quarters during her work as a "courier" for the Confederacy. A great deal of actual fighting in skirmishes also took place in the vicinity of Leesburg, the most significant engagement occuring in 1861 at **Ball's Bluff.**

121

A few miles further south on U.S. 15 is the historic James Monroe estate, **Oak Hill**, designed by Thomas Jefferson and built in 1820-23 for the fifth President of the United States by James Hoban, the same man who was the architect of the White House and the U.S. Capitol in Washington. Monroe lived there both during his term of office (1817-1825) and afterwards until the death of his wife in 1830. Lafayette stayed there when he visited the United States in 1825. It is said that James Monroe often commuted between the unfinished White House and Oak Hill, on horseback without military escort, carrying in his saddle-bags, government papers and important dispatches.

Oak Hill is just to the west of U.S. 15, ten miles south of Leesburg and two miles north of **Gilberts Corner** (the intersection of U.S. 50 and U.S. 15), and is plainly visible from the highway. It is privately-owned and is only open to the public on such special occasions as Virginia Garden Week in April.

Halfway between Oak Hill and Leesburg on U.S. 15, on the right side headed north, stands **Oatlands**, the country seat of George Carter, designed by him in 1800. This handsome mansion, with its box garden and 261-acre farm, was a gift of Mrs. David Finley and Mrs. Eustis Emmet to the National Trust for Historic Preservation and is open to the public daily from April through October. Oatlands is an example of Georgian architecture and comfortable country living during the 19th century and is noted for its lovely gardens.

In the heart of **Leesburg**, on Va. 7, within half a block of the typically southern courthouse square with its gun-toting Confederate soldier on granite, stands the **Laurel Brigade Inn**. This long-established dining place is not only quaint and quiet, but serves good food in the old southern tradition. A 3-mile jog north on U.S. 15, from the traffic light at the main intersection in front of the courthouse square, carries you past the turn-off to **Ball's Bluff National Cemetery** to fascinating **White's Ferry**. Ball's Bluff is small and unpretentious as Civil War cemeteries and battlefields go, and so is White's Ferry in comparison to the huge steam and diesel ferryboats threading the Hudson River at New York. But what White's Ferry lacks in size and horsepower, it more than makes up in charm and serenity in a truly old-world setting. The "Jubal Early", the ferry's only craft carries an absolute maximum of six cars on each ten-minute crossing of the peaceful and tree-lined Potomac, from Virginia riverbank to the concrete ferry-slip apron on the Maryland shore. It is one of the last self-propelled cable ferries in the United States, and a trip across the quiet waters of the Potomac River here on the "Jubal Early" (named after a famous Confederate general) is a treat to be remembered by the whole family—the young people in particular—since, like the covered bridge of bygone days, it is a fast-fading landmark.

Virginia State Travel Service

White's Ferry

Charming **Waterford**, the old colonial milltown which was only recently restored and which, over the past ten years, has become a mecca each October for visitors from far and near to its fall festival, lies a few miles to the northeast of Va. 9 on Va. 662, and is well worth visiting at any time of year. The restored houses, the quaint streets, the art galleries, and the antique and gift shops are an irresistible lure for those in search of antiquity, unhurried peace, and an occasional bargain in old art treasures. During festival time, local foods and delicacies—such as preserves, sweetmeats, and country bread and cookies—are sold along with paintings, bric-a-brac, metalwork, and woodcravings. In conjunction with the annual "Waterford Homes Tour and Crafts Exhibit," similar items are offered along the streets of Leesburg at the "Cart Mart" held on the first Saturday in October.

On top of all of this historical background, the Leesburg section has long been a major bastion of agriculture, horse breeding, cattle, and the fox hunt, a wealthy and worthy

123

rival of **Middleburg** and **Upperville,** a few miles to the west. Arthur Godfrey maintains his big "spread", **Beacon Hill Farm,** at Peonian Springs, about one mile northwest of Leesburg, along Va. 7. He also has his own private airfield on the grounds to supplement the **Leesburg** municipal airport which bears his name. Godfrey Field, Northern Virginia's finest municipal airport is 1½ miles east of Leesburg on Va. 643. Visitors are always welcome.

Morven Park, on the northern outskirts of Leesburg, formerly the home of Westmoreland Davis, Governor of Virginia from 1918-1922, is reached from Va. 7 or from U.S. 15 over a series of narrow streets and secondary roads as detailed in the suggested tour of the area to follow. Only recently, Morven Park was deeded by the Davis family to the Commonwealth of Virginia as a public recreation park and both the enormous porticoed house and formal gardens are being restored to their former glory. The chief attraction of this 1,200-acre public pleasaunce is not the main house, but the superb box and other extensive formal gardens, as well as the International Equestrian Institute and the carriage collection headquartered in the old groom and stable area.

For additional information on this area stop in Leesburg at the little museum, 14 W. Loudoun Street and its next door Chamber of Commerce office.

SUGGESTED TOUR: 90 Miles — 3½ to 4 Hours Round Trip from Winchester. (Add ½ Hour for Round Trip on White's Ferry)

Take Va. 7 east out of Winchester to **Berryville** and continue east on Va. 7 past **Castleman's Ferry** at the Shenandoah River bridge, across **Snicker's Gap** to **Round Hill** and **Purcellville.** 4 miles beyond Purcellville, at **Clarks Gap,** where Va. 7 joins Va. 9, turn left onto Va. 9 for one mile to the next right-hand fork in the road, which will be Va. 662. Follow Va. 662 for 3 miles to **Waterford.** Upon entering town, bear left and remain on Va. 662 (Factory Street) to Second Street and Main Street. **The Old Mill** and **Mill Shop** is at the foot of Main Street (Open on Saturdays and Sundays, 12:00 noon to 5:00 p.m., June through September.)

To reach **Leesburg** from this delightfully-restored mill town, retrace your route back to Clarks Gap, turn left onto

124

Va. 7 and drive the remaining 3 miles to Leesburg. You will pass the Arthur Godfrey estate, **Beacon Hill Farm,** on your left, about one mile past Clarks Gap on Va. 7.

Virginia Chamber of Commerce
Leesburg Courthouse

In Leesburg the **Laurel Brigade Inn** will be on your left just before you reach the main intersection in front of the old **Loudoun County Courthouse.** To reach **Ball's Bluff National Cemetery** and **White's Ferry,** turn left here, at the main traffic light, onto U.S. 15 and head north. Approximately 1 mile north of the town limits on U.S. 15, there is a state historical marker on your left which describes the Battle of Ball's Bluff. Opposite this maker, you will see a road marked Va. 837. Turn right onto Va. 837 and proceed to the stone marker at the fork in the road. Bear to the

125

right at this fork and continue on a dirt road 1½ miles to the cemetery. Although Ball's Bluff has the unique distinction of being the smallest United States, military cemetery (27 graves and a flagpole), a stinging engagement was fought there, beside the Potomac, in October 1861, a battle on which hinged the opening of the entire Piedmont to the Union forces. Return to U.S. 15 and continue 2 miles north to the turn-off for **White's Ferry**, which is on your right and is well marked. You may want to take the "Jubal Early" on the ten-minute crossing to the Maryland side of the Potomac.

After leaving White's Ferry, retrace your route back to U.S. 15 and Leesburg. Watch for the sign to Morven Park on your right. If you prefer to continue into Leesburg, turn right at the second cross street after entering the town limits (2 blocks north of Courthouse Square) onto W. North Street. After 2 blocks, turn right again at the dead end of North Street, in front of the cemetery, onto Old Waterford Road. Bear right at the next fork in the road, onto Morven Park Road which will take you over a hilly winding route to the main gates of **Morven Park**. Continue down the avenue of trees and follow the arrows to the parking lot for the main house, botanical gardens, and Equestrian Institute.

On leaving Morven Park, retrace your route back to U.S. 15. Keep south on U.S. 15 out of **Leesburg,** and continue

Howard Allen

approximately 6 miles to the entrance gates of **Oatlands** which will be on your left and is well-marked. After visiting Oatlands, continue south on U.S. 15 and 5 miles past **Oak Hill**, home of President James Monroe, which will be on your right. One mile beyond Oak Hill, on the left side of the road, you will find a descriptive marker. Stop at this marker for an unobstructed view of the beautiful hill top mansion.

Continue south to the intersection of U.S. 15 and U.S. 50 at **Gilberts Corner**. Turn right, onto U.S. 50 west, for **Aldie, Middleburg,** and **Upperville**. Continue west on U.S. 50 past **Paris** and over **Ashby Gap** and the **Byrd Bridge** across the Shenandoah to **Winchester**. En route, on both U.S. 15 and U.S. 50, you will be passing through some of the finest and most famous horse country in the entire world. This area will be covered in the next tour.

6. MIDDLEBURG—UPPERVILLE AREA

This loop through Fauquier and Loudoun counties takes you through the heart of the fabulous "Virginia hunt country", where the blooded horse is king, closely followed by the purebred Hereford and Angus, plus the lowly, but highly profitable, sheep and lamb. You will motor past the very cream of the thoroughbred horse farms, second in importance in the production of fine horseflesh only to the Ocala region in central Florida and the Lexington-Paris area in Kentucky. But they are second to none in prestige, beauty and decorum. This section of the Old Dominion boasts such magic names in fox hunting as Middleburg, Piedmont, and Orange County. The Orange County Hunt was only recently brought to world prominence by the presence of Mrs. John F. Kennedy as an active, riding member. The anxious Secret Service men, if they accomplished nothing else, drove the distinguished local citizens to distraction by their presence—all on top of the influx of unwelcome weekend visitors come to get a glimpse of the President or to see his First Lady on horseback, or both of them going to Sunday worship at the **Middleburg Community Center.**

Among the wealthy and distinguished list of local landowners is an expatriate from Pittsburgh and Rolling Rock, Mr. Paul Mellon. The Mellons, besides building up an

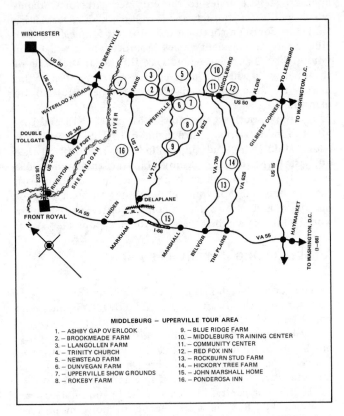

MIDDLEBURG – UPPERVILLE TOUR AREA

1. – ASHBY GAP OVERLOOK
2. – BROOKMEADE FARM
3. – LLANGOLLEN FARM
4. – TRINITY CHURCH
5. – NEWSTEAD FARM
6. – DUNVEGAN FARM
7. – UPPERVILLE SHOW GROUNDS
8. – ROKEBY FARM

9. – BLUE RIDGE FARM
10. – MIDDLEBURG TRAINING CENTER
11. – COMMUNITY CENTER
12. – RED FOX INN
13. – ROCKBURN STUD FARM
14. – HICKORY TREE FARM
15. – JOHN MARSHALL HOME
16. – PONDEROSA INN

enviable stable of racehorses at their **Rokeby Farm** near Upperville, have donated to the community a magnificent stone church in Upperville, which you will see on your left at the center of town as you drive east on U.S. 50 towards Middleburg. Another generous Mellon public enterprise in the area is the well-equipped **Middleburg Training Center** to the northwest of that community on Va. 611.

As you leave **Upperville,** headed east towards Middleburg (8 miles), just beyond Colin McLeod's **Dunvegan Farm** and Mrs. A. C. Randolph's **Oakley,** you pass on your right the **Upperville Horse Show** grounds. It is the site of the more-than-a-century-old **Upperville Colt** and **Horse Show** (oldest in the United States) and is nestled in the shade of a grove of ancient oaks beside U.S. 50.

The late Mrs. Isabel Dodge Sloane's **Brookmeade Farm,**

128

beside U.S. 50 just west of Upperville, was long known for its winners of many of the nation's top races. Many people with half an ear to the ground socially and at the tracks have heard of **Llangollen Farm's** colorful proprietress, Liz Altemus Whitney Tippett. Other top breeding and racing stables include **Newstead Farm** and **Blue Ridge Farm** in the Upperville area, and **Hickory Tree Farm** near Middleburg.

Other "musts" for the sightseeing newcomer to the section are a stop for at least a noggin of ale at the taproom of the **Red Fox Tavern,** which has been in continuous operation since 1746; a quick look around the **Middleburg Community Center** where President Kennedy worshipped on Sundays; and if you are looking for fine antiques, stop at any one or all of the Middleburg shops along Washington Street (U.S. 50) for a tempting array of period pieces guaranteed to burn a hole in your pocketbook. But above all, don't fail to pause on U.S. 50 at the top of **Ashby Gap** (sometimes called the Paris Gap), just west of the little community by that name, for a good look at the view on a clear day in both directions—east and west. It is one of the scenic gems of the entire Valley and Blue Ridge, with a superb panoramic view of the Piedmont plateau, the Bull Run Mountains to the east, and an equally breathtaking view of the northern Shenandoah Valley stretched out at your feet like a tapestry to the west.

SUGGESTED TOUR: 75 Miles — 3 Hours, Round Trip From Winchester.

Take U.S. 50 east from Winchester at the end of Millwood Avenue, for Paris, Upperville, and Middleburg. If it is a clear day, be sure to pause at the brink of **Ashby Gap** for the view east across the Piedmont. U.S. 50 will take you directly past **Annandale Angus Farm** and **Brookmeade Farm.** Before reaching Upperville, just beyond Brookmeade, approximately two miles to your left on Va. 619, are **Ayrshire Farm** and **Llangollen Farm.** U.S. 50 through Upperville passes **Trinity Episcopal Church** on your left. On your right beyond town are **Duvegan** and **Oakley** farms the **Upperville Colt and Horse Show grounds,** and Va. 623 leading (approximately 2 miles) to **Rokeby Farm** and **Blue Ridge Farm.**

Continue three miles east of Upperville and one mile beyond the village of Atoka, just off U.S. 50, where in

129

1863 Mosby organized his famous band of Rangers. To your left is Va. 611, which leads two miles north to the entrance to the **Middleburg Training Center**. The young horses being trained at the track are well worth seeing in the early morning hours. Just beyond the turn-off to Va. 611, you can see on the right from U.S. 50 the unpaved entrance road leading through the woods to where President and Mrs. John F. Kennedy built their weekend retreat.

At Middleburg on your left is the **Community Center** where the President attended church on Sundays during 1961 and 1962. Although temporarily used for church services, it has served area residents and children since 1948 as a recreation and meeting area. Open 9:30 a.m. to 5:00 p.m. Closed Mondays. At the main Middleburg intersection is the **Red Fox Inn** ("the Second Oldest Tavern in the United States").

Return from Middleburg on U.S. 50; after it becomes a dual-lane highway just west of the city limits, turn left onto Va. 709 for a drive through beautiful country to Marshall. After about a 5 mile drive **Rockburn Stud Farm** will be on the left, as you head south towards Belvoir and Va. 55. At the intersection of Va. 55 and 709 at Belvoir (no town, just a restaurant—country store), turn right at the Fauquier Livestock Exchange on Va. 55 for Marshall.

Three miles west of Marshall, Va. 55 becomes I-66 for 3 miles. The **John Marshall Home**, indicated by a state historical marker, is visible to your right far back from the road. Bear right on Va. 17 where it separates from I-66 and Va. 55 and head toward Paris. The town of **Delaphane** is just to your right as you cross the railroad tracks. Another 3 miles north on Va. 55 brings you to the intersection of Va. 17 and U.S. 50 again. Turn left on U.S. 50 for the climb back past Paris over **Ashby Gap**, and your return to Winchester.

Howard Allen

7. CLARKE AND WARREN COUNTY FARMS

If it is the more agrarian, off-the-beaten-track tour you are looking for, past superb farms, limestone gazing-land, big barns, and old manor houses, this will be the "run" for you. This tour is especially recommended in clear sunny weather in spring when the lambs, the calves, and the young foals are racing gaily about the pastures. The whole pocket contained in this area, enclosed by U.S. 50 to the north, U.S. 522-340 to the west, and the Shenandoah River and the Blue Ridge to the east and south, is breathtakingly beautiful farm country. It is threaded by excellent paved, gravel, or dirt roads and ringed by towering mountains—the Blue Ridge to the north and east, the Alleghenies far to the west and the Massanuttens, with the sharp loom of Signal Knob in the foreground, to the southwest. What is more, the area is entirely foolproof for the motorist. All roads in this ten-mile long and five-mile wide section eventually lead out to the main highways, U.S. 50 or 522-340. There is also one paved secondary road (Va. 624 — Va. 647) leading into **Front Royal** by the back route, across the low water bridge over the Shenandoah and thence into town through Happy Creek.

The romantic and colorful place-names of the big farms and estates of the old landed gentry stem from either the family tree of the founders or the whim of the early owners: **"Lucky Hit"**, **"Redgate"**, **"Federal Hill"**, **"Mt. Zion"**, **"Mt. Ida"**, and **"Mt. Republic"**, just to name a few. Most of these larger manor houses, with a few notable exceptions, were built after the period of the first home-steaders, Scotch-Irish brought in by Robert McKay and son. Among the exceptions are **Antrim Farm**, the home of Joshua Antrim McKay, and just to the west of U.S. 522-340 near Cedarville on Va. 628, **Cedarbrook Farm,** which originally was the log cabin dwelling of Aubrey Lee McKay. Beside U.S. 522 at Cedarville stands the home of Robert McKay, Jr., built in 1732 and said to be the oldest homesteader's house still standing in the Valley. It was used as a military hospital during the battle of Cedarville in 1862. Of special historical interest, in addition to the McKay homes, are Washington's surveying headquarters at **Greenway Court** and the remains of the old country store at **Milldale**.

The name **Milldale** originates from the two long-gone

131

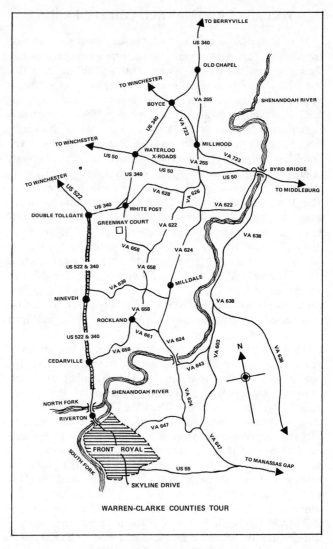

WARREN-CLARKE COUNTIES TOUR

gristmills whose waterwheels were set beside the stream, a minor tributary of the nearby Shenandoah. **Rockland's** name is attributed to the endless limestone outcroppings in the fertile soil where the succulent bluegrass grows so richly in season. **White Post** came from the tall white wooden column still standing at the hamlet's only cross road, put there in 1748 under the supervision of George Washington.

132

White Post

Double Tollgate derived its name from the twin toll houses at the intersection of the old post roads which are now U.S. 522 south from Winchester and U.S. 340 southwest from Berryville.

Lovely **"Erin"** with its classic Doric columns, built in 1844 by Colonel David Funsten of Irish descent, stands two miles north of **Cedarville** on U.S. 522-340 at Nineveh, on the east side of the dual-lane highway. The house is still occupied by the colonel's descendants. **Redgate Farm** was long one of the top registered Angus cattle breeding farms in the area. Now it is devoted chiefly to the rearing of fine thoroughbred horses as are nearby **Antrim Farm** and **Lucky Hit** at White Post. But whether the crop is apples, peaches, sheep, cattle, or fine horseflesh, all of these farms are well worth driving past, if only to enjoy their neat mint condition, their rolling fields and oak-studded copses enclosed by orderly fence-rows. The **Blue Ridge Hunt** meets here to steeplechase these same snake-fenced hedgerows in late fall and early winter. Although it is plain to see, from the well-kept lawns, barns, and houses, that, for the most part, this is a rich man's world, it is there for you to drive past and enjoy—scot-free—at your motoring pleasure. So are the mountains, the river, and the shaded winding gravel country roads which are always beautifully maintained and free of heavy or speeding traffic.

SUGGESTED TOUR: 45 Miles - 2 Hours, Round Trip From Front Royal.

Take U. S. 522-340 north out of Front Royal across the Shenandoah River bridges, and continue 9 miles to Double Tollgate. Turn right at the traffic light on U.S. 340 and continue 3 miles to the **White Post** exit on your right. At the White Post wooden pylon, turn right again and go south on Va. 658 for exactly 1.1 miles to the gravel lane on your right which leads to the site of **Greenway Court** and Washington's fieldstone surveying headquarters behind the new house built on the ruins of Lord Fairfax's summer home. Retrace your route to the pylon at White Post. Turn right at the post and proceed on Va. 628 for 2½ miles to its

133

Virginia State Library

Only remaining structure, Greenway Court

intersection with Va. 626. Turn right and follow Va. 626 to
Va. 622 (nearly 1 mile). Turn left on Va. 622 and continue
1 mile to Va. 624. Turn right (on south) here and stay on
Va. 624 for the next 6 miles down the valley floor to the
right turn onto Va. 661 for **Rockland.** At Rockland, turn
left onto Va. 658 and follow 658 to U.S. 522-340, the
dual-lane highway, at **Cedarville.** The **McKay House** will be
directly opposite you, across the highway, set on a slight
rise behind the church. It is half fieldstone and half
clapboard over huge walnut logs. Turn left into the
southbound lane at Cedarville for the short drive back to
Front Royal.

There are any number of variations of this tour in this
quiet pocket bounded by highways U.S. 50, 522-340, and
the Shenandoah River. Any road you take to your right, or
east and south, off either U.S. 522-340 or U.S. 340 beyond
Double Tollgate, will take you into the quiet farmland bowl
of peace and plenty. Similarly, any road you take out of

this pocket will eventually lead you back onto either of the main highways. You really can't get lost for long in these 30 square miles of agrarian nirvana.

To take a tour of the **Shenandoah Riverbank**, head east on Va. 622 (after following the first part of the tour

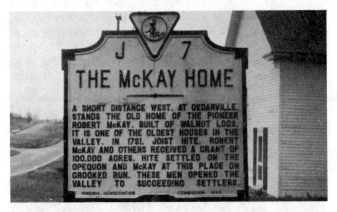

described above); then cross its intersection with Va. 624, which runs north and south, and, after about 1½ miles, you will reach a curve to the left which brings you out on the west bank of the Shenandoah River. Follow Va. 622 north along the tree-lined riverbank to the **Harry Flood Byrd Bridge** which carries U.S. 50 across the river. Here a curve in the dirt road just past and under the bridge takes you up to join U.S. 50 on the upper level. From here you can either follow U.S. 50 west, all the way back to Winchester, or, by turning left at the first traffic light beyond the bridge **(Waterloo Crossroads)**, you can follow U.S. 340 back to Front Royal (19 miles).

Incidentally, for you avid golfers, there is an excellent eighteen-hole public course with is own swimming pool 1 mile east of **Rockland** on Va. 658. It is called **The Shenandoah Valley Golf Club** and the greens fees per day are reasonable, with or without electric golf carts. The view from the course is superb, but the course is apt to be crowded on nice summer weekends.

8. STRASBURG–MIDDLETOWN AREA

Strasburg, settled by Germans largely from Alsace, was long famous not only for its Indian fighters, but for its fine

135

pottery. **Middletown,** settled by both Germans and Swiss, was known for its fine clocks, watches, and precision instruments used in both surveying and celestial navigation. Today, Strasburg is a rather sleepy agricultural town with only two major industries, printing and small boat building. Middletown, on the other hand, is becoming better-known each year for its fine cuisine at the delightful **Wayside Inn,** and its professional stock company at the nearby **Wayside Theatre.** Theater-goers and overnight guests arrive by the busload in season, and an evening at the theatre, with dinner before or supper afterwards, has become quite the "thing to do". There is also a gift shop, an art gallery, and a generous display of antiques at the Wayside Inn.

Wayside Theatre

There are several places of great historic interest in the area, all easily accessible from the highway. South of Middletown on U.S. 11 (the old Valley Pike), halfway to Strasburg, stands historic **Belle Grove,** now property of the National Trust for Historic Preservation. Belle Grove was built by Major Isaac Hite, Jr., grandson of one of the Valley's first settlers, Joist Hite, in 1794. Major Hite was a distinguished Revolutionary-War officer and a graduate of the College of William and Mary, where he was the first member elected to Phi Beta Kappa by the charter members.

Belle Grove is open to the public, April through October, and stands in the center of the site of the Battle of Cedar Creek, which took place during the Civil War. In the engagement the house served as the headquarters of General Philip Sheridan.

James Madison, who was Hite's brother-in-law, and his bride, Dolley, stayed at Belle Grove on their honeymoon trip. Thomas Jefferson made refinements to the plans for Belle Grove, although he did not design it. Belle Grove is built of squared local limestone blocks, while **Long Meadows**, built in 1845 by Hite's cousin, General George Bowman, son of the builder of "Harmony Hall," is constructed of brick with long wooden porches in the country manner.

This was Indian country, hence the rash of forts, as well as the Indian burial grounds recently uncovered beside George Bowman's "Harmony Hall", better-known as **Fort Bowman,** about 2 miles north of Strasburg. Fort Bowman is dry-masonry built of native fieldstone, and its cellar served as the area stronghold against the Indians. **Fort Stephens,** north of Strasburg, beyond Lebanon Church and beside Cedar Creek, was built of brick and is the only Indian fort in the area still in an excellent state of preservation.

Signal Knob, high above the valley floor at the northern tip of the Massanuttens, like a ship's prow, and overlooking Strasburg, was used during three wars as a lookout and military semaphore station, from which it derives its present name. The ambitious hiker can reach Signal Knob by a trail climbing from a point just east of where Va. 55 crosses the North Fork of the Shenandoah River.

To the west of Strasburg, on Va. 55, loom the towering peaks of the Appalachian Mountains, frequently referred to as the Shenandoah Mountains. The 23 miles to **Wardensville,** West Virginia from Strasburg is an up and down affair through mountain scenery. Approximately 3 miles southwest of Wardensville you cross **Lost River,** which disappears beneath the mountains for 2 miles to surface again as the **Cacapon River.** If you should add this 60-mile West Virginia loop to your tour, you will be driving through pleasant, hilly, but not rugged, country from Wardensville to Gore. The first 10 miles of this stretch of W. Va. 259 will take you along the Cacapon River. This is great apple and peach orchard country, and is extremely quiet and remote.

137

If you have not taken the drive from Winchester to
Front Royal, now is the time to do so, since the run from
Double Tollgate south to Front Royal is one of the scenic
highlights of the entire Valley, with mountains ringing you

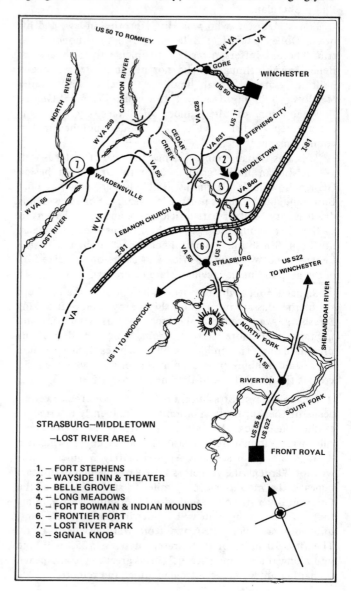

STRASBURG—MIDDLETOWN
—LOST RIVER AREA

1. – FORT STEPHENS
2. – WAYSIDE INN & THEATER
3. – BELLE GROVE
4. – LONG MEADOWS
5. – FORT BOWMAN & INDIAN MOUNDS
6. – FRONTIER FORT
7. – LOST RIVER PARK
8. – SIGNAL KNOB

138

from a hazy distance on all sides. Perhaps the most breath-taking view on a clear day is the 3-mile stretch of U.S. 522 between the tiny hamlets of **Nineveh** and **Cedarville**.

SUGGESTED TOUR: 38 Miles - 2 Hours. (**Add 60 Miles for West Virginia Loop**)

Leave **Front Royal** on U.S. 522-Va. 55 North. Cross the bridge over the South Fork of the Shenandoah River and turn left onto Va. 55 west at **Riverton** for **Strasburg**. Continue 10 miles to Strasburg on Va. 55. Beside the Southern RR tracks in the former railroad station, generously donated to the cause, stands the community museum. One of the largest and most comprehensive historical museums in the northern Valley, the **Strasburg Museum** is well worth half an hour's stop-over. On view are artifacts, old photographs, hand tools, machinery of long ago, and other interesting exhibits of ancient arts and handicrafts. Continue northwest from Strasburg on Va. 55.

At Lebanon Church (5 miles), turn right at the curve by the post office onto Va. 628. Drive north 3 miles on Va. 628 to the bridge over Cedar Creek. At the far side of the highway bridge, you can see **Fort Stephens** on the farmhouse lawn to your left. Continue on Va. 628 to Va. 631 (about 2 miles). Bear right onto Va. 631 and continue 4 miles to **Stephens City**. Here Va. 631 joins U.S. 11. Turn right and head toward **Middletown.**

In Middletown, the **Wayside Inn** will be on your right on U.S. 11, which is Middletown's main street, and the **Wayside Theater** is about a half-mile past the Inn. Note the highway marker indicating, just west of town, **Old Stone Fort** used for defense against Indians.

From Middletown, continue south on U.S. 11 one mile to **Belle Grove**, which is on the right. After visiting Belle Grove, continue south on U.S. 11 for two miles towards **Strasburg**. Just before you reach the down-hill curve where U.S. 11 briefly becomes dual-lane across Cedar Creek, turn left onto Va. 840, a hard-surfaced road. Drive 1 mile to the junction of Va. 840 and Va. 611. Turn right onto Va. 611, which is a dirt road. Approximately 1 mile southwest on Va. 611 will bring you to **Long Meadows** on your left, at the bottom of a hill just before Cedar Creek enters the North Fork of the Shenandoah River.

139

To reach nearby **Fort Bowman,** or "Harmony Hall", return to U.S. 11 and continue south to the interchange with I-81 just north of Strasburg. Cross over I-81 on the dual-lane overpass and turn left into the Sunoco station. Just to the north of the service station, there is a gravel road which bears to the right. This road (Frontage Road) leads to Fort Bowman. The fort is temporarily closed to the public while undergoing restoration, but you can catch a glimpse of it from behind the service station. It sits on a slight rise of Cedar Creek bottomland. Fort Bowman should be open to the public in the near future.

Return to U.S. 11 and continue to **Strasburg.** At Strasburg, you will see on your right an historical marker which identifies the **Frontier Fort,** a house used as a fort during Indian attacks (1755). If you wish to return to Front Royal at this point, turn left at the first traffic light in Strasburg onto Va. 55 for the 10-mile drive to Front Royal. As you drive toward Riverton and Front Royal, you will see the dramatic loom of the Massanutten Mountain range and **Signal Knob** to your right.

If, however, you elect to take the West Virginia mountain tour to **Wardensville, Lost River,** and **Gore,** turn right at the blinker light, one block before the traffic light in Strasburg, from U.S. 11 onto Va. 55 and head west toward Lebanon Church and Wardensville (23 miles.)

Continue on W. Va. 55 through Wardensville to **Lost River Roadside Park** (3 miles). From this park, you can walk across the bridge, down a path to your left about a quarter of a mile to the area where Lost River disappears under Sandy Ridge to emerge as the Cacapon River on the other side of the mountain. Return to Wardensville, and continue to the intersection of W. Va. 55 and W. Va. 259. Bear left onto W. Va. 259 and head towards Gore (20 miles).

At Gore, turn right again onto U.S. 50 for the 14 mile drive back to Winchester. At Winchester, follow U.S. 50 through the city to U.S. 522. Turn right onto U.S. 522 for the scenic 18-mile drive back to your starting point, Front Royal.

9. FORT VALLEY AREA

There are two theories as to how **Fort Valley** got its name. The first, and the simplest, is that it was named after

Powell's Fort, located along the western ramparts of the towering Massanutten Mountains. The second theory is that, as a natural and easily fortified bastion, it was the place to which George Washington was contemplating an ultimate retreat with the remnants of his frozen Continentals in that dark year of 1777 after his miserable winter at Valley Forge.

Fort Valley is still quite isolated and only sparsely farmed, with the cold, spring-fed waters of lovely Passage Creek purling down its center. Today it is ringed on all sides by the magnificent **George Washington National Forest** whose plentiful flora and fauna are carefully protected by the Park Service, and whose mountain streams, still pure and unpolluted, are rife with ferns and mountain laurel. One look at the entrance gorge as you arrive on Va. 678 from the turnoff at **Waterlick** and you can readily see why George Washington knew, from his surveying days, that this would be an advantageous stronghold. Just inside this northern entrance to Fort Valley lies the **Elizabeth Furnace Recreation Area** with its restored pre-revolutionary iron furnace, picnic tables and gladed parks, rustic outdoor amphitheater, and extensive camping grounds. There is excellent trout fishing in season where Passage Creek tumbles through the entrance gorge to join the North Fork of the Shenandoah River below Waterlick, and the foliage is especially striking during the fall when the trees turn red and gold.

There are many side roads and hiking trails leading into and sometimes crossing the hollows and gorges along the west side of the Massanuttens. All of them are scenic, with numerous fords across mountain streams. For the hiker, the 4-mile trail leading upward from Elizabeth Furnace to Signal Knob is most rewarding. In the spring and early summer, there is a wealth of dogwood and redbud blossoming and, later, mountain laurel, azalea, and rhododendron.

The most notable side road branches off Va. 678 about 10 miles beyond Elizabeth Furnace and leads into **Little Fort Valley** and to **Powell's Fort Camp** or to **Little Fort Recreation Area**. From the latter, the more adventurous can continue over the mountain ridges, past the **Observation Tower**, overlooking the seven bends of the Shenandoah, and make a corkscrew descent into the environs of **Woodstock**. The road from **Kings Crossing** to Edinburg (Va.

141

675 to your right) is paved all the way, but not nearly so unspoiled and lovely.

There are four small towns running down the center of Fort Valley: **Dilbeck, Seven Fountains, Detrick** and **Kings Crossing.** None of them have more than a scattering of houses, a few churches, a gas pump, and a general store. The first 18 miles along the Fort Valley Road (Va. 678), after you pass Elizabeth Furnace, is cultivated and highly productive farmland. A superb view from the summit of Va. 675 on the southeastern Massanutten rim is one of the outstanding attractions of the entire area. On a clear day, you can see all the way across the floor of the Luray Valley to the serried Blue Ridge beyond, with Luray nestled in its green setting in the distance and some of the serpentine bends of the South Fork of the Shenandoah River 2,000 feet below.

The last 10 miles, at the southern end of the valley, are far more forested and almost totally devoid of human habitation. You may elect to keep straight ahead on the gravel road through the forest instread of bearing left with Va. 675 up and over the eastern rim of the Massanuttens. This road is comfortably navigable at moderate speeds and has its own lovely vista towards Luray. It is well worth the extra mileage to where the road joins U.S. 211 at the top of the 1,845 foot pass (New Market Gap) between Luray and New Market.

One thing is certain: either route you take, the wooded drive straight ahead through the depths of George Washington National Forest, or the thrilling climb on Va. 675 above Luray, will be delightfully free of other cars and heavy traffic, even on the weekends at the height of the summer season. This is all unspoiled country, still virtually unknown to the sightseeing tourist.

SUGGESTED TOUR: 70 Miles - 2½ Hours Round Trip From Front Royal. (Add Another Hour to Visit Skyline or Luray Caverns Enroute)

Take U.S. 340-522 north out of Front Royal. At the intersection of U.S. 340-522 and Va. 55 near Riverton, turn left onto Va. 55 west towards Strasburg. Follow Va. 55 about 5 miles west to Waterlick. Turn left onto Va. 678, the Fort Valley Road, which passes the turnoff (Va. 613) to the **State Fish Hatchery** and leads directly into the north

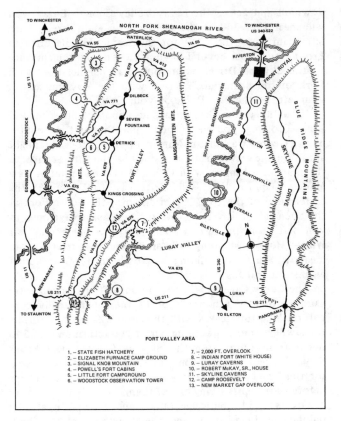

FORT VALLEY AREA

1. – STATE FISH HATCHERY
2. – ELIZABETH FURNACE CAMP GROUND
3. – SIGNAL KNOB MOUNTAIN
4. – POWELL'S FORT CABINS
5. – LITTLE FORT CAMPGROUND
6. – WOODSTOCK OBSERVATION TOWER
7. – 2,000 FT. OVERLOOK
8. – INDIAN FORT (WHITE HOUSE)
9. – LURAY CAVERNS
10. – ROBERT McKAY, SR., HOUSE
11. – SKYLINE CAVERNS
12. – CAMP ROOSEVELT
13. – NEW MARKET GAP OVERLOOK

gorge of the valley at **Elizabeth Furnace.** Be sure to look for the "Indian tree" at the right edge of the road near the entrance gates to the recreation grounds at Elizabeth Furnace. After a stop-over to visit the restored iron furnace, continue down Fort Valley on Va. 678, past **Dilbeck, Seven Fountains, Detrick** and **Kings Crossing.** Or, turn right just after Dilbeck, at Va. 771 and the sign for **Powell's Fort Camp** (4 miles). Another turn from Va. 678, a few miles further to the right, Va. 658 at Detrick, will lead to the **Little Fort Recreation Area** and to the **Woodstock Observation Tower.** Reverse your route to rejoin Va. 678 and turn right for Kings Crossing.

At Kings Crossing, Va. 675 from Edinburg crosses Va. 678. Bear left onto Va. 675 which swings over the crest of the mountain to Luray. If you continue by this route

143

downhill and across the Luray Valley floor to **Luray**, you
will meet U.S. 340 at the stoplight on Main Street. Turn
left again onto U.S. 340 for the scenic 25-mile drive to
Front Royal, just beyond **Skyline Caverns** and the entrance
to the **Skyline Drive**. Your route will parallel the South
Fork of the Shenandoah River, with the Massanutten on
your left and the Blue Ridge on your right.

If, at the well-marked crossroads about 3½ miles beyond
Kings Crossing, you elect to continue throught the depths
of the George Washington National Forest, proceed straight
ahead on the gravel road maintained by the Park Service, to
the junction (9 miles) with U.S. 211 at the summit of **New
Market Gap** for the 8-mile drive east to Luray. At the
eastern end of the U.S. 211 bridge over the South Fork of
the Shenandoah River, be sure to keep a sharp eye open to
your left, along the east riverbank, for the stone-and-mortar
White House, standing all alone in the river-bottom
meadow. This old building was built in 1760 as a fort
against the Indians.

The **Luray Caverns** will be on your left just as you enter
Luray proper. An hour's tour of these perpetually cool
natural limestone caves with their remarkable rock formations will be most rewarding. Or, if you return on U.S. 340
north from Luray, see the Skyline Caverns near Front
Royal. Take your pick, but unless you are sorely pressed
for time—and especially if you have never visited caverns
before—don't miss seeing one of them.

On U.S. 340 between Luray and Front Royal, the
redbud, or Judas trees, and the dogwood are in bloom
around the end of April or early in may. The area along the
roadside, particularly from **Rileyville** north, has become
nationally famous for them. If you possibly can, plan to
make this 25-mile drive in the spring when these two
marvels of the forest are at their best.

10. FRONT ROYAL – LURAY AND SKYLINE DRIVE AREA

Front Royal is probably best known as the northern
entrance to the world-famous **Skyline Drive**, but it has a
few other claims to fame besides the slogan on the local
license plates—"Where the Skyline Drive Begins". For one
thing, it was one of the most important crossroads and
trading posts in the Valley from the time of the area's first

144

settlement in 1734. It was a key transshipment point for
land-borne freight and produce, from pack horse and
Knoxville wagon to river barge and raft. In 1862, one of the
important engagements of the Civil War was fought here in
a surprise encounter between Generals Jackson and Banks.
Front Royal is also a large livestock center with one of the
biggest markets in the east for both horses and beef cattle.
Since 1939, it has been the location of the largest
single-component rayon plant in the world, the American
Viscose plant of the FMC Corporations, which employs
over 2,000 people. All in all, today, Front Royal finds itself
one-third country farm town, one-third mill town, and
one-third tourist recreation center.

The **Balthis House** on Chester Street is the oldest
building in town. Almost right next to it are the **Confederate Museum** and the town library. The old U.S. Calvalry
Remount Station, now the **Beef Cattle Research Station,** is
run jointly by the U.S. Department of Agriculture and the
Virginia Polytechnic Institute (VPI). To reach it, take U.S.
522 south out of Front Royal, using either the by-pass or
the old route along Royal Avenue through town, The
Research Station's 4,000 acres and cluster of barns and
buildings lie 3 miles south of the city limits, halfway up to
the 1,350-foot summit of **Chester Gap.** Visiting hours:
Monday through Friday, 9 a.m. to 4 p.m. The **AIFLD
(American Institute for Free Labor Development)** head-

145

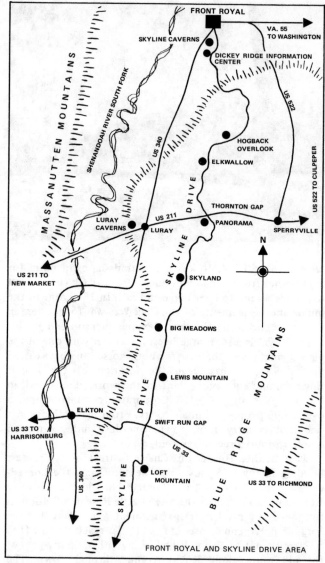

FRONT ROYAL

VA. 55
TO WASHINGTON

SKYLINE CAVERNS

DICKEY RIDGE INFORMATION
CENTER

US 522

HOGBACK
OVERLOOK

ELKWALLOW

US 522 TO CULPEPER

SHENANDOAH RIVER SOUTH FORK

MASSANUTTEN MOUNTAINS

US 340

SKYLINE DRIVE

THORNTON GAP

LURAY
CAVERNS

US 211

LURAY

PANORAMA

SPERRYVILLE

US 211 TO
NEW MARKET

N

SKYLAND

SKYLINE DRIVE

BIG MEADOWS

LEWIS MOUNTAIN

BLUE RIDGE MOUNTAINS

DRIVE

ELKTON

US 33 TO
HARRISONBURG

SWIFT RUN GAP

US 33

US 340

SKYLINE

LOFT
MOUNTAIN

US 33 TO RICHMOND

FRONT ROYAL AND SKYLINE DRIVE AREA

quartered just to the east of Front Royal along the Happy
Creek Road (Va. 647 to Va. 606, three miles east of town),
may be of interest to members of your party. Sponsored
jointly by the State Department, the Department of Labor,

and the AFL-CIO, the AIFLD trains labor leaders from under-developed countries.

Before taking the **Skyline Drive**— a "must" for every vistor to tbe Blue Ridge and the Valley—you may want to visit the **Skyline Caverns,** one of the most fascinating of the many underground caverns in the Valley. There are eating facilities and a gift shop, as well as a miniature railroad and picnic tables in the shade.

Once you are on the Skyline Drive be sure to stop at the **Dickey Ridge Information Center,** 5 miles from the entrance. It contains a complete small museum of the topography, geological structure, flora and fauna of the national park. In summer, continuous free illustrated lectures are given in a small theater at the rear of this attractive rustic building. Also, don't miss the superb view on a clear day across the South Fork and Luray Valley, to the neighboring Massanutten and beyond from the **Hogback Mountain Overlook** (3,385-foot elevation). Generally, although the Skyline Drive itself is some 105 miles long, set in 194,000 acres of parkland, the first 32 miles to the Luray Interchange at **Panorama** give an ample picture of the whole and, in my opinion, are the most scenic and lovely part of the entire Drive.

Overnight accommodations — reservations are advisable in summer — are available at both **Big Meadows** and **Skyland,** beyond the Panorama Interchange. Also, there are camping grounds as well as guest cottages for rent by the week in season. Food, gas, and restrooms are available at other selected points along the entire drive, notably **Elk Wallow, Thornton Gap** (Panorama), **Swift Run Gap,** and **Loft Mountain** near the end of the Drive. Turn-offs, overlooks, rest areas, picnic grounds, and restroom facilities are scattered in rustic settings throughout the Drive. A 35-mph speed limit is strictly enforced in the interest of safety and the park wildlife. A second visitors' information center, the **Harry F. Byrd Information Center,** has recently been added at Big Meadows to supplement the one at Dickey Ridge. Like the center at Dickey Ridge, the Byrd Information Center features slide lectures, contour maps, and wildlife and geological displays of the park area. Ranger-guided hikes are available at Matthews Arm, Skyland, Big Meadows, Lewis Mountain, and Loft Mountain. Riding horses are available at Big Meadows and Skyland. Visitors are also always welcome at the **Park Headquarters**

147

at the western edge of the park at the foot of Big Stony Mountain along U.S. 211 near Luray.

Luray boasts the world-famous **Luray Caverns** where the recently-installed Great Stalacpipe Organ produces concert quality music by creating stereophonic effect from the different positions of the stalactites in the area. The Caverns are open every day all year. At the same site is **Car and Carriage Caravan** (open daily from mid-March to Christmas) where the story of transportation is illustrated by an excellent selection of restored carriages and automobiles. At the nearby **Luray Singing Tower**, carillon recitals are given on Tuesdays, Thursdays, Saturdays and Sundays. Food and rest facilities as well as gift shop are close at hand, and there are an ample number of good motels in the area, including the charming Mimslyn.

Take South Royal Avenue (U.S. 340) south out of Front Royal to the **Skyline Drive** Northern Entrance (just beyond the city limits). The **Skyline Caverns** are about a mile south of the entrance to the Drive on U.S. 340. After a visit to the caverns, return to the Drive; the tollgate (admission per car — $2.00) is well past the turn-off from U.S. 340. Follow the Skyline Drive for the first 32 miles to the Luray Interchange at Panorama where you turn right, or west, onto U.S. 211 for the 8-mile downhill drive to Luray.

If you wish to visit the **Luray Caverns**, continue straight through town on U.S. 211 (Main Street) west to the far end of town or take U.S. 211 by-pass west. The **Luray Caverns**, the **Car and Carriage Caravan**, and the **Luray Singing Tower** will be on your right. The entrance is clearly marked. If you are making a roundtrip, turn left (north) at the intersection of U.S. 211 and U.S. 340. Continue north on U.S. 340 along the Luray Valley floor for the 25 magnificent scenic miles between two sets of mountains (the Massanutten and the Blue Ridge) back to Front Royal.

11. CATTLE COUNTRY

The area which contains the greatest concentration of the big cattle "spreads" in this superb bluegrass grazing section of the Old Dominion lies in Fauquier, Warren and Rappahannock counties, southeast of the big horse and cattle-buying center, Front Royal. This scenic upland country features, besides magnificient mountain views, many cattle ranches, varying from 1,000 to 5,000 acres, with barns, silos, and working pens. They are all owned and operated as both a business and a hobby by men of wealth while the actual work and management is done by professional "fitters" and herdsmen. There is a strong emphasis on purebred cattle for the sales and show rings. The "English" breeds — Hereford, Aberdeen Angus, and Shorthorn — predominate, and each farm has its own corral

149

of cow ponies to handle the stock on its rolling green acres.

Among the best-known cattle farms in the region are **Mulberry Hill,** (formerly owned by an executive of Ford Motor Co.); **Still House Hollow Farm,** in the Ralph Matthiesen family; and **Fairfield Farm,** belonging to the Marriott clan, who also own and operate the Marriott Motor Hotels and Hot Shoppes which dot the mid-Atlantic states. **Cobbler Mountain Farm** is owned by the widow of Colonel John Tyssowski — "Uncle John" to many of his former friends and associates. He was a shy and retiring World War I hero who married a member of the Woodward family of the Woodward & Lothrop store chain in the Washington, D.C. area. There are many other smaller livestock farms scattered about the area, but these "big four", all in Fauquier county, will serve to give you an idea of how championship quality beef cattle are bred and raised in the lush pastureland of this sector of the Blue Ridge. Since all of

them are concentrated along one set of roads in the same mountain valley, a tour of them will prove both scenic and interesting.

Suggested Tour of the Area: 37 Miles, 1½ Hours, Round Trip from Front Royal.

Take U.S. 522 south out of **Front Royal,** via either the By-Pass or South Royal Avenue, for **Chester Gap** and **Flint Hill.** Halfway up the 3-mile scenic climb to the 1,350-foot summit of Chester Gap, you will pass the 4,000-acre **Beef Cattle Research Station** which, until the end of World War II, was a leading U.S. cavalry remount station. It was also a large K-9 Corps training center, handling several thousand war dogs at a time. The Beef Cattle Research Station, operated on federal land jointly by the Department of

150

Agriculture and the Animal Husbandry Division of Virginia Polytechnic Institute, is open to the public Monday through Friday, 9:00 a.m. to 4:00 p.m. Visits to the various breed test centers are available by request at the administration building.

As your car climbs to the Gap, the main ridge of the Blue Ridge Mountains extends to your right; at the summit, South Mountain rising out of the Piedmont Plain can be seen on the left and the gradually diminishing nubs of the Blue Ridge foothills to the east. As you descend the far slope of Chester Gap on U.S. 522, you will come to a side road to your left, 5 miles beyond the Beef Cattle Research Station. This is the first paved road branching off U.S. 522 past the summit of Chester Gap. It is Va. 635, and it will take you past Marriott's **Fairfield Farm** and **Fiery Run Ranch,** behind South Mountain, to Va. 688 at **Hume,** a distance of approximately 10 miles. Turn left, or north onto Va. 688 and continue for 5 miles, past **Still House Hollow Farm** and **Mulberry Hill Farm** to **Markham.** Here you turn left again, over the bridge and onto Va. 55 for the return trip to Front Royal.

At **Linden,** 5 miles west of Front Royal, just before the post office, you will pass on your left a memorial marker to the first discoverer of the Valley, John Lederer. Linden is in the **Manassas Gap,** which Lederer used to enter the Valley. The western gorge of the Manassas Gap, overlooking Front Royal just east of the town, affords a superb view of the Massanutten Mountains and the main floor of the Valley (especially if you mentally erase the smoking chimneys of the American Viscose plant and the Riverton Lime Company).

An alternate route for a longer tour of the cattle country, doubling the mileage and elapsed time (55 miles – 3 hours), is as follows: take the same departure route from Front Royal on U.S. 522 over Chester Gap to the Va. 635 turn-off, one-half mile before **Huntly,** and proceed to **Hume.** At Hume, turn right, or south onto Va. 688 to Orlean. From Orlean, continue on Va. 688 to its intersection with U.S. 211 where you turn left to **Warrenton.** At the Warrenton By-Pass, be careful to bear left at the fork to Va. 17. Follow Va. 17 towards **Marshall.**

On Va. 17, between the Warrenton By-Pass and Marshall, you will pass on your left, as you leave Warrenton, the site of the annual Gold Cup timber races, as well as several big

Lewis Allen

Typical Virginia Cattle Auction

horse and cattle farms. **Meadowville Farm** is on your right. Approximately 4 miles before Marshall, at **Old Tavern**, Va. 17 turns sharply left. From here, Va. 17 passes **Belvoir Farm** on your right, **Dondoric Farm** and lovely **Sudley** on your left.

At the stoplight in Marshall, turn left on Va. 55. Approximately 4 miles beyond Marshall is the **John Marshall House**, which you can see in the distance on your right, just before Va. 17 leaves I-66-Va. 55. At the end of this dual-lane stretch of I-66-Va. 55, turn left onto Va. 729. After approximately 3 miles, Va. 729 jogs right past the entrance to **Cobbler Mountain Farm**. Continue about 2 miles to the junction of Va. 729 with Va. 688. Here you may choose one of two return routes to Front Royal.

The first will take you past **Mulberry Hill Farm** and **Still House Hollow Farm**. Turn left from Va. 729 onto Va. 688 and continue 3 miles to **Hume**. At Hume, turn right onto Va. 635 and continue to U.S. 522. This 7½ mile stretch will take you again past **Fairfield Farm**. Turn right again onto U.S. 522 and return to **Front Royal**.

If you wish to return directly to Front Royal from Cobbler Mountain Farm, take Va. 729 to Va. 688 and turn right. Take Va. 688 for 3 miles to Markham. At Markham, turn left onto Va. 55 and continue through Linden to Front Royal.

12. WARRENTON AREA

Warrenton sits astride several of the main routes leading into the Valley from the east and south. Although the most direct route, one of the most beautiful is U.S. 211, especially westward from the Warrenton by-pass to **Massies Corner**. At any of several intersections on the Warrenton by-pass, a left turn leads you uphill into the quaint and unspoiled community which is one of the last remaining strongholds of the "horsey set".

Warrenton, like Woodstock, Berryville, and Front Royal, has its county courthouse, it's "lawyers' row", and a mounting number of antique, gift, and saddlers' shops. The quaint old **Warren Green Hotel**, behind the courthouse square, has been converted into county government offices. On this site once stood the Norris Tavern, which was the scene of a magnificent banquet tendered to General Lafayette by the citizens of Fauquier on his visit to the

153

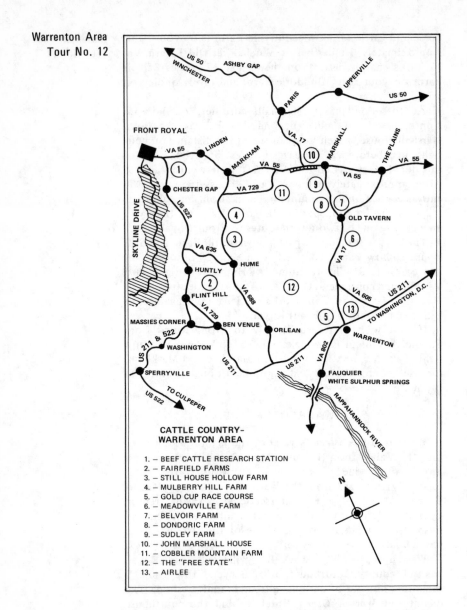

**CATTLE COUNTRY-
WARRENTON AREA**

1. — BEEF CATTLE RESEARCH STATION
2. — FAIRFIELD FARMS
3. — STILL HOUSE HOLLOW FARM
4. — MULBERRY HILL FARM
5. — GOLD CUP RACE COURSE
6. — MEADOWVILLE FARM
7. — BELVOIR FARM
8. — DONDORIC FARM
9. — SUDLEY FARM
10. — JOHN MARSHALL HOUSE
11. — COBBLER MOUNTAIN FARM
12. — THE "FREE STATE"
13. — AIRLEE

United States in 1825. After its conversion to the Warren
Green Hotel, General McClellan bade farewell to his officers
there in November, 1862, when he was relieved of the
command of the Army of the Potomac.

The early history of the Warrenton area can be traced to 1606 and Captain John Smith's exploration of the Rappahannock River where he found an Indian village just north of the present site of nearby Fauquier Springs. Later, the settlement of Warrenton — originally known as Fauquier Court House — grew up in the vicinity of the first courthouse (1760). Its name was changed soon afterwards to Warrenton, in honor of General Joseph Warren, the hero of Bunker Hill. (In the Valley, Warren County was also named for the general.) Warrenton played a big role in the maneuvering of both armies during the Civil War and was also a key base for the Grey Ghost of the Confederacy, Colonel John Mosby, who is buried here.

The three loveliest drives in the Warrenton area are U.S. 211, west through handsome estates and horse farms dotting the Blue Ridge foothills; Va. 17, south from either The Plains or Marshall; and southwest on Va. 802 to Fauquier White Sulphur Springs.

Va. 17 south takes you, in rapid succession as you drive from Marshall, past lovely **Sudley** and **Dondoric** on your right and **Belvoir Farm** on your left. Approximately 2½ miles after Va. 17 turns sharply right at Old Tavern, you will find Dr. Fritz Howard's **Meadowville Farm** on your left. After the turn-off to your left (Va. 605) for **Airlee**, the **Gold Cup Racecourse** is on your right as you head into Warrenton.

As you drive along Va. 17, near Meadowville Farm, to your right is the Rappahannock Mountain Range, the eastern border of the legendary area known as "The Free State". The name of this somewhat isolated 12-mile square south of Marshall is attributed to its post-revolutionary tenants, and their descendants, many of whom were pugilistic, law-defying characters, who successfully resisted any attempts at collection of rents or taxes. Today, with good county roads, there is little trace of the earlier conditions which gave the section its name and reputation, but there are still colorful tales of Charlie Ashby, known as "King of the Free State" during the latter 19th century, and others, including the giant Tim Bray, whose cabin site was on Wild Cat Mountain.

Today, Warrenton is perhaps best known by its not-too-distant neighbor, Washington, D.C., for the annual **Virginia Gold Cup Point-to-Point** race meet held early each May (the premiere timber race of the Virginia spring season). The prominent **Airlee Foundation,** Dr. Murdock Head's international conference center, is also located north of the town and can be reached via Va. 605 from either Va. 17 or U.S. 211. Airlee covers some 1,200 acres and has become a mecca for intellectuals the world over. It plays host to meetings of leaders of government, industry, science, education, and religion and has an international house, a motion picture-TV production facility, a medical research center and a 600-acre game preserve.

The Fauquier Springs Road (Va. 802) takes you, in only 6 miles, past the **Warrenton Training Center** and such lovely

Virginia State Library

Fauquier White Sulphur Springs

farm estates as: **Waverly Farm, Clover Croft, North Wales,** formerly owned by Walter P. Chrysler, Jr., **Whiffletree Manor, Kilmaurs, The Oaks, Woodbourne,** and **Canterbury** farms. Just before Va. 802 crosses a narrow bridge over the Rappahannock River is **Fauquier White Sulphur Springs,** once a fashionable resort dating back to the late 1700's. The Virginia Assembly held its sessions here during the summer of 1849. Today, relatively few landmarks reflect its former splendor, but the old **Baptist Meeting House** (1794) still stands, and near the entrance gates to the Fauquier Springs Country Club is the old **Fauquier Springs Coach House Tavern.**

All of the countryside surrounding Warrenton is lovely, especially in the springtime when it very much resembles

the English rural landscape, and all of it is liberally dotted
with large farms and country estates of permanent residents, many of whom commute by car to Washington. Like
its neighbors, Middleburg, The Plains, and Upperville, it is
the land of the horse, the purebred ram and bull, and of
stationwagons sporting either fox or thoroughbred on the
"bonnet".

**Suggested Tour of Area: 30 Miles — 1 Hour, or 90 Miles —
3 Hours, Round Trip from Winchester or Front Royal.**

Take either Va. 55 out of **Front Royal** or U.S. 50 out of
Winchester, heading east. From Winchester, turn right off
U.S. 50 at Paris and follow Va. 17 to **Marshall** and
Warrenton. From Front Royal, follow Va. 55 east to
Marshall. Turn right on Va. 17 at Marshall (the blinker
light) for Warrenton. For **Airlee,** turn left, off Va. 17, onto
Va. 605, two miles before you reach the Warrenton by-pass.
From Airlee, continue on 605 and turn right onto U.S.
29-211 for the one-mile drive to Warrenton.

For the Fauquier Springs Road tour (12 miles roundtrip)
take Va. 802 southwest out of Warrenton to **Fauquier
White Sulphur Springs** and the Rappahannock River and
return via the same route.

To return to Front Royal or Winchester, take U.S. 211
west. A 20-mile drive will bring you through lovely farm
and mountain scenery to **Ben Venue.** Turn right at Ben
Venue on Va. 729, or continue 3 miles to **Massies Corner**
and turn right on U.S. 522 through Huntly, and across
Chester Gap back to Front Royal or Winchester.

13. RAPPAHANNOCK COUNTY AREA

With all its considerable wealth in thoroughbred horses,
orchards, cattle, and long-established county "names" and
families, there is still one section of this northern valley
area of Virginia which tops even the celebrated and
exclusive Piedmont hunt country areas around Leesburg,
Warrenton, and Middleburg in conservative prestige. And
mind you, it does so largely without the assistance of "new
Yankee blood" — and money. Rappahannock County is the
last unbreached stronghold north of Roanoke dedicated

solely to true-blooded Virginians; it is a blue-blooded, self-contained, and largely self-sustained agricultural area. It is zealously guarded from contamination by outsiders and, therefore, is surprisingly ingrown and "unspoiled" by outside influences.

The terrain, which lends itself to this insular attitude of exclusion, is beautiful, rugged, mountainous, rocky, and unyielding. Some of the most magnificent scenery to be found in the entire Blue Ridge is here. Threaded by numerous mountain streams, watered by the swift-running Thornton and Rush Rivers, this section is largely dedicated to fruit-growing, horses, sheep, and cattle — and to the self-preservation of its "first families." The towns, **Flint Hill, Sperryville**, and "Little" **Washington**, are completely southern and provide a delightful glimpse backward into the valley of Virginia that once was. As you roll along U.S. 52, U.S. 211, Va. 3, or Va. 231 — the only good paved roads in the county — the wild, hilly mountain scenery is overpowering, especially in clear weather. The Blue Ridge, with the Skyline Drive on top, forms the western boundary of the county. The Rappahannock River forms the northern boundary. Running north and south in the center of the county, closely paralleling the Blue Ridge, is a lower range known as the Madison Hills.

It is the upper part of Rappahannock County, from the Warren County line atop **Chester Gap** to just below **Sperryville**, that is the most scenic, although the 25-mile drive down the **Thornton Valley** on Va. 231 is almost equally rewarding. **Flint Hill** is one of the most delightful little towns left in the entire valley. **Washington** is full of old houses, stray hound dogs, and somnolence. This "first

Washington of all" the 28 Washingtons in the United States was surveyed and platted by George Washington in 1749.

Ben Venue is a wonderfully preserved working farm estate which stands beside the highway with its ancient brick slave quarters intact in a superb setting. **Huntly** has its attractions, tiny as it is, and so does the rugged **Rush River Valley** behind and to the west of Washington, with its old tumbled-down log cabins, its stately farm estates, and its water source high up in the Shenandoah National Park. The view as you approach Sperryville from either direction, north or east, on U.S. 522, is one is one of the scenic wonders east of the valley. Nestled at the foot of the Blue Ridge with its towering pinnacles of **Hawksbill** and **Stony Mountain**, Sperryville is in an almost Alpine setting. Nearly everywhere you look as you drive through the northern section of the county, you are ringed by rolling hills and steep mountains, peace and contentment, poverty and bucolic charm, and all the fruits of current agriculture.

First discovered by John Lederer on his initial trip of exploration in 1669, later discovered by Colonel William Catlet, and then staked out by Colonel Cadwalader Jones as his private fur-trading ground with the Indians in 1673, the region was first officially settled by a hardy band of Englishmen of Scotch-Irish descent under the leadership of Colonel Francis Thornton, in whose honor the mountain gap to the west of Sperryville, the valley and the river winding down its center are named (the F.T. Valley as it is now called). Colonel Thornton's family home can be seen from Va. 231. This original band of early settlers was joined shortly htereafter by a group of displaced German immigrants.

Such odd-sounding place names as Banco, Syria, Yager Mountain, and Criglersville attest to the diversity of the first white inhabitants of the region. **Graves Mountain Lodge**, in the tiny hamlet of **Syria**, just beyond **Criglersville**, is very Tyrolean in appearance and atmosphere, nestled among the lower slopes of the Blue Ridge, and it serves excellent country fare throughout the year. However, the peak of its season is during the summer months. If you bring your fishing rod and a Virginia fishing license, you will have a choice of dropping a line in the Rose, Robinson or Hughes Rivers or in one of the trout streams that tumble down the slopes from the Shenandoah National Park.

159

**Suggested Tour: 110 Miles — 4½ Hours, Round Trip from
Front Royal.**

Leave Front Royal on U.S. 522 for Chester Gap and
Flint Hill. At the southern town limits of **Flint Hill,** turn

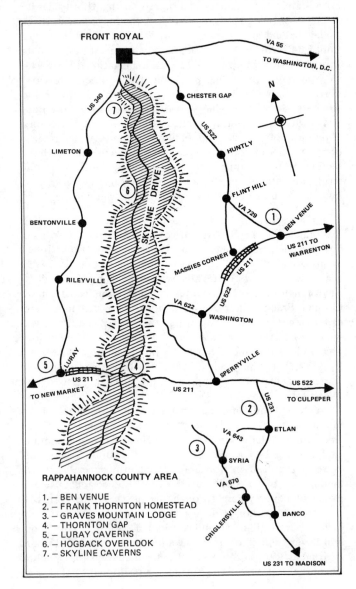

FRONT ROYAL

VA 55

TO WASHINGTON, D.C.

N

US 340

CHESTER GAP

⑦

US 522

LIMETON

HUNTLY

SKYLINE DRIVE

⑥

FLINT HILL

VA 729

BEN VENUE

①

BENTONVILLE

US 211 TO
WARRENTON

MASSIES CORNER

US 211

RILEYVILLE

US 522

VA 622

WASHINGTON

LURAY

⑤

④

SPERRYVILLE

US 211

US 522

TO NEW MARKET

US 211

TO CULPEPER

US 231

②

ETLAN

VA 643

③

SYRIA

VA 670

CRIGLERSVILLE

BANCO

US 231 TO MADISON

RAPPAHANNOCK COUNTY AREA

1. — BEN VENUE
2. — FRANK THORNTON HOMESTEAD
3. — GRAVES MOUNTAIN LODGE
4. — THORNTON GAP
5. — LURAY CAVERNS
6. — HOGBACK OVERLOOK
7. — SKYLINE CAVERNS

left off of U.S. 522 onto Va. 729 for the 4-mile drive
through the mountain gorges to **Ben Venue,** a completely
restored working plantation. At Ben Venue, turn right onto
U.S. 211/Va. 522 for 2 miles to **Massies Corner.** Follow
U.S. 522 to its turn-off to "little" **Washington.** At
Washington, turn right onto Va. 622 for the 10-mile loop
through the **Rush River Valley.** Part of this route is over a
winding, unpaved road that skirts the edge of the Shenandoah National Park and then follows the Covington River
to where Va. 622 rejoins U.S. 522 just before Sperryville.
At this junction, turn right again and continue to Sperryville.

At **Sperryville,** continue on past the cemetery on U.S.
52 to the east end of town. Just beyond the cemetery,
turn right onto Va. 231, which is the F.T. Valley Road.
Continue 6 miles on Va. 231, past the **Francis Thornton
Homestead** which is on your left. It stands, with its out
buildings, on a rise of the valley floor and can be identified
by a row of white columns on its facade. Continue to
Banco (approximately 12 miles). On your right, at the first
gas station and general store at the north end of tiny Banco,
turn right onto Va. 670 for **Criglersville** and **Syria.** Graves
Mountain Lodge, near Syria, is 3 miles beyond Criglersville,
just off Va. 670 to your left.

After lunch at Graves Mountain Lodge, reverse your
route and turn left at Syria onto Va. 643. This is a 6-mile
drive through rugged farm and mountain scenery around
the base of **Old Rag Mountain** to **Etlan,** where you turn left
onto Va. 231 for the return drive to Sperryville. At
Sperryville, turn left onto U.S. 211 for **Thornton Gap** and
the **Skyline Drive** trip to Front Royal. If it is a clear day, be
sure to stop at the **Hogback Overlook** on the Skyline Drive
for the magnificent view at the 3,385-foot elevation of the
seven serpentine bends in the Shenandoah River below.
Continue along the Skyline Drive to Front Royal.

14. THE VALLEY PIKE

This 100-mile stretch of the Valley Pike (U.S. 11) down
the center of the main valley, and its expressway counterpart, I-81, does not lend itself to brief tours, except for a
few side trips we will mention as we go along. We have
described Winchester, Stephens City, Middletown, and

161

Strasburg in some detail in other sections; so we can move south from Strasburg towards our starting point: historic Woodstock, seat of Shenandoah County.

From Strasburg, you may wish to start your tour with a pleasant side trip away from historic places and buildings. As you head south on I-81, turn off at Exit 73 (Toms Brook); then turn again on Va. 651 for one mile west to Mt. Olive. Turn left at Mt. Olive onto Va. 623 south for a 12-mile scenic drive through rolling farm country to Va. 42 at Columbia Furnace. Turn left on Va. 42 for the 6-mile drive east back to I-81, U.S. 11, and Woodstock.

If, however, you take U.S. 11 from Strasburg, just two miles before Woodstock, on the short dual-lane stretch of highway beside Pugh's Run stands an old coaching tavern known as Halfway House. **Woodstock** is perhaps best known for its county courthouse, the oldest in continuous use anywhere west of the Blue Ridge. Nearby is the Museum of Shenandoah County with an unusual collection of pioneer artifacts. Woodstock was first named Mullerstadt in honor of its founder, Jacob Muller, who came down from Pennsylvania in 1752 to lay out the town on land granted to him by Lord Fairfax.

It is also famed for its fighting parson, the Reverend Peter Muhlenberg, who in 1776, after a rousing sermon from the puplit, lead his German Lutheran congregation off to fight in the Revolutionary War.

Be sure to stop long enough at Woodstock for a look at the **Shenandoah County Courthouse** (1791) and Lawyers' Row behind it. There are similar Lawyers' Rows throughout the Valley, notably at Winchester and Lexington, but those at Woodstock are the best—and surely the quaintest— examples in the entire area. Although many of them are no longer used as lawyers' officer, in the old days they were conveniently adjacent to both the local courtroom and the judge's chambers.

For a superb panorama of the Valley and the famous horseshoe bends of the North Fork of the Shenandoah River, turn at Court House Square and follow Va. 758 east for 4 miles to the **Woodstock Observation Tower** on the crest of Massanutten Mountain. From there you may join the latter part of the Fort Valley tour, or return to Woodstock. On U.S. 11 about 3 miles south of Woodstock, you will pass on your left a state historical market indicating the site of the last Indian massacre (or outrage, as

162

the local historians called them) in the area (1766). Also nearby, on your left, just beyond Narrow Passage Creek, is another old post house from the stagecoach days. **Renner's Ordinary**.

Edinburg comes next on U.S. 11 and was the site of the first Civilian Conservation Corps (CCC) camp under President Franklin D. Roosevelt. There is now **Camp Roosevelt** in George Washington National Forest, a recreation area in the Massanutten Mountains, open from April to October (and you pass the entrance to it during the latter part of the Fort Valley tour on Va. 675). The CCC also helped start the construction of the Skyline Drive and many facilities in Shenandoah National Park, 20 miles to the east. During the War of 1812, there was a gun factory just west of where

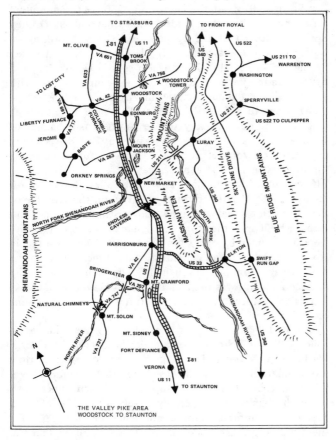

THE VALLEY PIKE AREA
WOODSTOCK TO STAUNTON

163

rifles and muskets for the American army were manufactured. It used the plentiful water power of the nearby
North Fork of the Shenandoah River and its tributaries.

Mt. Jackson, which is 6 miles further south on U.S. 11,
was first known as Mt. Pleasant, but changed its name after
the War of 1812 to honor Andrew Jackson, hero of the
Battle of New Orleans. If you like old water-powered
gristmills, iron furnaces and some of the most striking and
remote farm and mountain scenery in the entire Valley,
there is a highly rewarding side tour from Mt. Jackson
which requires only an extra hour's driving.

Leave Mt. Jackson on Va. 263 west for 8 miles through
lovely country, much of it along quiet streams flowing
toward the Shenandoah River — Mill Creek, Crooked Run,
and Straight Run. At the end of Va. 263 are the mountain
valley resorts at Basye, and, 2 miles beyond, at **Orkney
Springs,** situated at the edge of the George Washington
National Forest and beneath Big North Mountain. Orkney
Springs is one of the oldest health spas in the Valley, and
Bryce Mountain at Basye is a year-round resort with
some of the best skiing facilities in Virginia.

At Basye turn onto Va. 717 for the 8-mile drive through
verdant mountain scenery to the tiny German hamlet of
Jerome. Just as you leave Basye on Va. 717 drive slowly
and watch on your left for the old iron ore furnace hugging
the hill near a small stream bridge crossing. At Jerome, Va.
717 continues to the right along the valley floor beneath
high peaks to **Liberty Furnace** (1817), on the left side of
the road. Both the water-powered gristmill, and the iron
furnace built into the stone-faced side of the adjoining hill,
were in commercial operation until 1906. There are picnic
grounds and a cool and delightful wooded meadow with the
mill stream running through it. The house above the
furnace and mill was built in 1941 by Captain S. G. Clark,
who also restored the mill and furnace to their present
condition.

From Liberty Furnace Va. 691, a gravel side road,
follows "Little" Stony Creek to its headwaters in George
Washington National Forest and climbs over Devil Hole
Mountain to Lost City in West Virginia. Continue on Va.
717 past the entrance to Camp Strawderman, where you
reach the banks of "Big Stony Creek, which Va. 717-675
follows to **Columbia Furnace,** and continue on Va. 675 for
the 5-mile drive east to **Edinburg.** This trip can be taken in

Liberty Furnace Grist Mill

reverse, starting at Edinburg and ending at Mt. Jackson, but
the scenic views are far more striking when you begin the
trip from Mt. Jackson.

Surrounding **New Market** is some of the finest fertile
land in the Valley. **The Bushong House,** just north of town.
was the center of one of the many bloody Civil War battles
in the Valley. This one featured 247 young cadets from the
Virginia Military Institute 75 miles to the south. Their
heroic charge on May 15, 1864 is recreated by an inspiring
12-minute motion picture which is shown in the new **Hall
of Valor,** an impressive museum and visitor center. Well
displayed exhibits present a panoramic survey of the entire
Civil War, and there is a second film that depicts Stonewall
Jackson's famed Valley Campaign. The 160-acre **New
Market Battlefield Park** is just off I-81 at Exit 67.

Just south of New Market at the edge of town is a state

165

historical marker which indicates the southwestern boundary of Lord Fairfax's five million-acre royal land grant.
Near here on the left is the modern Shenvallee Lodge,
Motel, and Golf Course, which features many other
recreational facilities. Two miles further south brings you
to the stone gates of the paved road leading to **Endless
Caverns**, one of the best known and largest caverns in the
Valley. Open year round, the caverns have a coffee shop,
art museum, and camping and picinic facilties. Also on your
left just off U.S. 11 is **Court Manor**, built about 1830 as
Moreland Hall.

About 15 miles further south is **Harrisonburg**, formerly
known as Rocktown. The county seat of Rockingham
County, Harrisonburg is a bustling agricultural, cultural,
and industrial center, in an area especially known for its
fine turkeys and poultry. Harrisonburg is also the location
of Madison College, which was formerly the State Normal
School of Women, but is now co-educational and confers
degrees in all of the liberal arts.

Seventeen miles east of Harrisonburg on U.S. 33 is
Elkton (once called Conrad's Store), the point where
General Stonewall Jackson began his Valley Campaign in
1862. Seven miles further east on U.S. 33 brings you to its

Viginia State Library

166

Fort Defiance Church

junction with Skyline Drive at **Swift Run Gap** (2,365 ft.) where Lederer first glimpsed the Valley in 1669, and where Governor Spotswood and his "Kinghts of the Golden Horseshoe" crossed the Blue Ridge Mountains in 1716. **Grand Caverns**, discovered in 1804 and opened to the public two years later, are located 16 miles south of Elkton on U.S. 340. The shield formation are particulary interesting. Stonewall Jackson quartered troops in the caverns during the Civil War and held religious services in its "Cathedral Hall" before the Battle of Port Republic nearby.

Eight miles south of Harrisonburg on U.S. 11 at Mt. Crawford, Va. 257 takes you west 3 miles to **Bridgewater College**, which is run by the Church of the Bretheren, or Dunkards as they were once called. West of Bridgewater, 4 miles off Va. 42 at Mt. Solon, is **Natural Chimneys**, a remarkable rock formation, almost the scenic equal of Natural Bridge, 90 miles to the south on U.S. 11. This geological natural wonder, over 100 feet high, consists of seven hugh towers of colorful stone. **Mt. Solon** is also well-known for its annual jousting tournament held the third Saturday in August in a nearby field. This event has been contested here every year since 1821.

At Fort Defiance, approximately 10 miles south from Mt. Crawford on U.S. 11, is **Augusta Stone Church.** The church, completed in 1747 by Scotch-Irish Presbyterian settlers, was also prepared to serve as a fort during the frequent raids which characterized the French and Indian War. Just beyond the grove of trees surrounding Augusta Stone Church is **Augusta Military Academy** (1865), with a very handsome collection of crenellated buildings. One of the reasons that there are so many military schools in the Valley is the legacy of the Civil War and the many important battles fought in the area. Another is the propinquity of the Virginia Military Institute at Lexington, for which they served as preparatory schools at one time.

Three miles further south is Verona, near Staunton where both the American Safety Razor main plant and Westinghouse Electric Corporation Air Conditioning Divisions are located. Between Verona and Staunton, on the right side of U.S. 11, spreads the impressive expanse of the Ingleside Motel and Restaurant, with its fine golf course, swimming pools, clubhouse, and extensive dining and banquet facilities.

Staunton is a very hilly town, much like Harpers Ferry,

167

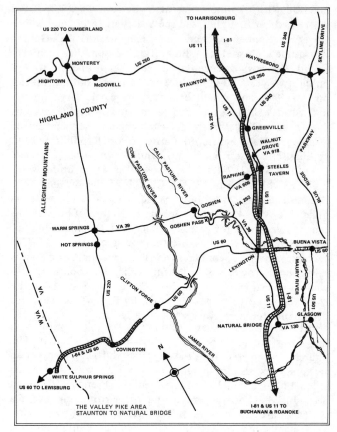

THE VALLEY PIKE AREA
STAUNTON TO NATURAL BRIDGE

but there the similarity ends. Where Harpers Ferry was a
ghost town transformed by the National Park Service into
Harpers Ferry National Historical Park, Staunton is a
thriving cultural and industrial community, constantly
growing at the instigation of its wide-awake city fathers and
citizens. Sparked by the appearance of the Virginia Central
Railroad back in 1854, it has been growing ever since, both
industrially and as an agricultural center. Gypsy Hill Park,
located in the northern section of the city, is one of the
largest and most beautiful parks in Virginia. The city has a
cluster of educational institutions within a few blocks of
each other in the downtown area: **Mary Baldwin College**
(1842), **Stuart Hall,** a girls' finishing school (1843),

168

Staunton Military Academy (1860), and the **Virginia School for the Deaf and Blind.**

Staunton's most famous son was the 28th President of the United States. The **Woodrow Wilson Birthplace**, the old Presbyterian manse, at the corner of N. Coalter and Frederick Streets, is now a national shrine, open daily to

Virginia Chamber of Commerce
Woodrow Wilson Birthplace

visitors. A documentary film is shown, and there are exhibits, a beautifully restored garden and a gift shop.

Today, Staunton's first settler, Captain John Lewis, would scarely know it. His home, **Bellefont**, stands on a high hill just northeast of town. The building, which was as much a fort as a dwelling, is believed to be the oldest house

169

in the Shenandoah Valley. Staunton's rich heritage is reflected in other historical buildings, such as **Kalorama** (1737), home of William Beverley, grandson of the area's first land grant patentee. Originally (1738-70) Augusta County was a Crown grant to William Beverley and extended from the Blue Ridge west to the Mississippi River. During the Revolutionary War, Staunton was capital of the state when the Virginia Assembly convened for eleven days in Trinity Church after fleeing Richmond and Charlottesville pursued by the British. **Trinity Church** (1855) is the third church of the same name built on its site at Church and Beverley Streets.

Somewhat outside our valley bailiwick, high up to the west of Staunton are the rolling ridges of the Appalachians on the West Virginia state line, lies Highland County. Both

Virginia Chamber of Commerce
Sugar Maple, Highland County

McDowell and Monterey, the county seat, on U.S. 250 are famous not only for the surrounding unspoiled mountain wilderness and superb scenic views, but also for sugar maples and the product that are derived from the sap—or "water", as the natives call it—maple syrup and maple sugar candy. The syrup is made fresh in early spring, and a Maple Sugar Festival is held to celebrate the "sugaring"—usually on two weekends in March. The sugar maples thrive in the brisk mountain air. The clear atmosphere is also ideal for scientific observation. Highland County's borders are within a few miles of the famous Sugar Grove Observatory, which boasts one of the largest radio-telescopes in the western world.

Six miles north of Monterey, on U.S. 220, is the Virginia Trout Company on whose pond there is flyfishing 7 days a week and where fresh frozen trout can be bought at the processing plant. Two miles further, turn left on Va. 642 for Blue Grass Valley and lovely mountain country. This 10-mile loop leads back to U.S. 250 at Hightown, 6 winding miles above Monterey. It takes a hardy soul to drive the hilly, twisting curves of the 45 miles to Monterey, but the trip is well worth it. In town there is a courthouse, general store, crafts shop, and antiques galore—plus wildlife in abundance, sparkling streams, and lovely, lofty mountain peaks.

Waynesboro, 15 miles to the east of Staunton on U.S. 250, is another busy industrial and agricultural center. Although not a "valley town" in the strict geographical sense, it nestles under the face of nearby Rockfish Gap at the southern entrance to the Skyline Drive. Its life is very much in keeping with the friendly tempo of the other communities in the lowlands along the Shenandoah River. General Electric and Du Pont both have large plants in Waynesboro. Four miles east of Waynesboro, at the southern end of Skyline Drive and the beginning of Blue Ridge Parkway is **Swannanoa**, an Italian Renaissance palace and gardens, headquarters of the University of Science and Philosophy, which is open year round and well worth a visit.

Southwest of Waynesboro via U.S. 340 and 11, about one mile west of Steeles Tavern, between U.S. 11 and I-81, lies **Walnut Grove Farm**. Cyrus McCormick, inventor of the grain reaper, was born here. The house, mill, and workshop have been restored and are maintained by the Virginia

171

Polytechnic Institute which operates the farm as an agricultural experiment station. To reach this historic site from U.S. 11, turn right on Va. 606 at the "McCormick Memorial Wayside" sign for .8 of a mile and turn right again onto Va. 918. There is a parking area for visitors and an attractive picnic area near the mill and workshop-museum. Just beyond Walnut Grove is the village of Raphine, where James Gibbs invented the sewing machine.

Lexington, 15 miles further south, is at the crossroads of U.S. 60, 11 and I-81, and the view from the north or east along any of these scenic highways is just about as spectacular as any to be seen in all of Virginia. Surrounded by steep mountains to the northwest, west, and south, the approach to Lexington gives very much the same effect as the approach to Sperryville in Rappahannock County. Lexington is famous, too, for VMI, the **Virginia Military Institute**, whose crenellated walls have housed many a national hero either as student or instructor - often both. Many famous figures were here, such as George C. Marshall as a cadet and Stonewall Jackson as a teacher. Formal parades of the VMI Corps of Cadets are held each Tuesday and Friday afternoon during the school term. Visitors are welcome at the parades which begin at 4:20 p.m. during the winter months and at 5:00 p.m. in the spring.

Virginia Chamber of Commerce
VMI Parade

As you enter Lexington from the north, immediately beyond and adjoining VMI, is **Washington and Lee University.** A "must" for all visitors is its famous **Lee Chapel,** today restored as a shrine and museum. . It contains some of the finest portraits of General Robert E. Lee, George Washington, and the Marquis de LaFayette, as well as Lee's office and furniture and other items of the period. The chapel houses the famous Valentine recumbent statue of General Lee and the crypt in which he and other members of his family are buried. Both Lee and Washington were instrumental in the development of the University. In 1798 Washington endowed it with 200 shares of his James River Canal Company stock, from which gift the school still derives income, and Lee furthered its growth with funds borrowed on his personal signature. The Stone ruins of the parent of Washington and Lee University, **Liberty Hall Academy,** erected in 1793, can be seen just west of Lexington off U.S. 60. When the school moved to Lexington it was renamed Washington College, and in 1870 after General Lee's death while president of the college, it became Washington and Lee University.

Another great general of the Confederacy, Stonewall Jackson, was a resident of Lexington for ten years and is buried in the town cemetery on S. Main Street. It is now called **Stonewall Jackson Memorial Cemetery** and two former governors of Virginia, James McDowell and John Letcher, are also buried there. Jackson's home on Washington Street near the Courthouse is now open to the public daily as a museum. One of the oldest buildings in the community is the **Alexander-Withrow House,** built about 1790, located on the corner of Main and Washington Streets. This old landmark, with its diamond-shaped brick pattern, has served as a private residence, school, post office, and as a store. Tours of the Lexington area are conducted daily during the summer months from 9:00 a.m. to 4:00 p.m. weekdays and 1:00 p.m. to 3:00 p.m. Sundays, leaving on the hour from the **Visitor Information Center,** 401 South Main Street. The tour covers some sixteen points of interest in Lexington and eight out-of-town places. Several self-conducted county tours are also available.

West of Lexington on scenic Va. 39 lies beautiful **Goshen Pass** where the Calfpasture River becomes the Maury and flows through the last Allegheny range to

173

Virginia State Travel Service
Goshen Pass

Lexington and to the floor of the Valley. A 15-mile drive
along the smooth, paved highway follows the banks of the
Maury River as it rushes among rugged boulders from the
timbered mountains of George Washington National Forest.
Another few miles bring you to a river-gorge park, a fern
and pine-girt fairy wonderland. Here is an **anchor monument** to Commodore Matthew Fontaine Maury, a **VMI**
instructor known as the "Pathfinder of the Seas" for his
work in charting ocean currents. The area is especially
beautiful in autumn and in spring. Maury, who had often
wandered in the area, requested from his deathbed that his
body be carried through Goshen Pass when the rhododendron was in bloom.

174

From Lexington, the Maury River flows to Buena Vista and southward to **Glasgow** where the James River cuts through the Blue Ridge Mountains. Here at Balcony Falls is the junction of the James and Maury Rivers, also the site where an old James River Canal branched up the Maury to Lexington.

Eight miles to the west, on U.S. 11, and 15 miles south of Lexington is **Natural Bridge.** Considered by Thomas Jefferson to be one of the seven natural wonders of the world, he came often from Monticello, his home at Charlottesville, to view and admire this 90-foot natural stone span bridging a 215-foot gorge. In 1774, Jefferson bought Natural Bridge and the surrounding 157 acres from King George III of England for 20 shillings "of good and lawful money". Today people from all over the world come to see this great landmark which stands at the foot of the Shenandoah Valley. From the cluster of motels, shops, and restaurants around U.S. 11 at the top of the gorge, it is but a short walk to the point down around the bend where Natural Bridge towers above Cedar Creek.

At Natural Bridge, our Valley Pike tour comes to an end, but U.S. 11 and I-81 continue south through **Roanoke,** the largest city in Virginia west of Richmond, and into

Virginia Department of Highways

I–81 South of Lexington

Southwestern Virginia, as the southern half of the vast Valley of Virginia is called. The Blue Ridge Parkway winds its way along the mountain crests down into Tennessee, and U.S. 11 and I-81 carry you to the city of **Bristol** on the Virginia-Tennessee border. About 100 miles west of Bristol is the famed Cumberland Gap on the Wilderness Road, which like its northern Valley counterpart, Cumberland, Maryland on the Cumberland (National) Road, was used by countless settlers, frontiersmen, and explorers as a gateway to the American west.

HISTORIC, SCENIC AND RECREATIONAL

All admission rates and hours listed are subject to change and should be verified.

HISTORIC HOMES, GARDENS, AND MUSEUMS

Winchester Area (Tour 2)

Abram's Delight (1754) — Rouss Spring Drive, off Millwood Ave. (U.S. 50-522), Winchester. Home of early settler, Abraham Hollingsworth, completely restored and furnished with relics of the 18th century. Open May-Nov., 9 to 5 daily; 2 to 5 Sundays. Adults, 75¢; children, 25¢.

Stonewall Jackson's Headquarters — 415 N. Braddock St., Winchester. General Jackson and staff occupied this house during the winter of 1861-62 before his famous Valley Campaign. Open all year, 9 to 5 daily; 10 to 6 Saturdays; 10 to 4 Sundays. Adults, 75¢.

Frederick County Courthouse (1840) N. Loudoun Street, Winchester. Recently restored with superb interior. Open 9 to 5 daily. No admission fee.

George Washington's Office — Corner of S. Braddock and W. Cork Sts., Winchester. First used by Washington while surveying for Lord Fairfax (1748) and later (1756-58) when commanding troops in the French and Indian War. Open May 1 — Nov. 1, 9 to 5 daily. Adults, 50¢; children under 12, free.

Charles Town — Harpers Ferry Area (Tour 4)

John Brown Museum in Gerard B. Wager Building (1836-38) — Corner of Shenandoah and Potomac Sts., Harpers Ferry National Historical Park, just off U.S. 340 at Shenandoah River bridge. The story of the

177

George Washington's Office

abolitionist's life is told through exhibits. Open 9 to 5 daily. No admission fee.

Jefferson County Courthouse (1836) — Washington Street in the center of Charles Town. The scene of the John Brown Trial. Once block east on the corner of Washington and Samuel Streets is the **Jefferson County Museum** with the wagon which carried Brown to the place of his execution and other interesting exhibits.

Harper House (1775-82) — the oldest surviving structure in Harpers Ferry. Robert Harper, builder and millwright, operated a ferry at the junction of the two rivers, and the town took its name from this service. The new house was built on high ground to avoid the periodic floods, but Harper died before it was completed. George Washington and Thomas Jefferson visited the house later when it was an inn. Now restored and refurnished in period pieces, it is open to visitors in the summer.

Leesburg Area (Tour 5)

Morven Park (1780's) — Two miles north of Leesburg on Va. 698. 1,200 acre estate with extensive boxwood gardens, nature trails, International Equestrian Institute, antique carriage collection, and huge Greek revival style mansion, home of Va. Gov. Westmoreland Davis during early 20th century. Open April 1 - Oct. 31, Wed.-Sun.; 10 to 5 Wed.-Sat.; 1 to 5 Sundays. Adults, $1.75, students, 75¢.

Oatlands (1800) — Six miles south of Leesburg on U.S. 15. Outstanding Federal period home, built by George Carter, grandson of Robert "King" Carter, beautiful boxwood and formal gardens, equestrian center with hunt race course. A property of the National Trust for Historic Preservation. Open April 1 - Oct 31, 10 to 5 daily; 1 to 5 Sundays. Adults, $1.00; children, 50¢.

Sully Plantation (1794) — On eastern edge of Dulles Airport, Va. 28, ½ miles from U.S. 50 intersection. Home of Richard Bland Lee, early member of the Phi Beta Kappa Society. Open, except Dec. 25, 10 to 5 daily. Adults, 50¢; children, 25¢.

Waterford — Quaker settlement dating to 1733. 7 miles NW of Leesburg on Va. 698 or 3 miles north of Va. 9 on Va. 704. During the 3-day annual October Home Tour and Crafts Exhibit, homes are open, antiques, arts and crafts and home-cooked foods are on display and for sale. The Mill, operated as a craft shop, is open 12 to 5 Sat. and Sun. during the summer months.

Middletown-Strasburg Area (Tour 8)

Belle Grove (1794) — One mile south of Middletown on U.S. 11. Built of locally cut limestone by Maj. Isaac Hite, a revolutionary officer and grandson of early settler, Joist Hite. Thomas Jefferson was involved in its architectural design. A property of the National Trust, open April 1 - Oct. 31, 10 to 4 daily, 1 to 5 Sundays. Adults, $1.00; children 50¢.

Strasburg Museum — Located in the old railroad station, on King Street (U.S. 55) at the eastern edge of Strasburg. Indian artifacts and fossils; displays from farmers' homes and barns from Civil War and railroad eras; blacksmith, cooper and potter shops. Open May-October, 10-4 daily; 1 to 4 Sundays; during July and August also, 7 to 8:30. Adults, 50¢; children, 25¢; family group, $1.25.

Warren Rifles Confederate Museum — 95 Chester Street, Front Royal. An impressive display of Civil War relics of Stonewall Jackson, Col. Mosby and his Rangers, Belle Boyd, etc. Open 9 to 6 daily. Adults, 75¢; children under 12, free.

Marler

Belle Grove

Luray Area (Tour 10)

Car and Carriage Caravan — Located near entrance to Luray
Caverns. "History on Wheels" featuring 75 authentic
restorations of carriages dating from 1625 and cars from
1892. Open March 16 - June 15, 9 to 7:30; June 16 -
Labor Day, 9 to 8:30; Labor Day - Nov. 15, 9 to 7:30;
Nov. 16 - March 15, 9 to 5:30. To both Caverns and
Caravan, adults, $4.00; children (7-13), $2.00.

Waynesboro Area (Tour 14)

Forest Hill Gardens — 656 Cherry Ave., Waynesboro, off
U.S. 250, 11 miles east of Staunton. Approximately 2
acres of terraced gardens, featuring azaleas, rhododendron
and over 1,500 boxwood. Open May to October. Adults,
$1.00; children, 50¢.

Swannanoa (1913) — U.S. 250 four miles east of
Waynesboro at junction of Skyline Drive and Blue Ridge

Parkway. Rennaissance-type marble palace full of art reproductions with terraced sculpture gardens and splendid mountain views. Open (summer) 8 a.m. to dusk, daily; (winter) 9 to 5. Adults, $1.00; children, 50¢.

Staunton Area (Tour 14)

Woodrow Wilson Birthplace (1856) — 24 N. Coalter Street, Staunton. Substantial brick house in which the 28th President of the United States was born in 1856. A varied and interesting collection of Wilson mementos including his Pierce Arrow limousine. Visitors are shown an inspiring film, "Spokesman for Tomorrow". Attractive gift shop and Victorian gardens. Open 9 to 5 daily, closed Sundays of December, January, and February. Adults, $1.00; children, 50¢.

Lexington Area (Tour 14)

Walnut Grove Farm — Between Staunton and Lexington and U.S. 11, near Steeles Tavern, and I-81, Exit 54. The farm is used as an Agricultural Research Station. The site where Cyrus McCormick perfected the reaper in 1831 has been designated a National Historical Landmark. The original red brick house has been restored along with the grist mill and blacksmith shop which features a

Virginia Chamber of Commerce
McCormick Shrine

reproduction of the original reaper. Open May 1-Oct 15, 9 to 5 daily. No admission fee.

Stonewall Jackson's Home — 8 E. Washington St., Lexington. The only home ever owned by the famous Confederate leader, now open to the public as a museum. Open 8:30 to 4:30, daily. Adults, 50¢; children, 25¢.

Lee Chapel (1866) — On Washington and Lee University campus, Lexington. Constructed under Lee's supervision while he was president of the college. Also houses the Lee Museum and crypt in which are buried the General and other members of the family. Open Nov. - April, 9 to 4 daily, 2 to 5 Sundays; May - Oct., 9 to 5 daily; 2 to 5 Sundays. No admission fee.

The VMI Museum — in Lexington at VMI in Jackson Hall. The Barracks were built 1848-50, burned in 1864, and rebuilt 1870-73. The museum displays memorabilia depicting the history and growth of the Virginia Military Institute and its contributions to Virginia and the nation's history. Open, except Dec. 25, 9 to 5 daily; Saturdays and Sundays, 2 to 5.

George C. Marshall Research Library — At the edge of the VMI Parade Ground in Lexington. The building features a special electric map on World War II as well as Marshall Plan exhibits. Open 9 to 4 daily; Sunday 1 to 4. Stays open one hour later May-Sept. Adults, 50¢; children under 12, school groups and military, no admission charge.

HISTORIC MILLS, INDIAN FORTS, TAVERNS & IRON FURNACES

HISTORIC MILLS:

Millwood Area (Tour 3)

Burwell-Morgan Mill (1782-1785) — At Millwood on Va. 723. Restored and open as a museum.

Shepherdstown Area (Tour 4)

Thomas Shepherd Grist Mill (1739) — On Town Run which now runs under Main Street. The largest and oldest water wheel built.

Aldie Area (Tours 5 & 6)

Aldie Mill (1807) — Recently operating, on U.S. 50 at Aldie,

6 miles east of Middleburg. Nearby is the home of the builder of the mill, Charles Fenton Mercer, noted abolitionist.

Middletown Area (Tour 8)

Kline's Mill (1798) — Between Middletown and Stephens City, approximately 1½ miles, east of U.S. 11 and I-81. Turn east on Va. 735; then right on gravel road, Va. 709, for one mile. Or 3 miles from Middletown, east on Va. 627, then left on Va. 636 and Va. 709.

Strasburg Area (Tour 8)

Old Mill Tavern (1797) — At the south edge of Strasburg on U.S. 11.

Broad Run Area (Tours 11 & 12)

Beverley Mill (1799) — Off Va. 55 at Thorofare Gap, 9 miles east of Marshall.

Woodstock Area (Tour 14)

Liberty Furnace (1817)

Beverley Mill

183

Steele's Tavern Area (Tour 14)
Grist Mill (1825) — At McCormick's Birthplace.

INDIAN FORTS:

Strasburg Area (Tour 8)
Fort Stephens (1754) — On Va. 628 at Cedar Creek.
Frontier Fort (1755) — On U.S. 11, Strasburg. The old Hupp
  homestead used as a fort against the Indians.
Fort Bowman (1750) — North of Strasburg between I-81 &
  U.S. 11.

Luray Area (Tour 10)
White House Fort (1760)

TAVERNS AND INNS:

Winchester Area (Tour 2)
Red Lion Tavern (1753)

Leesburg Area (Tour 5)
Laurel Brigade Inn (1834)

Middleburg Area (Tour 6)
Red Fox Tavern (1728)

Middletown Area (Tour 8)
Wayside Inn (1797)

Warrenton Area (Tour 12)
Warren Green Hotel (1820)

Woodstock Area (Tour 14)
Halfway House (1798)
Renner's Ordinary (1792)

Staunton Area (Tour 14)
Steele's Tavern (1798)

IRON FURNACES:

By the 1850's, many of the Valley iron ore extractors,
along with those in nearby Maryland, Pennsylvania and
New Jersey, had been closed as steel production moved

westward. Several of the Valley furnaces, however, were reactivated during the Civil War for a brief period.

Berkeley Springs Area (Tour 1)
Washington Furnace (1795) — On U.S. 522 between Berkeley Springs, West Va. and Hancock, Md.

Winchester Area (Tour 2)
Opequon Furnace (1784)

Harpers Ferry Area (Tour 4)
Harpers Ferry Furnace (*circa*, 1850)

Fort Valley Area (Tour 9)
Elizabeth Furnace (1800)
Powell's Fort Furnace (1825)

Woodstock Area (Tour 14)
Jerome Furnace (1820)

AND A COVERED BRIDGE:

Mt. Jackson — New Market Area (Tour 14)
Meems Bottom Bridge (1817-93) — At the North Fork of the Shenandoah River about 2 miles south of Mt. Jackson. Turn west from U.S. 11 on Va. 720 to the river. Accessible also from Exit 68 of I-81 east to U.S. 11; then one mile north to Va. 720. A single-span 204-foot covered bridge, which still carries traffic over its wooden planks. Its massive arch supports and stone abutments were hewed and quarried from nearby materials. Several bridges preceded the present one. Stonewall Jackson burned the Shenandoah bridge at this same site to cut off advancing Union troops, and another was destroyed by the flood of 1870.

BATTLEFIELDS

During its 300-year history, the Shenandoah Valley has been the scene of numerous major battles, plus countless minor engagements, both during the French and Indian War and during the Civil War. No formal fighting took place in the Valley itself during the American Revolution, although as we have seen, many Revolutionary War leaders, soldiers and heroes came from the Valley, and Fort Valley (Tour 9) was at one time considered as a fort of final refuge by George Washington.

Historical markers throughout the Valley commemorate colorful events during the time of the "Indian outrages" and massacres. There are also markers at the sites of stockades which the early settlers erected to defend themselves against the Indians. But, for the most part, the State Historical Markers along the Valley roadsides deal with the Civil War and such notable figures as Stonewall Jackson, Turner Ashby, John S. Mosby, Belle Boyd, and many others. These markers are complemented by many blue and gray roadside signs and battle maps erected by the Civil War Centennial Commission during the years 1961-65.

Thousands of tourists and historians visit the Shenandoah Valley battlefields each year, and an excellent starting point for your tour is the **Hall of Valor** at **New Market Battlefield Park** (Tour 14). The 160-acre park lies between U.S. 11 and the Shenandoah River, and is accessible from

Colonial Studio

Hall of Valor

I-81, just north of New Market. At its center is the spectacular, Hall of Valor, a memorial to the 247 VMI cadets who turned back the invading Federal forces on May 15, 1864. There is an annual reenactment of the battle on the Sunday preceding May 15, and every day visitors can view an awards-winning film commemorating the event.

Excellent exhibits in the Virginia Room survey the entire National Parks
course of the Civil War and serve as orientation to the
various Valley battlefields. Another motion picture depicts
Stonewall Jackson's famous Valley Campaign. Open daily,
except Christmas Day, 9 to 5. Adults, $1.00; children
(7-13), 50¢; special group rates. Tel: 422-8353.

Stonewall Jackson's Valley Campaign (1862) can easily
be followed by car to eleven strategic points along U.S. 11
and U.S. 340. Museums, roadside maps and historical
markers relate the battles of Kernstown, Cedar Creek,
Fisher's Hill, New Market, Lacey Spring, Cross Keys,
McDowell, Port Republic, Front Royal and Winchester
(Tours 2, 8, 10, & 14). At Harrisonburg, in the Municipal
Building on Main Street, there is a comprehensive Electric
Map with lights and narration. It traces the tactical
brilliance with which Jackson marched his little army 630
miles in 39 days, harassing Union armies while protecting
the "Breadbasket of the Confederacy."

In **National and Confederate Cemeteries** a few blocks
east of Winchester's main business area nearly 8,000
soldiers from both sides lie buried (Tour 2). Most of them
were casualties of the Civic War battles fought in the
Winchester area.

Ball's Bluff Cemetery overlooking the Potomac near
Leesburg (Tour 5), is the smallest national military
cemetery in the United States and is the site of the key
Battle of Ball's Bluff (1861).

Across the Potomac River from Shepherdstown (Tour 4)
and 5 miles east of Sharpsburg, is **Antietam National
Battlefield Site**. The battle (1862) in which more than
23,000 Union and Confederate troops were killed,
prevented General Robert E. Lee from carrying the War
into the north. The 787 acre area features a visitor center,
observation tower and such famed landmarks as Burnside
Bridge and "Bloody Lane." The visitor center is open every
day except Thanksgiving and Christmas.

NATIONAL PARKS

There are two national parks in the area which offer a
variety of recreational facilities.

187

SHENANDOAH NATIONAL PARK — 193,646 acres of superb Blue Ridge Mountain forest land, valleys, and streams, with mountain peaks up to slightly over 4,000 feet in elevation. The park is threaded with 130 miles of paved public roads, many ranger side roads (usually closed to visitor traffic) and over 200 miles of scenic trails for hikers. The famous Skyline Drive and one of the most attractive sections of the 2,000 mile Appalachian Trail are also to be found here. The Drive begins just south of Front Royal and winds 105 panoramic miles through the Park to its southern boundary at Rockfish Gap; thereafter, it joins the equally scenic Blue Ridge Parkway, which continues south and west to the Great Smoky Mountains of North Carolina and Tennessee.

Wildlife and wild flowers abound in the spring, when red bud, pink and snowy-white dogwood, mountain laurel, azalea, trillium, and hepatica cover the mountainside; in summer wild lilies, blueweed, Indian pipe, thimbleberry, an occasional rhododendron and flowering plants of many kinds take over. In fall, the whole area turns a blazing riot of color starting with the Virginia Creeper, as the first frosts hit the hardwoods, and the bright fruits of the dogwood, white baneberry and sumac add to the brilliance of goldenrod, asters, yarrow and fireweed. The most lavish

Phil Flournoy

From the Skyline Drive

displays usually occur between October 10 and 20, and, not surprisingly, this is the period of the largest concentration of visitors to the park. Please remember not to pick flowers or other plants or injure the vegetation. Leave them for others to enjoy.

There is no hunting allowed inside the park, which serves as a major game preserve. All forms of wildlife are protected, pets must be kept on leash, and hunting weapons are prohibited. The park's wildlife includes bear, fox, deer, raccoon, and bobcat, as well as the more common rabbit, skunk, woodchuck, and possum. Trout fishing is permitted and is very popular in the many stocked mountain streams throughout the area. A Virginia fishing license is required.

Horseback riding along the trails is a favorite sport for many, with horses available from the stables at Big Meadows and Skyland. Hiking and nature study are two other favorite pastimes throughout the park, with numerous ranger-guided walks scheduled during the summer at Dickey Ridge, Matthews Arm, Skyland, Big Meadows, Lewis and Loft Mountains. (See Hiking for further details.)

Throughout the summer, there are illustrated ranger lectures and campfire programs and from early spring to late autumn, exhibits of the park's geology and ecology at the Dickey Ridge Information Center, near the northern end of Skyline Drive, and at the Byrd Visitor Center at Big Meadows in the central section.

Mileposts along the drive are numbered from north to south, and park features, facilities and services are keyed to these mileposts. The Virginia Skyline Company, Inc., Box 191, Luray, Virginia 22835, tel: (703)743-5108, operates Skyland and Big Meadows Lodges and their cottages and the cottages at Lewis Mountain, which accommodate 800 guests in the park's central district. Write or telephone for reservations well ahead of time. The company also serves as park concessioner for restaurants, gift shops, service stations and riding stables; and offers facilities for campers, such as grocery and camping-supply stores, shower and laundry buildings, ice and wood sales. Picnicking is permitted only in the eight designated areas listed below, which have water, fireplaces and grills. There are trash receptacles in all picnic and parking areas. Don't be a litterbug.

189

Principal facilities at stops on the Skyline Drive, measured by miles from the north entrance near Front Royal, are:

4.6 mi. - **Dickey Ridge Visitor Center**— Exhibits and programs. Information, bookstore, maps. Restrooms. Picnic ground nearby. Telephone. Open daily April through October.

22.3 mi. - **Matthews Arm Campground** — Tent and trailer sites. Showers, laundry and firewood. Hikes and campfire programs.

24.1 mi. - **Elkwallow Wayside** — Picnic grounds. Coffee shop, gift shop. Camper supplies. Gasoline. June through October. Tel: 599-2253.

31.5 mi. - **Thornton Gap** — Entrance Station and U.S. 211 interchange. Park headquarters 4 miles west near Luray. Panorama Restaurant open all year; gift shop and gasoline service station. Tel: 599-2265.

36.7 mi. - **Pinnacles** — Picnic grounds. Appalachian Trail junction.

41.7 mi. - **Skyland** — Hotel-cottage accommodations for 400. Dining room, handicraft shop, riding horses. April to early November. Tel: 599-2221. Stony Man Nature Trail and Whiteoak Canyon Parking.

51.0 mi. - **Big Meadows Wayside.** — Byrd Visitor Center. Exhibits, programs, information. Coffee shop, gift shop, camper supplies. Gasoline service station. April through October.

51.3 mi. - **Big Meadows** — Hotel-cottage accommodations for 250. Dining room, handicraft shop, riding horses. May through October. Tel: 599-2221. Picnic grounds, camp and trailer sites, open all year. Showers, laundry, firewood, ice sales in summer. Swamp Nature Trail; campfire programs.

57.6 mi. - **Lewis Mountain** — Indoor-outdoor cottages. Tel: 599-2294. Picnic grounds. Campground with trailer sites. Firewood, limited camper supplies. June through September.

62.9 mi. - **South River Picnic Area** — Picnic grounds. 2½-mile round trip trail to falls.

65.7 mi. - **Swift Run Gap.** — Entrance Station and U.S. 33 interchange.

79.8 mi. - **Loft Mountain** — Coffee shop, gift shop, camper supplies. Picnic grounds. Campground with trailer sites, laundry, firewood, ice. Hikes and campfire programs. Gasoline service station. June to mid-October.

83.5 mi. - Browns Gap — Dundo picnic grounds.

105.4 mi. - Rockfish Gap — South entrance station and U.S. 250 interchange. 5 miles to Humpback Rocks Visitor Center on Blue Ridge Parkway.

Above all, the great appeal and drawing power of Shenandoah National Park and its Skyline Drive are the superb panoramas from the succession of seventy-five parking overlooks, each with its own safe turnout and parking area, guarded by stout stone ramparts. Another dramatic feature of the Drive is Mary's Rock Tunnel cut straight through 700 ft of rock. The 105-mile procession of outstanding views and vistas draws over 2,300,000 visitors to the park annually. The largest single influx comes during the fall coloring season, but every pleasant summer weekend draws its share of sightseers.

In my opinion the most beautiful section of the Drive is the first 31 miles from the northern entrance, with its steady but carefully engineered climb from the floor of the Valley to the towering heights (3,385 feet) of Hogback Overlook, and then the gradual descent to 2,300 feet at Thornton Gap (Panorama). First, on your drive, is a stop at the Dickey Ridge Information Center, and then, as the Drive winds from one side of the Blue Ridge to the other, a look over the lovely, fertile Luray Valley with the winding horseshoe curves of the Shenandoah River skirting the beetling flanks of the green Massanutten range opposite. Soon there is a peek to the other side, across the Piedmont Plain and its bumpy scattering of nubbly receding foothills. Shenandoah Valley Overlook, Signal Knob, Gooney Manor, Hogwallow Flat, Browntown Valley, Range View, Hogback, Piney River, Jeremy's Run, and Pass Mountain Overlooks— the views along here are second to none. Everytime you look, there is another small valley town or crossroads nestling at your feet amid criss-cross patterns of fields and forest, streams and pastures, ribbonlike country roads and green copses. Although this is not the highest section of the Drive, it has always been my favorite, with the Browntown Bowl on one side, Huntly, Flint Hill, and "Little" Washington, on the other; then the clean sweep below as you swirl downgrade from aloft, to either the town of Luray to the west, or to the east to Sperryville and the rugged rocky terrain of Rappahannock County.

One day— a fine clear day, preferably, of course—is all that is needed to tour either one or two sections of the Skyline Drive, including your drive from any nearby city such as Winchester, Washington, Baltimore, Roanoke or Richmond. From any greater distance, however, I suggest you plan three days: one to reach the Valley, another for your leisurely tour of Shenandoah National Park and surrounding areas, and a third for your return home. Four days is ideal, allowing enough time to include some other scenic and historic spots listed in this travel guide.

The Park is open all year, but in winter, occasionally, severe weather conditions require that it be closed for safety reasons. During the winter months, even if the Drive is not officially closed to general traffic, driving is apt to be slow and slippery. By car, there are four main entrances to the park along the Skyline Drive:

North Entrance (Front Royal) — From U.S. 340 and 522 and Va. 55.

Thornton Gap (Mile 31.6) — From U.S. 211

Swift Run Gap (Mile 65.7) — From U.S. 33

South Entrance (Rockfish Gap) — From U.S. 250 and from the Blue Ridge Parkway

Entrance fee of $2.00 is collected from each car, usually from April through October. Drivers displaying the National Park's Golden Eagle Passport (cost $10.00) may enter without additional charge. Hikers may enter the Park free of charge at any point. There are no fees for camping in the designated campgrounds, but it is necessary to register at the campground entrance stations for assignment of tent and trailer sites.

Bring a camera and a pair of sturdy shoes for walking, and, if you have a pair of binoculars, they will add to your appreciation of the park. If you come in spring or fall, bring enough sweaters and warm clothes for the whole family. It gets chilly up in the mountains as the sun goes down. Most of the park facilities are closed in winter (November though May), but the restaurant at Panorama and the campground at Big Meadows are open the year round. Park rangers will help you in emergencies or with any special questions. Check one of the park's fifty outdoor bulletin boards for timely announcements or for schedules of activities. If you

Virginia State Travel Service

Shenandoah National Park

have questions prior to your arrival, write to the Superintendent, Shenandoah National Park, Luray, Va. 22835.

HARPERS FERRY NATIONAL HISTORICAL PARK — 100 acres, off U.S. 340 at Shenandoah River Highway bridge, Harpers Ferry, West Virginia. Watch for entrance sign. A fully restored, Federal period town, once a major railroad, canal, and river boat center at the confluence of the Potomac and Shenandoah Rivers, and site of John Brown's infamous raid on the Federal Arsenal in 1859. Curio shops, museums, and John Brown's fort on premises. Frequently flooded by the rampaging rivers in the past, this unusual hillside community has been faithfully and tastefully restored to its mid-19th century condition by the National Park Service. There is no entrance fee.

Harpers Ferry National Historical Park

The Park headquarters and visitor center are in the restored old Stagecoach Inn near the public parking area. Along the Shenandoah River shore, beyond the parking area, are picnic grounds. At the visitor center, which is open daily, you can see exhibits and obtain information. There are abandoned old mill races, formerly used to power the waterwheels driving the lathes in the arsenal, and remains of the small U.S. Arsenal destroyed when Union forces burned the arsenal buildings in 1861. The nearby Master Armour's House has been restored and is now a museum featuring the story of gunmaking. The U.S. Armory fire enginehouse, used by John Brown as a fort during the abortive 1859 raid, is near the point where the Shenandoah and Potomac Rivers meet, once the heart of town. From the Stone Steps, hand-carved into the natural rock, it is only a short walk to the upper level of Harpers Ferry and its oldest surviving structure, the Harper House, built by Robert Harper, the man for whom this town was named. His ferry and mill have long since disappeared. The celebrated Jefferson Rock is about a half mile further uphill. It was from this spot in 1783 that Thomas Jefferson extolled: "The passage of the Potomac through the Blue Ridge is perhaps one of the most stupendous scenes in nature . . . On your right comes up the

Shenandoah, having ranged along the foot of the mountain an hundred miles to seek a vent. On your left approaches the Potomac, in quest of a passage also. In the moment of their junction, they rush together against the mountain, rend it asunder, and pass off to the sea. . . . This scene is worth a voyage across the Atlantic."

Harpers Ferry National Historical Park

John Brown's Fort in its original setting, Harpers Ferry

NATURAL WONDERS

There are a number of natural wonders located throughout the Valley, the most popular of which are Natural Bridge and the numerous underground caverns or caves. Most of the caverns are very artistically lighted, maintain a year-round temperature of about $55°$, and have guided tours of approximately one hour through their subterranean wonderland of stalactites, stalagmites, and shimmering rock crystals. All of them have gift shops, restaurants, and picnic grounds nearby.

Harpers Ferry Area (Tour 4)

Harpers Ferry Caverns — 2½ miles northwest of Harpers Ferry National Park via U.S. 340. Discovered in 1967. Exit by electric cart from underground. Gift shop, snack bar, lounge, picnic area. Open daily all year. Summer 10

195

to 7; winter 11 to 4. Adults $2.50; children (7-13) $1.50; under 7 free.

Strasburg Area (Tour 8)

Battlefield Crystal Caverns – U.S. 11, one mile north of Strasburg. A legendary refuge of Indians and a haven to soldiers during the Civil War.

Wardensville, West Virginia Area (Tour 8)

Lost River Canyon Roadside Park – On W. Va. 55-259, three miles southwest of Wardensville. Near here Lost River suddenly goes underground into a funnel-like opening to reappear five miles further north as the Cacapon River. From picnic area, cross bridge and walk left ¼ mile along river bank.

Front Royal Area (Tour 10)

Skyline Caverns – On U.S. 340, near entrance to Skyline Drive, one mile south of Front Royal. Open daily all year. Gift shop, snack bar, miniature railroad, unique calcite formations (anthodites). Annual Easter Sunrise Service. Hours vary with season. Adults $3.00, children (7-13) $1.50.

Luray Area (Tour 10)

Luray Caverns – On U.S. 211 at west end of Luray. Stalacpipe organ plays concert selections on stone formations. Gift shop, restaurant, antique car and carriage museum and carillon bell tower nearby. Open daily all year. Spring and fall 9 to 6; summer 9 to 7; winter 9 to 4; Admittance to Caverns and Car Caravan, adults $4.00; children (7-13) $2.00; under 7 free.

New Market to Staunton Area (Tour 14)

Shenandoah Caverns – On U.S. 11, between Mt. Jackson and New Market or take I-81, exit 68. Elevator service, picnic grounds, coffee and gift shops. Firetruck ride to covered bridge. Open daily all year. Spring and fall 9 to 6; summer 9 to 7; winter 9 to 5. Adults, $3.00; children (7-14) $1.50; under 7 free.

Endless Caverns – 3 miles south of New Market on U.S. 11 or 3½ miles east of I-81, exits 66 and 67. Camp and picnic grounds, lake, horseback riding, art museum, gift shop, restaurant. Open all year. June 11 - Labor Day, 9 to 7; Nov. 11 - March 10, 10 to 5; rest of year, 9 to 5. Adults $2.50; children (7-14) $1.25; under 7 free.

Massanutten Caverns—Keezletown, Va., 5 miles east of Harrisonburg via U.S. 338 & Va. 620. Gift shop and picnic grounds. Open daily, June 1 — Labor Day, 10 to 6. Otherwise Sat. & Sun. only. Adults $2.75; children (7-14), $1.50; under 7, free.

Grand Caverns (Weyer's Cave) — U.S. 340 at Grottoes, Virginia. First cave discovered in Virginia (1804). During Civil War, Stonewall Jackson quartered his troops here. Giftshop. Open daily, except Christmas, 9 to 4; May 10-Labor Day, 8:30 to 7. Adults, $3.00; children (6-12), $1.25; special group rates.

Natural Chimneys Regional Park —Between Harrisonburg and Staunton at Mt. Solon, 7 miles southwest of Bridgewater via Va. 42 and 747. Here, on the third Saturday of every August since 1821, a jousting tournament is held. Fascinating rock formations. Trail to highest point, 120 feet above surrounding plain. Nature trails, picnicking, camping. Open all year. $3.00 per car.

Virginia State Travel Service

Jousting at Natural Chimneys

197

Virginia State Travel Service
Natural Bridge

Goshen Pass Natural Area — On Va. 39, 12 miles NW of Lexington. Here the Maury River cascades through the pass for 3½ miles. Picnic tables, fishing permitted, and hunting in adjoining wildlife management area.

Natural Bridge — U.S. 11 and I-81 between exits 49 and 50, 13 miles south of Lexington. Hotels, gift shops, restaurants, tennis, swimming, ice skating, golf, shooting preserve, and camping nearby. Surveyed and initialed by George Washington; bought from King George III of England in 1774 by Thomas Jefferson, who eventually deeded it to the state of Virginia. One of the "Seven Natural Wonders of the World", 215 feet high. Open daily all year. "The Drama of Creation" pageant presented nightly. Combination day-night admission: Adults, $3.00; children (6-12), $1.50. Single visits: Adults, $2.00; children (6-12), $1.00.

CAMPING

The facilities available to the tent and trailer camper range from elaborate campsites complete with showers, electricity, laundry equipment, recreation areas, playgrounds, grocery stores and gift shops to the more primitive campsites usually associated with wilderness camping. Many campgrounds are operated by the state or federal government, but there are a growing number privately owned. Unless indicated by the word "primitive", all camping spots listed here have at least cleared campsites, drinking water, sanitary facilities, picnic tables and firepaces. Write or telephone for rates and further information. Privately-operated campgrounds are indicated by an asterik as are those special facilities for which there is an extra charge.*

Berkeley Springs Area (Tour 1)

Sleepy Creek Public Hunting Area — c/o George Lewis, Jones Spring, West Va. 25429. Tel: (304) 754-3855. State-operated; 25 primitive tent sites, 10 primitive tent or trailer sites. Drinking water, grocery store. Open all year.

Falling Waters Campsite* — c/o Dale A. Leatherman, Falling Waters, West Va. 25419. Tel. (304) 267-8815. 10 miles north of Martinsburg on U.S. 11. 25 standard tent or trailer sites. Electric hookup, water hookup, showers, dumping station, groceries. All year.

Coolfont Recreation* — c/o J. W. France, Berkeley Springs, West Va. 25411. Tel: (304) 258-1793. Cold Run Valley Road, 3 miles from Berkeley Springs. 125 standard tent or trailer sites. Electric hookup, water hookup, showers, laundry facilities, dumping station, groceries. All year.

Henry's Trailer Park*, — c/o Melvin E. Henry, RFD 1, Berkeley Springs, West Va. 25411. Tel: (304) 258-2510 or 258-1104. 11 miles south of Berkeley Springs. Electric hookup, water hookup, showers, dumping station, groceries. All year.

Tri-Lake* — c/o Albert Fanucchi, Berkeley Springs, West, Va. 28411. Tel: (304) 258-1331. Adjacent to Blue Ridge Fish Hatchery, U.S. 522 near Va. border. 120 tent or trailer sites. Electric hookup, dumping station, groceries. March-November.

Winchester Area (Tour 2)

Magic Mountain Recreation Area — Rte. 2, Winchester, Va. 22601. Tel: 667-8856. 5 miles west of Winchester on U.S. 50. 100 tent or trailer. *Electric hookup, *water hookup, flush toilets, dumping station, private lake, fishing, boating, babysitting service, outdoor games. March 1 - December 15.

Opequon Creek Family Campground — Rte. 1, Box 214, Berryville, Va. 22611. Tel: 955-2505. 7 miles north of Winchester on I-81 to Exit 83; then 4 miles east on Va. 672. 30 tent or trailer. Well, electric hookup, flush toilets, firewood, hot showers, dumping station, hunting, fishing. 1 mile to store. April-December.

Berryville-Boyce Area (Tour 3)

Willow Lake Campground* — Bluemont, Va. 22012. Tel: 955-1881. 14 miles southeast of Berryville. 50 sites, *electric hookup, *water hookup, dumping station, hot showers, flush toilets, firewood, fishing, swimming, boats for rent. 2 miles to grocery. May-November.

Charlestown-Harpers Ferry Area (Tour 4)

Mountain State,* — c/o Thomas W. Newcomer, Harpers Ferry, West Va. 25425. Tel: (304) 725-2066. U.S. 340 near Cliffside Motel, Harpers Ferry. 12 primitive tent or trailer. Drinking water, dumping station, groceries.

Mountain Lake*, – Paris, Va. 22130. Tel: 837-1261. Va.
606, 1 mile after crossing Shenandoah River on U.S. 50
from Winchester. 25 sites. Electric hookup, hot showers,
flush toilets, fishing and hunting, swimming, dumping
station. 3 miles to grocery store,. April-November.

Virginia State Travel Service
Camping in Shenandoah National Park

Fort Valley Area (Tour 9)
Elizabeth Furnace – c/o District Ranger, George
Washington National Forest, U.S. Forest Service,
Edinburg, Va. 22824. Tel: 459-4171. From Strasburg, 5
miles east on Va. 55; then 3 miles south on Va. 678. 25
combination tent and trailer. Showers, flush toilets,
firewood, fishing, hunting, nature trails, playgrounds,
campfire programs June 1-Labor Day. Grocery store 3
miles at Waterlick. April 1-December 1.
Little Fort – c/o District Ranger, George Washington
National Forest, Edinburg, Va. 22824. Tel: 984-4412.
From Front Royal, 7 miles on Va. 55; then 12 miles
south on Va. 678; then 3 miles west to area. 7
combination tent and trailer. Firewood, hunting, nature
trails. Grocery store 5 miles at Woodstock. All year.

Camp Roosevelt — c/o District Ranger, George Washington National Forest, Edinburg, Va. 22824. Tel: 984-4412. 9 miles west of Luray on Va. 675 or 9 miles east of Edinburg on Va. 675. 10 tent or trailer sites. Flush toilets, firewood, hunting, playground. Grocery store 5 miles at Kings Crossing. April 1-December 1.

Front Royal-Luray-Skyline Drive Area (Tour 10)

Deerpoint * — P. O. Box 320A, Front Royal, Va. 22630. Tel: 635-3984. From Front Royal, 1 mile south on U.S. 340; then 3 miles west on Va. 619. 70 tent or trailer. *Electric hookup, *sewer hookup, hot showers, flush toilets, dumping station, *air conditioners, *electric heaters, *swimming pool, fishing, hunting, outdoor games, grocery store. March 15-Nov. 30 (limited camping Dec. 1-March 14).

Gooney Creek Camp * — Goodeview, Inc., Box 1165, Front Royal, Va. 22630. Tel: 635-4066. 4 miles south of entrance to Skyline Drive on U.S. 340. 60 tent or trailer. Electric hookup, water hookup, hot showers, flush toilets, firewood, hiking trails, playground areas, boating, fishing, swimming. April-October.

Massanutten Camp Forest* — Route, 1, Front Royal, Va. 22630. Tel: 635-6061. U.S. 340 south 1 mile from Front Royal; then west 6 miles on Va. 619. 97 tent or trailer. Electric hookup, hot showers, flush toilets, dumping station, firewood, *swimming pool, nature trails, fishing, grocery store. All year.

Three Springs KOA Campground* — Box 274, Front Royal, Va. 22630. Tel: 635-2741. U.S. 340 south 2 miles from Front Royal. 65 sites. *Electric hookup, water hookup, hot showers, flush toilets, firewood, automatic washers and dryers, dumping station, nature trails, fishing, children's playground, camp store. March 15-November 30.

Big Meadows — c/o General Delivery, Luray, Va. 22835. 215 tent and trailer. *Hot showers, flush toilets, *automatic washers and dryers, sewage disposal station, *firewood, *ice, trout fishing in season, nature trails, campfire programs, *riding stables, grocery store and service station. All year.

Lewis Mountain — c/o General Delivery, Luray, Va. 22835. 32 tent or trailer. Flush toilets, *firewood, *ice, trout fishing in season, nature trails, campfire programs.

Grocery store 7 miles north at Big Meadows. May
15-October 31.

Loft Mountain — c/o General Delivery, Elkton, Va. 22827.
Tel: 559-2241. 64 walk-in, 167 tent or trailer. Flush
toilets, sewage dump station, *laundry, *showers, *ice,
*firewood, trout fishing in season, nature trails, campfire
programs, grocery store and service station. April 15-
October 31.

Matthews Arm Campground — c/o General Delivery,
Luray, Va. 22835. 186 tent or trailer. Flush toilets,
fishing in season, nature trails, campfire programs.
Limited supplies 2 miles from campground. April-
October.

Brookside Campground* — RFD 4, Luray, Va. 22835. Tel:
743-5698. 15 tent and trailer. Electricity, hot showers,
flush toilets, dumping station, restaurant, cottages, gift
shop and gasoline. April-October.

Rappahannock County (Tour 13)

Piney River Campsites — 11103 Cavalier Court, Apt. 10-L,
Fairfax, Va. 22030. Tel: 987-8153. 1 mile north of
Sperryville on U.S. 211, then west 3 miles on Va. 612. 40
tent or trailer. Hot showers, flush toilets, *firewood,
fishing, hunting, nature trails, concessioner, dumping
station. April 1-November 1.

Valley Pike (Tour 14)

Wolf Gap — c/o District Ranger, Edinburg, Va. 22824. Tel:
984-4101. Near Virginia line, just off W. Va. 23. 10
primitive camping units. Drinking water.

Endless Caverns Campground* — New Market, Va. 22844.
Tel: 422-3158. 3 miles south of New Market, exits 66 &
67 from I-81. 100 tent and trailer. Hot showers, flush
toilets electric outlets, lake with sand beach, boating,
fishing, swimming, *horseback riding, hiking, *caverns,
art museum, *restaurant, children's playground, *camp
equipment rentals, supply store. May 15-Oct. 15.

Rancho Travel Trailer Park & Campground* — Box 35, New
Market, Va. 22844. Tel: 436-3422. 1½ miles south of New
Market on U.S. 11. 65 sites. Electric hookup, hot showers,
flush toilets, firewood, ice, dumping station. Grocery
store in New Market. May 15-October 15.

Keyers Camping Ground* — Route 1, Shenandoah, Va.
22849. 50 tent, 20 trailer. Electric hookup, hot showers,
flush toilets, wash tubs, firewood, ice, fishing, fishing

supplies, boats for rent, hunting, nature trails. May 15-Oct. 15.

Gerundo Family Campground* — Route 1, Penn Laird, Va. 22846. Tel: 289-5351. 80 sites. Electric hookup, hot showers, flush toilets, automatic washers and dryers, firewood, ice, dumping station, fishing, swimming, *fishing supplies, hunting in season, nature trails, children's playground, grocery store nearby. April-October.

Todd Lake — c/o U.S. Forest Service, Bridgewater, Va. 22812. Tel: 828-2591. 17 miles west of Bridgewater. From Mt. Solon (see below), right on Va. 731 for 1 mile & 2½ miles on Va. 730; then north 1 mile on Va. 718, left for 5 miles on Forest Service Road 95. 20 tent or trailer. Flush toilets, firewood, swimming, hunting, fishing. Grocery stores at Stokesville, 3 miles. April-December.

Natural Chimneys Regional Park — Mt. Solon, Va. 22843. Tel: 350-2510. 4 miles south on Va. 42 from Bridgewater; then right on Va. 747 for 4 miles to Mt. Solon; right on Va. 731. 110 sites. Hot showers, laundry, electricity, flush toilets, swimming, dumping station, nature trails. All year.

Hone Quarry — c/o District Ranger, U.S. Forest Service, Bridgewater, Va. 22812. Tel: 828-2591. 11 miles west of Dayton on Va. 257. 10 combination tent and trailer. Firewood, fishing, hunting, nature trails, play field. Grocery store at Dayton. April-December.

North River — c/o District Ranger, U.S. Forest Service, Bridgewater, Va. 22812. Tel: 828-2591. 10 miles northwest of Churchville. 15 tent. Firewood, fishing, hunting, nature trails, play field. Grocery store at Churchville. All year.

Sherando Lake — c/o U.S. Forest Service, Lyndhurst, Va. 22952. Tel: 261-6105. From Waynesboro, Va. 624 for 4 miles; left on Va. 664 for 10 miles, then right on Forest Service Road 91 for 2 miles. 65 tent or trailer. Cold showers, flush toilets, *firewood, swimming, fishing, *boats for rent, hunting, nature trails, play fields, campfire programs. April 1-December 31.

Spring Valley Campground — Box 623, Staunton, Va. 24401. 6½ miles west of Staunton. U.S. 250 west 2 miles to Va. 732 for 2.4 miles to Va. 736 for 2 miles to campground. 20 tent, 20 trailer. *Electric hookup, *water hookup, hot showers, flush toilets, dumping station, firewood, hiking, fishing, camp store. April-December.

Shenandoah Acres Resort* — Stuarts Draft, Va. 24477. Tel: 337-1911. 60 sites. Electric hookup, laundry near-by, hot showers, flush toilets, firewood, ice, dumping station, swimming, outdoor sports, hunting in season, nature trails, horseback riding, *bicycles for rent. Grocery store, fishing, and golf nearby. April-November.

Senger's Mountain Lake Resort* — Greenville, Va. 24440. Tel: 337-1775. 160 tent and trailer. *Electricity hook-up, *water hookup, hot showers, flush toilets, automatic washers and dryers, dumping station, firewood, ice, swimming, fishing, *row boats for rent, *fishing sup-plies, hunting in season, nature trails, *cabins for rent, grocery store. All year.

Waynesboro KOA, Inc. — Route 3, Box 333, Waynesboro, Va. 22980. Tel: 992-2395. 4 miles north of Waynesboro on U.S. 340. 15 tent, 40 trailer. Electric hookup, water hookup, hot showers, flush toilets, automatic washers and dryers, firewood, ice, swimming pool, hiking, horseback riding, grocery store. April-October.

250 Camping* — c/o S. N. Nite, Route 1, Staunton, Va. 24401. Tel: 886-7975. Hot showers, flush toilets, firewood. Supermarket near campground. April-November.

Maplecrest Camping Area.* —c/o Charles L. Hooke, High-town, Va. 24444. Tel: 468-2381. Va. 640 south 2.7 miles from U.S. 250 at Hightown. *Electric hookups, central water, flush toilets, dump station, firewood.

Kirkpatrick's Campground* — P.O. Box 851, Lexington, Va. 24450. Tel: 463-5106. 6 tent, 7 trailer. *Electric hookup, *water hookup, flush toilets, hot showers, auto-matic washers and dryers, dumping station, firewood, *ice, playground, concessionaire. All year.

Douthat State Park — Clifton Forge, Va. 24422. Tel: 862-0612. 1 mile east of Clifton Forge on U.S. 60, then 5 miles north on Va. 629. 130 tent or trailer. Hot showers, flush toilets, wash tubs, dumping station, *firewood, ice, *trout fishing, *fishing supplies, *row boats, swimming, nature trails, *horseback riding, con-cessionaire, restaurant. June-October.

Circle H Campgrounds — RFD 1, Clifton Forge, Va. 24422. Tel: 862-3131. 50 tent, 75 trailer. *Electric

Hiking

hookup, hot showers, flush toilets, dumping station, *firewood, ice, swimming, fishing, hunting, hiking, *boat rentals, playgrounds, outdoor games, camp store. 1 mile to restaurant, antique shop, grocery store. All year.

Whispering Pines Camping Area* — RFD 1, Clifton Forge, Va. 24422. Tel: 862-3896. 125 sites. *Electric hookup, showers, flush toilets, *firewood, dumping station, swimming, fishing, hunting, nature trails. Grocery store 1½ miles. May-October.

Blowing Springs — District Ranger, George Washington National Forest, U. S. Forest Service, Hot Springs, Va. Tel. 962-2214. 8 miles west of Warm Springs on Va. 39. 12 combination tent and trailer. Pit toilets, firewood, fishing, hunting, nature trails, playfield. Grocery store at Warm Springs. April-December.

Peaceful River* — c/o I. N. Hobbs, Route 1, Millboro, Va. 24460. 11 miles east of Warm Springs, on Va. 39. 15 tent or trailer. Electric hookup, pit toilets, garbage disposal cans, firewood, fishing, hunting, boating, nature trails. Ice and grocery store 2 miles west at Millboro Springs. All year.

Natural Bridge Campground — Natural Bridge, Va. 24578. On U.S. 11, 3 miles from Natural Bridge; take Exit 50 from I-81. 5 trailer. Stay limited to overnight. Electric hookup, flush toilets, ice, grocery store. All year.

Cave Mountain Lake Recreation Area — Jefferson National Forest, U.S. Forest Service, Natural Bridge Station, Va. 24579. 9 miles from Natural Bridge on Va. 130 and Va. 759. 49 tent & trailer. Flush toilets, firewood, swimming, nature trails, food and camping supplies at snack bar. May 15-Sept. 15.

Hopper Creek Group Camping Area — c/o District Ranger, Jefferson National Forest, Natural Bridge Station, Va. 24579. 6 miles south of Natural Bridge Station on Va. 759. Groups up to 100. Drinking water, pit toilets, outdoor cooking facilities, firewood. All year.

HIKING

Hiking trails abound in the Valley and in the surrounding mountain areas. The popular **Appalachian Trail**, running down the central spine of the Appalachian Mountains from

Maine to Georgia is, of course, the granddaddy of them all. In West Virginia and Virginia, this well-cleared, white-blazed trail, for the most part, traverses publicly-owned land — Harpers Ferry National Historical Park, Shenandoah National Park and the George Washington and Jefferson National Forests.

As the Trail leads southward there are a number of blue-blazed side trails leading from picnic grounds and parking areas to the main trail. At Harpers Ferry (tour 4) the Trail crosses U.S. 340, and from there the Appalachian Trail goes south over Loudoun Heights for 6 miles to where Va. 9 crosses it at Keys Gap. From this point it is just over 13 miles by the Trail to Snickers Gap where Va. 7 crosses it west of Bluemont, Va. From here the hiker can walk 11 miles to its crossing with U.S. 50 at Ashby Gap. It is another 13 miles to Manassas Gap and Va. 55 at Linden. By the Trail, it is only 5.5 miles farther to Chester Gap and the junction of U.S. 522 leading to Front Royal. Less than 2 miles beyond is the edge of Shenandoah National Park. In all, the distance to the Park's border is 50 miles from the departure point near Harpers Ferry, and there are six shelters scattered at intervals along this section of the Trail.

For the next 94 miles the Appalachian Trail crosses and recrosses the Skyline Drive (Tour 10) although it avoids the Drive as much as the rather narrow ridge permits. U.S. 211 crosses the Park at Thornton Gap (milepost 31.5), and 8 miles north along the Trail is Range View Cabin, one of 5 Potomac Appalachian Club cabins in the Park. They are locked and their use is restricted to those who make reservations in advance through the Potomac Appalachian Trail Club, 1718 N Street, N.W., Washington, D. C. 20036. Two other Hiking Clubs also maintain the Trail in the Shenandoah Valley area and have programs of hikes, usually on weekends: Shenandoah-Rockfish Appalachian Trail Club, 1520 Mulberry St., Waynesboro, Va. 22980; and Natural Bridge Appalachian Club, Lynchburg, Va. 24503.

Shenandoah National Park has excellent hiking, with more than 250 miles of well-marked trails, including the 94 mile portion of the famous Appalachian Trail. The central section of the Park, from Panorama (milepost 31.5) to Swift Run Gap (milepost 65.7) where U.S. 33 crosses the Skyline Drive, contains many of the best hiking trails in the Valley area:

Mary's Rock, from milepost 33.5, 3.6 miles round trip

(approx. 3 hrs.). Broad sweep of scenery in every direction. Steady climb but easy return.

Little Stony Man, milepost 39.1, 1.5 miles (1 hour). Steep climb for 0.6 mile of forest trail. Splendid view of Shenandoah Valley.

White Oak Canyon, milepost 42.6, 5 miles (4 hours). Cool walk through woods; series of six waterfalls at end of trail.

Hawksbill Trail, milepost 45.6, 1.5 miles (1 hour). To summit of highest mountain in park; shady but steady climb.

Dark Hollow Falls, milepost 50.5, 1.5 miles (1 hour). A series of cascades easily accessible by trail from Big Meadows.

South River Falls, milepost 62.8, 3 miles (3 to 4 hours). A moderately strenuous hike to the most picturesque waterfalls in the Park.

There are longer hiking trails, the most notable being the climb of **Old Rag Mountain,** part of which is rocky, rough and steep. It is advisable to allow a full day for the trip up and back from Old Rag's boulder-strewn summit, but it is a rewarding experience on a clear day. There are magnificent views of the Piedmont farmlands below to the east and to the west, the eastern walls of the Blue Ridge. The two shelters on Old Rag Mountain are similar to those at intervals along the Appalachian Trail. They are simple structures open on one side facing a stone fireplace, available to campers traversing the Trail on a first-come-first-served basis.

During summertime, the Park Rangers also conduct a wide variety of naturalist, ecology and "explorer" hikes and walks. They proceed at about one mile per hour and begin at Dickey Ridge, Matthews Arm, Skyland, Big Meadows, Lewis Mountain, and Loft Mountain. There are also evening campfire programs led by Ranger Naturalists at most of these locations. Schedules of these hikes and other events vary somewhat from year to year. You can send for the annual list and schedule of "Visitor Activities" by writing Shenandoah National Park, Luray, Va. 22835.

In the Park, there are also year round Self-Guiding Trails with trailside markers which tell interesting facts about the flora, fauna and natural history of the area. Several of these have printed guide-booklets available from dispensers.

208

Traces Trail (2 miles) starts from the parking area at the amphitheater near entrance station to Matthews Campground, milepost 22.3. A leisurely walk with emphasis on the past and old mountain homesteads.

Stony Man Trail (2 miles) starts at parking area on the north entrance road to Skyland, milepost 41.8. Environmental awareness is stressed. On clear days there are spectacular views of the Shenandoah Valley 3,000 feet below.

Swamp Trail (2 miles) starts near Big Meadows Ampitheater parking area, milepost 51.3. There are superb views of the Valley and a variety of habitats including forest, meadow and mountaintop swamp.

The Deadening (1.3 miles) starts at the service station parking area across from the entrance road to Loft Mountain Campground, milepost 79.8. The theme is how Nature is healing the wounds inflicted on the Mountain by man.

The Pedlar District of the **George Washington National Forest** lies below Shenandoah National Park and extends roughly from Waynesboro to just east of Natural Bridge (Tour 14). Winding through the mountain crest of this part of the Forest is a 70-mile stretch of the Appalachian Trail with seven lean-to shelters comfortably spaced at convenient intervals.

Throughout the Forest there are numerous easy-to-follow, "family-type walks" which take an hour or less round trip. In the Fort Valley area (Tour 9) are:

Pig Iron Trail - near Elizabeth Furnace picnic ground. A story trail with exhibits and self-guiding booklet describing the history of Elizabeth Furnace and iron making.

Woodstock Tower - by car the approach from Fort Valley is on Va. 758 from Detrick. From the observation tower is the renowned view of the Seven-Bends-of-the-Shenandoah River.

In the area west of Harrisonburg — Staunton (Tour 14):

Ramsey's Draft - by car turn off U.S. 250 on Forest Service Road 68 near Mountain House picnic ground. The trail begins on the right just beyond the first stream crossing. A Natural Area of virgin timber, plants, flowers, wildlife, and birds.

Elkhorn Lake Dam - west of Bridgewater on Va. 730; then follow Forest Service Road 96 along the shore of a

209

Hiking   mountain lake to the top of the man-made dam. Wildlife, fishing, forest and mountain scenery.

Some mountain trails in the George Washington National Forest offer particularly rewarding scenic viewing points or forest attractions. Allow at least a half day for the round trip. Several notable ones of from 3 to 6 miles are:

Kennedy Peak — start near Camp Roosevelt on Va. 675 in Fort Valley (Tour 9). Follow the Massanutten Mountain Trail. Outstanding panoramas of the Shenandoah Valley and the Blue Ridge, Fort Valley and the Massanutten.

Nature Walk, Shenandoah National Park

Jerry Run - from Ramsey's Draft (see above) to Sexton Shelter. A relaxing hike beside a mountain stream through the quiet beauty of the forest.

Big Schloss — start at Wolf Gap on the West Va. Line (Tours 8 & 14). The first half mile is a climb; then the Mill Mountain Trail follows the crest of the ridge to a rock outcropping. Return by the same route.

There are many more hiking trails throughout the Valley, but perhaps these will suggest the variety offered and lead you to further hiking adventures.

CANOEING

Canoeing and kayak paddling on our Valley rivers and streams has become an increasingly popular pastime. More and more cars loaded down with these light craft buzz about the countryside in search of new streams to explore. The annual Whitewater Canoe Race Championships, held each spring in May on the South Fork of the Shenandoah River from a point near Rileyville (U.S. 340 between Front Royal and Luray) have greatly added to the popularity of the sport.

It is best to bring your own canoe or kayak, but canoes are available for rent at Rush's Bait Shop, Riverton, Va. 22651, beside the North Fork Dam. Canoes may also be rented five miles west of Luray off U.S. 211 to your right.

Public boat landings and launching ramps are identified in the following section on Boating. All of them have sand or gravel ramps, have parking areas and are also used for fishing and pleasure boats. Launching sites along minor creeks and rivers are not always well marked, but they are dependable for the varying canoe runs listed below. They are recommended by Randy Carter, canoe expert and author of **Canoeing White Water River Guide**. Before you start your canoe trip, be sure you know if the river is too low to run.

Strasburg — Middletown — Wardensville, West Va. (Tour 8)
Cacapon River from Wardensville, W. Va. 29 miles to Capon Bridge, through superb Shenandoah Mountain country. Safe for experienced canoeists.

211

Cacapon River from U.S. 50 bridge to Forks of Cacapon. More wild, unspoiled mountain country. Safe for experienced canoeists.

Lost River—Cacapon River from W. Va. 55 highway bridge 5 miles above Wardensville to just below Wardensville. A real thriller, severe white water, for professionals only. And only in spring flood season when Lost River comes above ground and circles the mountain.

Cedar Creek from Va. 628 bridge (Stephens Fort) 14 miles to low water bridge, 1 mile above Shenandoah River (Va. 635). Safe for good canoeists.

Shenandoah River, North Fork (Tours 8, 10 & 14)

On the 73 miles of the North Fork between Mt. Jackson and Front Royal, there are five major dams, which should be avoided by portaging around them. Otherwise there are few rapids and long slow loops of unexciting river. The famous "Seven Bends" are in the area around Woodstock. During summer dry weather the North Fork does not maintain a flow like the Shenandoah's South Fork.

Shenandoah River, South Fork (Tour 10)

This is the gem of them all, with the river winding down the Luray Valley to meet the South Fork at Riverton and Front Royal. The scenery is peaceful and beautiful along one of the finest fishing rivers in the east. There are numerous rapids as the river winds between the Massanutten and the Blue Ridge. Below Front Royal the river is less interesting and increasingly difficult near Harpers Ferry, but the scenery is superb as the Shenandoah and Potomac Rivers meet.

The Potomac is wonderfully scenic above Harpers Ferry, particularly its South Fork above Petersburg, West Va. But this is out of our territory and must be left here to the paddler's own exploring instincts.

Rappahannock River (Tour 12)

18 miles from U.S. 211 highway bridge near Waterloo to U.S. 15 bridge at Remington. Good section for inexperienced canoeists, some rapids, riverside is mostly farm land.

16 miles from Fletchers Mill at Sperryville to the low water bridge at Monument Mills (confluence of Hazel and Thornton Rivers). Beautiful, fast, narrow stream which can be run until about June 1. In some places no wider than a canoe, but it is the most scenic part of the entire Rappahannock.

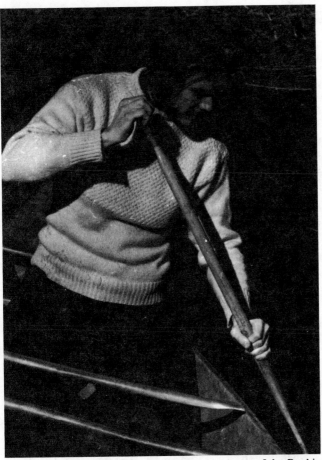

John Rankin

Canoeing

213

Stoney Creek (Tour 14)

15 miles from Va. 675 at Camp Strawderman to the Shenandoah River below Edinburg. A fast-moving, easy, small river, good for canoeing until about May 1.

Maury (Calfpasture) River (Tour 14)

The lower section from Rockbridge Baths 13 miles to Lexington (Limekiln Bridge, Va. 631). Spectacular scenery, worth the long drive to get there. Usually can be run until June 1, but it is fast water and rough going, definitely for experts only.

BOATING

There are few bodies of water for the larger types of outboard cruisers in this area. However, there are stretches of river, stream and lake safely and delightfully navigable to the small outboardpowered punt, canoe, or rowboat. The Shenandoah was navigable to flatboats and river scows as late as the 1870's, but then the water table fell as towns grew and used more water, and industry began moving into the area.

SHENANDOAH RIVER

Berryville — Boyce Area (Tour 3)

Castleman's Ferry — Northernmost launching-landing on the Shenandoah River, located on the east bank under the bridge where Va. 7 crosses the river. From Berryville 5 miles east on Va. 606 which circles under bridge to parking area and ramp.

Locke's Landing — On west bank, 5½ miles from Berryville via Va. 7 and 608 and then right on 621; or 3½ miles from Old Chapel via Va. 618 and 621.

Warren — Clarke County Area (Tour 7)

Morgan's Ford — On east bank, 4 miles north of Front Royal; located at end of low water bridge, off Va. 624.

Front Royal — Luray Area (Tour 10)

Riverton Landing — On west bank of the North Fork of the Shenandoah River, north of Riverton just before its confluence with the South Fork. From Front Royal take

U.S. 340 north, cross two Shenandoah River bridges and
turn immediately right on Va. 637 to river bank.

Front Royal Landing – On east bank of South Fork, southern edge of Front Royal, near city pumping station and Va. 619 bridge.

Karo Landing – On east bank of South Fork, 5 miles south of Front Royal. Large parking area and gravel ramp reached from U.S. 340 at the Gooney Run bridge.

Bentonville Landing – On west bank of South Fork. From Front Royal, 10 miles south on U.S. 340 to Bentonville, then right approximately one mile on Va. 613, cross bridge to parking area.

Hazard Mill Landing – On west bank of South Fork, approximately 4 miles upstream from Bentonville Landing. Reached after crossing Va. 613 bridge and left turn on FS 236 (George Washington National Forest) for 4 miles to concrete ramp.

Foster's Landing – On west bank of South Fork. From Front Royal 16 miles south on U.S. 340 to Rileyville, right on Va. 684 for one mile to Shenandoah River and one more mile to graveled ramp and parking lot.

White House Landing – On east bank of South Fork, 4 miles west of Luray, under White House bridge on Va. 211. Location is from Va. 646, along river, near White House Fort.

Elkton Area (Tour 14)

Grove Hill Landing – On east bank of South Fork, approximately 19 miles south of Luray on U.S. 340, left on Va. 650, for 1¼ miles after crossing the river at Grove Hill.

Elkton Landing – On east bank of South Fork and its most upstream launching point. Reached via U.S. 33 at west edge of Elkton.

Woodstock – Edinburg Area (Tour 14)

Chapman's Landing – On west bank of the North Fork, the only launching ramp on the North Fork above Riverton. At Willow Grove, approximately 1½ miles south of Woodstock on U.S. 11, turn east on Va. 672 to graveled parking lot and ramp.

Warrenton Area (Tour 12)

Lake Brittle — 5 miles east of Warrenton, off U.S. 29-211 at New Baltimore. Take Va. 600 and 793 to boat ramp. Concession stand, bait and tackle, rental boats and motors.

Harrisonburg Area (Tour 14)

Lake Shenandoah — 5 miles east of Harrisonburg, off U.S. 33 at Massanetta Springs. Take Va. 687 to boat ramp. Concession stand, bait, rental boats and motors.

Clifton Forge Area (Tour 14)

Douthat Lake — Douthat State Park, 5 miles north of Clifton Forge on Va. 629. Row boats and paddle boats for rent. No motor boats allowed on 90-acre lake. Lake stocked with trout, sandy beach and bathhouses.

HORSEBACK RIDING

The average rental fee for a well-broken horse and tack throughout the area is about $3.50 to $5.00 per hour. Livery stables which give riding lessons and the stables at The Homestead at Hot Springs charge slightly more. Some beautiful riding trails with superb forest and mountain scenery are located around Big Meadows and Skyland on the Skyline Drive in Shenandoah National Park. There are also some striking views on rides from Leisure Point near Woodstock, Cacapon State Park and Shenandoah Acres Resort near Stuart's Draft. Horses may be hired from other stables in the area, but here are some prominent riding facilities. To be on the safe side, it would be well to telephone ahead for riding reservations.

Berkeley Springs, W. Va. Area (Tour 1) — Cacapon State Park, Berkeley Springs, West Va., 25411. Tel: (304) 258-1022. Located 10 miles south of Berkeley Springs on U.S. 522. Stables open May-November.

Berkeley Springs, W. Va. Area (Tour 1) — Coolfont Recreation Area, Berkeley Springs, West Va. 25411. Tel:

Virginia State Travel Service
Shenandoah National Park

(304) 258-1793. Located 6 miles west of Berkeley Springs. Trail rides and week-long pack trips. Open year round.

Leesburg Area (Tour 5) — Morven Park International Equestrian Institute, Leesburg, Va. 22075. Tel: 777-2890. Located on Morven Park Road just north of Leesburg. Primarily for experienced horsemen training to be instructors in equitation and proper horse care. Indoor ring. Open year round.

Leesburg—Purcellville Area (Tour 5) — North Fork School of Equitation, Purcellville, Va. 22132. Tel: 554-7474. Class instruction for children & adults. Horses boarded. Weekend camp & Summer camp.

Middleburg-Upperville Area (Tour 6) — Orchard Hill Riding Stable, Unison, Va. 2141. Tel: 554-8255. From Middleburg, U.S. 50 west 2 miles, turn right on Va. 611; after 4½ miles turn left on Va. 630 to stable. Horse boarding & training. Horses for hire.

217

Horseback Riding

Luray Area (Tour 10) – S. H. Griffith Stables, U.S. 211, Luray, Va. 22835. Tel: 743-6322. At Hillside Motel on U.S. 211, 3 miles east of Luray. Open year round.

Shenandoah National Park (Tour 10) – Skyland Stables, Skyland Lodge, Luray, Va. 22835. Tel: 599-2211. Located on Skyline Drive at Milepost 41.8. Trail rides for adults & children, accompanied by experienced guides. Stables open May-October.

Shenandoah National Park (Tour 10) – Big Meadows Stables, Big Meadows Lodge, Luray, Va. 22835. Tel: 599-2221. Trail riding in Shenandoah National Park. Special group trips and rates. Stables open June-October.

Rappahannock Area (Tour 13) – Graves Mountain Lodge, Syria, Va. 22743. Tel: 923-4231. Trail rides accompanied by guide. Riding over farm and within nearby Shenandoah National Park. Open Memorial Day – November.

Woodstock Area (Tour 14) – Leisure Point, RFD 2 Woodstock, Va. 22664. Tel: 459-4154. Located on the 7 bends of the Shenandoah River; 4 miles east of Woodstock at shopping center, turn on Va. 758. Open May – September.

Harrisonburg-Staunton Area (Tour 14) – Kalvin Hill Farms, Route 1, Mt. Crawford, Va. 22841, Tel: 234-8311. 8 miles south of Harrisonburg.

Waynesboro Area (Tour 14) – Shenandoah Acres Resort, Stuarts Draft, Va. 24477. Tel: 337-1911. Located 15 miles east of Staunton & 11 miles west of Waynesboro. Open April-November.

Hot Springs Area (Tour 14) – The Homestead Stables, The Homestead, Hot Springs, Va. 24445. Tel: 839-5500.

White Sulphur Springs Area (Tour 14) – Green Brier Stables, Green Brier Hotel, White Sulphur Springs, West Va. 24986. Tel: (304) 536-1110.

218

BICYCLING

There are a number of quiet, unfrequented secondary roads throughout the area where bicycling can be safe, relaxed, scenic, and free of taxing steep grades. Some of the best stretches near our main tour areas are:

Front Royal Area (Tour 7)

Take Va. 624 north out of Milldale for 3.5 miles. Turn right on Va. 622. The last 2 miles of this route will take you along the west bank of the Shenandoah River to the Byrd Highway Bridge on U.S. 50. Trip distance 7.5 miles.

Or take Sixth Street out of Front Royal from the U.S. 522 By-pass. Turn east on Va. 647 (Happy Creek Road) for approximately 3 miles to Va. 624, which descends to the Shenandoah River. After 1.5 miles turn right onto Va. 643 just before the low water bridge at Morgan's Ford. Continue along the River to Va. 603, bear left past Howlesville where the route becomes Va. 638, and then 6 miles to the highway bridge at U.S. 50. This route takes you along the east bank of the Shenandoah River. Trip distance 15 miles.

Leesburg—C & O Canal Area (Tour 5)

Start from the access road north of Leesburg, which leads (one mile) to White's Ferry, site of General Jubal Early's crossing in July 1864, after his raid on the outskirts of Washington. Bicycle toll fare on ferry is 25 cents. The route from White's Ferry is up the C & O Canal Towpath, which follows the Maryland side of the Potomac River. The towpath is in good condition for moderate pace cycling and is shaded by trees for most of the distance. There are several old locks along the Canal and about midway is the Monocacy Aqueduct, a 500-foot span of white granite arches, built in 1833, which carries the canal over the Monocacy River where it enters the Potomac. A convenient point to be met and picked up is the public boat ramp just before the bridge which carries U.S. 15 across the Potomac River at Point of Rocks. Trip distance 15 miles.

Harpers Ferry—C & O Canal Area (Tour 4)

For another pleasant bicycle trip along the C & O Canal,

amidst historic settings, start with a visit to Harpers Ferry, where the Shenandoah and Potomac Rivers meet. From Harpers Ferry, access to the canal towpath is via the truss railroad bridge which has a wooden walk. Do not use the girder (upstream) railroad bridge which carries the mainline tracks. At the end of the truss bridge, before the tunnel mouth, descend the east embankment, cross the road and proceed 130 paces upstream to the footbridge atop Lock no. 33. There is water in some sections of the canal and the towpath is in good condition for easy cycling. At Antietam Aqueduct (9 miles) a detour may be made along Harpers Ferry Road to Sharpsburg and Antietam Battlefield (3 miles). A convenient pick-up point is Snyder's Landing, approximately 2 miles west of Sharpsburg and 4 miles upstream, on the Maryland side, from Shepherdstown. Trip distance 16 miles.

Fort Valley Area (Tour 9)

Take Va. 55 for 5 miles west from Front Royal to Waterlick. Turn left at Waterlick, heading south on Va. 678 past the magnificent gorge at Elizabeth Furnance and paralleling lovely Passage Creek down the center of Fort Valley. At the far end of Va. 678 at Kings Crossing (17 miles from Waterlick) continue south on Va. 675. At the point where Va. 675 turns left, uphill towards Camp Roosevelt, cycle straight ahead on the gravel road, Forest Service Road 274, to its juncture with U.S. 211 at the New Market Gap. For the last 12 miles you will be travelling through some of the finest forest land in all of the George Washington National Forest. Trip distance 29 miles.

Woodstock-Mt. Jackson Area (Tour 14)

Turn left off I-81 or U.S. 11 at Mt. Jackson onto Va. 263 to Basye (11 miles). At Basye turn right onto Va. 717 past Jerome (7 miles) and Liberty Furnace (2 miles). After a look at the old waterwheel gristmill at Liberty Furnace, continue to Va. 675 (2.5 miles). Turn right and follow alongside peaceful Big Stoney Creek to Columbia Furnace (3 miles). Here turn left on Va. 42 for the 5-mile pedal to Woodstock and back to I-81 or U.S. 11. Trip distance 30 miles.

Marshall-Orlean—Hume Area (Tours 11 & 12)

The bike route starts from the intersection of Va. 55 and 17 for one mile east along Va. 17, a heavily-trafficed road; so be careful. Turn right on Va. 691 and follow it for 10 miles through beautiful countryside (the "Free State"). Bear right at the "T" intersection and stay on Va. 691. Turn oblique right on Va. 688 and continue through Orlean and Hume (17 miles). Turn right on Va. 635 for 3 miles over gently rolling hills. Turn left on Va. 647 for 4 miles into Marshall, the starting point of the loop trip. Trip distance 35 miles.

GOLF

Listed below are private clubs, resorts and municipal or public 9 and 18-hole courses in The Valley and Piedmont areas. Hot Springs, with the Homestead resort complex, is considered "The golf capital of Virginia". Its Cascades Course has been called "the world's finest mountain course", and there are two other excellent 18-hole courses.

Martinsburg, W. Va. Area (Tours 1 & 4)
Woodbrier Golf Course (9), public

Winchester Area (Tour 2)
Carpers Valley Golf Course (18), private
Winchester Golf Club (18), private

Berryville — Millwood Area (Tour 3)
Shenandoah Retreat (9), private
Millwood Country Club (9), private

Leesburg — Purcellville Area (Tour 5)
Goose Creek Country Club (18), private
Leesburg Golf & Country Club (18), private
Loudoun Golf & Country Club (18), semi-private

Front Royal Area (Tour 10)
Front Royal Golf & Country Club (9), semi-private
Shenandoah Valley Golf Club (18), semi-private

221

Warrenton Area (Tour 12)
Fauquier Springs Country Club (18), private
Warrenton Country Club (18), private

Valley Pike Area (Tour 14)
Harrisonburg — Lakeview Golf Course (18), public
Spotswood Country Club (18), semi-private
New Market — Shenvallee Golf Club (18), Semi-private
Staunton — Gypsy Hill Golf Course (9), municipal
Ingleside Golf Course (19), resort
Country Club of Staunton (18), private
Waynesboro —Swannanoa Country Club (9), municipal
Waynesboro Country Club (18), private
Lexington — Lexington Golf Club (9), semi-private
Clifton Forge — Cliftondale County Club (9), semi-private
Hot Springs —Cascades Golf Course (18), resort
Lower Cascades Golf Course (18), resort
Homestead Golf Course (18), resort
White Sulphur Springs, W.Va. — three courses (18), resort

WINTER SPORTS

Winchester Area (Tour 2)
Shawnee-Land — Va. 614, 11 miles west of Winchester, 79 miles from Washington, D. C. 5 slopes and trails, 2 rope tows, snow-making equipment, ski school, ski shop and rental equipment, meals and rooms. Tel: 662-2820.

Rappahannock County Area (Tour 13)
Rappahannock Ski Area (formerly Big Devil) — Washington, Va., 112 miles from Washington, D.C. 40 miles from Winchester. 3 slopes for beginners to experts, double chairlift, T-bar, 2 rope tows, ski school, snow-making equipment, ski rentals; night skiing; season passes; cafeteria and snack bar; nearby lodging. Tel: 672-3316.

Valley Pike Area (Tour 14)
Bryce Mountain — South on I-81 to Mt. Jackson exit, then west on Va. 263 to Bayse. 50 miles from Winchester,

222

Virginia State Travel Service

Skiing

115 miles from Washington, D.C. Double chair lifts, 2 rope tows, 4 slopes, ski school, ski shop and rental equipment; ski chalet and condominium rentals. Semi-private on week-ends. Tel: 477-3171.

Massanutten Ski Area — Harrisonburg, Va., 100 miles from Washington, D.C. Night skiing, 4 double chairlifts, J-bar; vertical drop 795 feet; longest run, 5,600 feet. Tel: 289-2121.

Mountain Run Resort — Near New Market, Va. 730, east from I-81, Shenandoah Caverns exit. 50 miles from Winchester, 100 miles from Washington, D.C. Lodge, double chairlift, rope tow, 4 slopes, snowmaking equipment, ski rentals, ski school. For further information, Box 217, New Market, Va. 22844. Tel: 477-3149.

223

The Homestead Hotel and Cascades Inn — Hot Springs, Va. On U.S. 220, 145 miles from Winchester, 200 miles from Washington, D.C. 6 trails and slopes; trestlecar, T-bar and 2 rope tows; ski school, ski shops and rental shop, ice skating rink; skating school; restaurants; accommodations at hotel and inn. Tel: 839-5500, extensions 2607 and 2608.

HUNTING

The exact hunting seasons in each county of Virginia and West Virginia, and for each of the many types of game, vary from year to year. Information concerning seasons and regulations may be obtained at all game-checking stations and county courthouses in the area as well as from newspapers and sporting goods stores. The seasons vary considerably between the regions east and west of the Blue Ridge, but, in general, the hunting seasons for the areas covered in this book are:

September—Dove, woodcock, snipe.

October — Raccoon, squirrel, opossum. Bow and arrow season starts on deer and bear. Commercial shooting preserves open.

November—Deer, bear, turkey, rabbit, Bobwhite quail, grouse, woodcock, snipe, raccoon, squirrel, opossum.

December—Bear, rabbit, raccoon, squirrel, opossum, dove, grouse, Bobwhite quail.

January — Rabbit, raccoon, squirrel, opossum, grouse, Bobwhite quail. End of most seasons.

March — Commercial shooting preserves close.

April-May—Spring turkey gobbler season (3 weeks).

Bow and arrow is a legal weapon for all species, including migratory game birds, and may be used in regular seasons as well as the special archery season (October-November) which precedes the regular hunting seasons for deer and bear. For trapping seasons and regulations, it is advisable to check in each county. Beaver, for example, may be trapped in Virginia generally in January and

February, except in Clarke and Warren Counties where they may not be trapped at any time. In West Virginia, the beaver-trapping season usually starts in November and runs into February. Foxes may be trapped in Virginia usually from mid-November to the end of January, but in some counties they may be trapped the year around. In Clarke, Fauquier, Loudoun, and Rappahannock Counties, however, the trapping of foxes is prohibited, and in those counties they may be hunted with dogs only.

There is an excellent "Virginia Hunters Guide" available from either the Virginia State Game Commission, Box 1642, Richmond, Va. 23213 or from the Virginia State Travel Service, 911 East Broad Street, Richmond, Va. 23219 or from its branch information centers (see "For Further Information"). The Commission's "Summary of Virginia Game Laws" is published during the summer each year and is distributed to license agents and sporting goods stores throughout the state. It contains season dates, bag limits and basic hunting regulations for the ensuing season. A similar publication, "West Virginia Hunting & Trapping Regulations" is published annually by the West Virginia Department of Natural Resources, Game and Fish Division, Charleston, W. Va. 25305.

Hunting licenses may be obtained from the clerk's office in county courthouses or from many sporting goods stores. Fees vary and are subject to yearly change; so check for exact information concerning regulations and fees for the particular area in which you wish to hunt. Some counties require a special stamp to hunt bear and deer in addition to other licenses. In Virginia the "license year" is July 1 through June 30 of the following calendar year, but in West Virginia licenses are valid from January 1 through December 31.

Licensed hunting in season is permitted in the **George Washington National Forest**. All persons are required to have a National Forest Permit to hunt, trap, or fish on National Forests in addition to other licenses. This permit (stamp) is available from all local agents for $1.00. Further information on facilities and regulations for George Washington National Forest can be obtained from its headquarters in the Federal Building, Harrisonburg, Va. 22801. Tel: 434-3841.

Hunting is never permitted in the Shenandoah National Park nor on posted property. No one is allowed to hunt

225

with firearms or other weapons on Sunday, and it is also unlawful to hunt from automobiles or other motor-driven vehicles. Artificial lights may be used only in hunting for raccoon, skunk and oppossum.

In addition to the George Washington National Forest, hunting is permitted in the following public areas:

Berkeley Springs (Tour 1) **Sleepy Creek Public Hunting & Fishing Area**

Madison County (Tour 13) **Rapidan Wildlife Management Area,** 332 acres.

Augusta-Rockbridge Counties (Tour 14) **Little North Mountain Wildlife Management Area,** 16,603 acres.

Bath-Alleghany Counties (Tour14) **Gathright Wildlife Management Area** 18,392 acres

Highland County (Tour 14) **Highland Wildlife Management Area** 17,753 acres

Rockbridge County (Tour 14) **Goshen Wildlife Management Area** 16,236 acres

Rockingham County (Tour 14) **Wunder Wildlife Management Area** 1,313 acres
Detailed information concerning these areas be obtained from the Virginia State Game Commission at the above address.

These are also several shooting preserves in the area:
Warrenton (Tour 12) **Granville Shooting Preserve** Write: J. M. Nash, Box 2, Warrenton, Virginia 22186

Harrisonburg (Tour 14) **Melrose Hunting Preserve** Write: Bill V. Neff, P.O. Box 1050, Harrisonburg, Va. 22801

Natural Bridge (Tour 14) **Thunder Ridge Shooting Preserve** Write: R. N. Horn, Natural Bridge Station, Va. 24579

A special nonresident license to hunt on shooting preserves only is obtainable.

FISHING

Both forks and the full length of the Shenandoah River are Virginia's most famous freshwater fishing streams. Annually thousands of anglers come to its pools and shallows to fish for the highly-prized smallmouth bass and the equally ferocious channel catfish. However, there are other game fish in the Shenandoah: namely, redbreasted sunfish, crappies, carp, and suckers. But it is the fighting bass that brings the fishermen from far and near each season.

There is an old legend about how the first smallmouth bass came into the Shenandoah River. Old-timers hereabouts say that an engineer on the Norfolk & Western Railroad, which parallels the South Fork for fifty miles between Elkton and Front Royal, lived in this area and was an avid angler. He trapped or netted a "passel" of bass in a stream in southwest Virginia, dumped them into the water compartment of the coal tender attached to his steam locomotive, and came north pounding up the right of way until he reached the train viaduct at Overall. Here he paused long enough to drain his tender, releasing the fish into the river; then he moved just beyond the viaduct for a refill under the railroad water tank. Whether this is true or not, we have the bass. Come try your luck on the South Fork.

There are many fine freshwater game-fish rivers and streams, creeks and lakes, ponds and potholes throughout the area. Here are some choice spots:

Shenandoah River North Fork (Tours 8 and 14). Between Mt. Jackson and Woodstock; and between Strasburg and Front Royal. — Largemouth and smallmouth bass; rock bass, crappie and pickerel.

Shenandoah River South Fork (Tour 10) Between Overall at the Page-Warren County line and the south end of Front Royal above the Viscose plant. — Largemouth bass, pickerel, smallmouth bass, rock bass, walleye.

Shenandoah River below Front Royal (Tours 3, 7 and 10). Between the low water bridge at Morgan's Ford (Va. 624) and White Horse Rock at Castleman's Ferry. — Largemouth bass, pickerel, walleye, rock bass, smallmouth bass.

227

Virginia Chamber of Commerce

Cacapon River (Tours 1 and 8) From Wardensville, W. Va. north to the Potomac west of Berkeley Springs. — Trout, bass, perch, sunfish, crappie and carp.

Opequon Creek (Tour 2) Va. 622 & 628 west of Winchester. Smallmouth bass.

Cedar Creek (Tour 8) Va. 55 west and Va. 678 to Lebanon Church. From the Star Tannery to Shenandoah River.— Smallmouth bass, rock bass, brown trout and rainbow trout.

Passage Creek (Tour 9) Va. 678 into Fort Valley. The trout section of this clear, cold mountain stream over rock ledges is one of the most scenically picturesque in the entire Valley and is stocked by the U.S. Forest Service. Brook trout, rainbow trout, brown trout, particularly from Elizabeth Furnace to Waterlick.

Rush River (Tour 13) U.S. 522 South to Little Washington; then west on Va. 622. One of the scenic gems in the entire area. Remote and peaceful. Trout, bass and perch.

Thornton River (Tour 13) U.S. 522 south to Sperryville. Brook and rainbow trout in headwaters beneath Thornton Gap; bass and perch, Fletcher Mill to Monument Mill.

Rappanhannock River (Tours 12 and 13) Va. 522, Va. 17 and U.S. 29. With its headwaters just below Chester Gap, in the mountain area, the best fishing on this stream is between Waterloo and Remington. Bass, sunfish and some pickerel.

Jackson River (Tour 14) Along the West Virginia line. U.S. west from Staunton to Monterey, or Va. 39 west to Warm Springs from Goshen. Smallmouth bass, rock bass, pickerel, and brook, brown and rainbow trout.

Calfpasture-Maury Rivers (Tour 14) Va. 39 at Goshen Pass, north of Lexington. Smallmouth bass, rock bass, pickerel.

Shenandoah National Park — Skyline Drive (Tours 10 and 14). Open to trout fishing only. Residents and nonresidents who wish to fish in the Park may purchase a special 3-day license for $3.00. Good trout fishing may be found at Piney River (milepost 22), Jeremy's Run (milepost 24.3), Thornton River (milepost 31) Rapidan River (milepost 51.3), Big Run (milepost 81).

George Washington National Forest (Tour 14) There are a number of lakes and ponds, all stocked with trout and open from the first Saturday in April through December 31. Some of the most notable are: Todd Lake (10.7 acres), Elkhorn Lake (54 acres), Upper Sherando (8 acres), Lower Sherando (26 acres) and Clifton Forge Reservoir (16 acres). Some also contain bass and bluegills. A $1.00 National Forest Stamp is required in addition to the proper fishing license.

Virginia residents have the choice of purchasing for $3.50 a state license to fish only or to purchase for $2.00 a license to hunt and fish in the county or city of residence only. Non-residents of Virginia may purchase a non-resident fishing license for $10.00, which conveys the same priveleges as a resident license. They may also obtain for $5.00 a trout license to fish in designated waters stocked with trout. In West Virginia a resident has the choice of a statewide fishing license for $3.00 or a combined hunting and fishing license which costs $5.00.

For more detailed information write to Department of Natural Resources, Wildlife Resources Division, Charleston, West Va. 25305 for *West Virginia Fishing Regulations* or to Virginia Commission of Game and Inland Fisheries, P.O. Box 11104, Richmond, Va. 23213 for *Virginia Fishing Regulations*. It and the attractive and informative booklet, *Let's Go Freshwater Fishing in Virginia*, may also be obtained from the Virginia State Travel Service offices.

ANTIQUE SHOPS

Berkeley Springs Area (Tour 1)
H. Tom Seely — Winchester Road (U.S. 522). Tel: (304) 258-2343
Waterview Workshop — Lick Run Road. Tel: (304) 258-9813

Winchester Area (Tour 2)
Bradley's Antiques — 2970 Valley Avenue (U.S. 11). Tel: 667-4426
Boyd G. Headley Auctioneers & Antiques — N. Frederick Rd. Tel: 662-6350.
Mark S. Headley — Senseny Road. Tel: 955-2022
Peter Stephens Shop — 35 N. Braddock St. Tel: 667-7835.
Plain Dealing Antiques — 210 S. Loudoun Street. Tel: 667-8057
L. F. White, Repairing & Restoring — 1225 Berryville Avenue. Tel: 667-4334.

Berryville — Boyce Area (Tour 3)

Battletown Antiques — 117 E. Main St., Berryville. Tel: 955-2399

Charles Town — Harpers Ferry Area (Tour 4)

Rickel's Antiques — 504 Euclid Ave., Charles Town. Tel: (304) 725-2761

Bolivar Country Store Antiques — Washington Street, Bolivar. Tel: (304) 535-2141

Daniel's Antiques — 1141 Washington Street, Harpers Ferry. Tel: (304) 535-2218

Stone House Antiques — Potomac Street, Harpers Ferry.

Leesburg Area (Tour 5)

The Aldie Attic — U.S. 50, Aldie.

Antiques Etcetra — S. Wirt Street, Leesburg. Tel: 777-7300

By-Gone-Days Antique Shop — Corner of Va. 7 & 641. Tel: 777-1988

H. M. Kirk — Va. 7 East, Purcellville.

The Gallerie — 26 W. Market Street, Leesburg. Tel: 777-1048

White Horse Antique Shop — U.S. 15, 3 miles south of Leesburg. Tel. 777-3023

Anne B. Akre — Waterford. Tel: 882-3404

Middleburg — Upperville Area (Tour 6)

Argos Gallery — E. Washington St., Middleburg.

The Golden Horseshoe — U.S. 50, Upperville. Tel: 592-3470

Mrs. Greer of Middleburg Ltd. — E. Washington St., Middleburg. Tel: 687-6363

The Pheasant's Eye — W. Washington St., Middleburg. Tel: 687-7711

Delaplane Store — Va. 712 & U.S. 17, Delaplane. Tel: 364-2754.

Clarke and Warren County Area (Tour 7)

Campbell's Antique Shop — U.S. 50, 7 miles east of White Post. Tel: 837-1351

Roberts Antiques — White Post. Tel: 837-1766.

Strasburg — Middletown Area (Tour 8)
Harvey's Antiques — U.S. 11, Stephens City.
Wayside Antiques — U.S. 11, Middletown. Tel: 869-3344.

Front Royal — Luray Area (Tour 10)
Alden's Antiques — John Marshall Highway, Front Royal. Tel: 635-4202
McLaughlin's Furniture & Antiques — 296 South St., Front Royal. Tel: 635-5809
"The Roses" Antiques & Art Gallery — 126 S. Royal Ave., Front Royal.
Shenandoah Gifts & Antiques — 1516 Shenandoah Avenue, Front Royal. Tel: 635-9092
Simonpietri's Gifts & Reproductions — 55 S. Royal Ave., Front Royal. Tel: 635-3558
Valley View Antiques & Furniture — U.S. 522-340 between Nineveh & Cedarville.
Duke and Fran's Antiques & Country Store — 24 E. Main St., Luray. Tel: 743-3491
The Luray Trading Post — 1230 E. Main St., Luray. Tel: 743-6943

Linden — Marshall — Warrenton Area (Tour 11 & 12)
The Attic — U.S. 55, Marshall. Tel: 364-7881
Elmer Martin — U.S. 55. west of Linden.
New Baltimore Crafts & Antiques — New Baltimore. Tel: 347-9362.
Beverly Mill Antiques — Va. 55 at Broad Run, 9 miles east of Marshall.

Rappahannock County Area (Tour 13)
That Sperryville Emporium — Intersection U.S. 211 & 522, Sperryville.
The Washington Country Store — Washington. Tel: 675-3788.

Valley Pike Area (Tour 14)
Daniel Burner, Auctioneer — U.S. 11, Woodstock. Tel: 459-3141
Racey Furniture Shop, Reproductions — Woodstock. Tel: 459-4441
Elouise D. Ritenour — U.S. 11 north of Woodstock. Tel: 459-3010
Mrs. Mary E. Corbin — Edinburg. Tel: 984-4879

Shenantiques — Shenandoah Caverns, Mt. Jackson. Tel: 477-3115

Fixit Shop — New Market. Tel: 422-3606

H. B. Long, Jr. — New Market. Tel: 422-3777

Corner Cupboard Antiques — 95 N. Liberty St., Harrisonburg. Tel: 434-8581

The Craft House 212 S. Main St., Harrisonburg. Tel: 434-8073

Foster's Antique & Coin Shop — 61 E. Elizabeth St. Harrisonburg. Tel: 434-6377

Suter's Craft Shop, Reporductions — U.S. 11, south of Harrisonburg. Tel: 434-2131

Harrisonburg Antique Flea Market (Sat. & Sun.) — Exit 62 & I-81, Harrisonburg. Tel: 434-5991

Carson Knupp, Reproductions — Mt. Crawford. Tel: 434-7217

The Odd Shop — 103 N. Main St. Bridgewater. Tel: 828-3577

Beverley E. Wolfe — U.S. 33, Elkton. Tel: 298-4171

Dean Wilson Antiques — U.S. 11, Fort Defiance. Tel: 886-7822

Fadeley's Shop — 608 W. Beverley, Staunton. Tel: 886-2452

Antique & Collector's Shop — 28 South New Street, Staunton.

Jolly Roger Haggle Shop —27 Middlebrook Ave., Staunton. Tel: 886-9527

Treasure Chest — 804 W. Beverley, Staunton. Tel: 886-9537

Tuts Log Cabin — W. Beverley St. Extended, Staunton. Tel: 886-9747

The Crackerbarrel — 260 N. Commerce Ave., Waynesboro. Tel: 942-4746

Henry's Antique Shop — 604 E. Main St., Waynesboro.

Turtle Lane Gift Shop — Va. 250, Churchville, Tel: 886-9313

Bath Hampton Antiques & Accessories — west of Goshen on Va. 42 & 39 at Millboro. Tel: 997-5393

Goodharts Second Hand Shop — 7 N. Jefferson St., Lexington. Tel: 463-7559

Millers Antiques — 101 W. Nelson St., Lexington. Tel: 463-5678

Antiques by Bradford — Natural Bridge Station. Tel: 291-2217

233

GOOD EATING IN UNUSUAL SETTINGS

Berryville — Boyce Area (Tour 3)

Battletown Inn — On Va. 7, near traffic light at Berryville. Tel: 955-1348.

Charles Town — Harpers Ferry Area (Tour 4)

Scollay Hall — At Middleway, just off W. Va. 51, eight miles west of Charles Town. Tel: (304) 725-7428. 1890 house in delightful village surroundings. Lunch and dinner country style and the Legend of Wizarde Clippe.

Bavarian Inn — On the Potomac, near Rumsey Bridge, Shepardstown. Tel: (304) 876-6070. German cuisine.

Middleburg — Upperville Area (Tour 6)

The Red Fox Tavern — U.S. 50, Middleburg. Old world dining in colonial surroundings. "The second oldest inn in the U.S." Tel: 687-2771

Middletown Area (Tour 8)

The Wayside Inn — On U.S. 11, at Middletown. Tel: 869-2578. Antiques and 18th-century atmosphere. Dining and beverages in The Boot and Hat Room. Overnight lodgings. Beverages and snacks at the Curtain Call beside Wayside Theatre one block away.

Skyline Drive Area (Tour 10)

Panorama Restaurant — Panorama (milepost 31.25), U.S. 211 interchange. Tel: 599-2265. Fine view of Luray Valley. Open year round.

Skyland Lodge — (milepost 41.7). Superb view of Luray Valley from dining room. Tel: 599-2211. Open mid-April to November. Hotel-cottage accommodations for 400. For reservations: Virginia Skyline Company, Inc., P. O. Box 191, Luray, Va. 22835. Tel: 743-5108.

Rappahannock County (Tour 13)

Graves Mountain Lodge—Syria, Va. 22743. Tel: 923-4231.
From Banco on Va. 231 to Va. 670 two miles west to
Syria and ½ mile beyond. Country meals in Swiss-style
chalet. Open Memorial Day to November 29 daily. April
and May weekends only.

Mt. Jackson Area (Tour 14)

Sky Chalet—Mt. Jackson, Va. 22842. Tel: 447-2236. Ten
miles from Mt. Jackson, near Bryce and Orkney Springs.
Dining and mountaintop swimming pool in superb
mountain setting.

Woodstock Area (Tour 14)

Narrow Passage Inn — On U.S. 11, two miles south of
Woodstock. Tel: 459-4770. Antiques, southern dishes,
and wonderful views of the Shenandoah River and the
Massanutten Mountain range.

CREAM OF THE CROP TOURS,
SCENIC DRIVES &
UNFORGETTABLE GOLD STAR PLACES

Everybody has his own opinion as to what is historic and
what is beautiful in the Valley and the Piedmont. No
matter where you go or what you do in this lovely area,
you will not be disappointed. These are my favorites, and I
hope they will be yours too.

Cream of the Crop Tours:

The Berryville—Boyce Area tour
The Clarke and Warren County Farms tour
The Fort Valley Area tour
The Front Royal-Luray and Skyline Drive Area tour
The Rappahannock County Area tour through the "F.T.
Valley"

235

Scenic Drives

U.S. 522 from Double Tollgate to Front Royal (12 miles), especially the breathtakingly beautiful 3-mile stretch between Nineveh and Cedarville.

On a clear day, the first 32 miles of the Skyline Drive from its northern entrance at Front Royal to the Panorama Interchange above Luray.

The trip down the center of Fort Valley on Va. 678 through Passage Creek Gorge at Elizabeth Furnace and to Luray via Va. 675, with a stop at the 2,000-foot panorama overlook.

U.S. 522 south from Front Royal over Chester Gap (1339 feet) to Huntly, Flint Hill, and Sperryville.

Va. 688 from Markham to Hume and Orlean past the big cattle 'spreads'.

The approaches from the northeast to both Sperryville (U.S. 522 and 211) and Lexington (I-81, U.S. 11 & Va. 39).

Gold Star Places

The panorama to the east from the summit of Ashby Gap on the drive on U.S. 50 from Winchester to Upperville and Middleburg.

The twin river gorges at Harpers Ferry where the Shenandoah and Potomac Rivers meet.

White's Ferry above Leesburg, just off U.S. 15.

Old Chapel, just off U.S. 340, 3 miles south of Berryville.

Shepherdstown, West Virginia, for a glimpse of pure nostalgia.

Huntly and Flint Hill, on U.S. 522, south of Front Royal.

236

Harewood, home of Samuel Washington, on W. Va. 51, west of Charles Town.

Wayside Inn in Middletown on the Valley Pike (U.S. 11).

Glen Burnie in Winchester, when it is open for the annual garden tour in April.

New Market Gap (George Washington National Forest) where Forest Service Road 274 from Fort Valley joins U.S. 211.

The Red Fox Inn in Middleburg on U.S. 50.

The overlook at Hogback Mountain (elevation 3,385 feet) on the Skyline Drive (Front Royal-Luray section) with its superb view of the seven bends in the South Fork of the Shenandoah River.

ANNUAL EVENTS

Here is a list of the major events taking place in the Valley and the Piedmont. Exact dates vary slightly from year to year. For further information and exact dates of events taking place in Virginia, write Virginia State Travel Service, 911 Broad St., Richmond, Va. 23219.

MARCH

Highland County Maple Sugar Festival, Monterey

MARCH-APRIL

Easter Sunrise Services, Skyline Caverns & Natural Bridge

APRIL

Oatlands Point-to-Point Races, Leesburg
House and Garden Tour, Martinsburg, Shepherdstown, Charles Town, Harpers Ferry, West Va.
Historic Garden Week in Virginia, Loudoun, Fauquier, Warren, Clarke, Frederick Counties, Lexington, Staunton, Waynesboro

237

Apple Blossom Parade

MAY

Shenandoah Apple Blossom Festival, Winchester
The Virginia Gold Cup, Warrenton
White Water Canoe Race, Front Royal
Reenactment of the Battle of New Market, New Market
    Battlefield Park
Hunt Country Thoroughbred Stable Tour and **Art Auction.**
    Upperville

JUNE-SEPTEMBER

Wayside Theater, Middletown
American Oberammergau Passion Play, Strasburg

JUNE

Antique Show, Winchester
Coin Sale, Eastern Numismatic Association, Winchester
Antique Car Rally, Skyline Caverns, Front Royal
Upperville Colt & Horse Show, Upperville

JULY

Farm Craft Days, Belle Grove, Middletown

238

AUGUST

Shenandoah Valley Music Festival, Woodstock & Orkney
Springs
National Championship Country Music Contest, Warrenton
Natural Chimneys Jousting Tournament, Mt. Solon
Country Fairs, Front Royal, Winchester, Berryville
State Fair of West Virginia, Lewisburg

SEPTEMBER

County Fairs, Woodstock, Harrisonburg, Staunton

OCTOBER

Waterford Homes Tour & Crafts Exhibit, Waterford
Festival of the Leaves, Front Royal
Highland County Fall Foliage Festival, Monterey
Bluemont Craft & County Fair, Bluemont

FOR FURTHER INFORMATION

Shenandoah Valley Travel Association, 1900 N. Coalter St.,
Staunton, Va. 24401. Tel: 885-5145
Berkeley Springs-Morgan County Chamber of Commerce,
201 Fairfax St., Berkeley Springs, West Va. 25411. Tel:
(304) 258-2543
Berryville-Clarke County Chamber of Commerce, 411
Walnut St., Berryville, Va. 22611
Broadway—Timberville Chamber of Commerce, P.O. Box
91, Broadway, Va. 22815. Tel: 896-7413
Clifton Forge Chamber of Commerce, P.O. Box 87, Clifton
Forge, Va. 24422. Tel: 862-4969
Front Royal—Warren County Chamber of Commerce, 14
W. Main St., Front Royal, Va. 22630. Tel: 635-3185
Harrisonburg—Rockingham Chamber of Commerce, 155 N.
Main St., Harrisonburg, Va. 22801. Tel: 434-3862
Highland County Chamber of Commerce, Monterey, Va.
24465
Jefferson County Chamber of Commerce, 200 E. Washing-
ton St., Charles Town, West Va. 25414. Tel: (301)
725-5514

Lexington-Rockbridge County Chamber of Commerce, 401 S. Main St., Lexington, Va. 24450. Tel: 463-5375

Loudoun County Chamber of Commerce, P. O. Box 427, Leesburg, Va. 22075. Tel: 777-2176

Luray Chamber of Commerce, 47 W. Main St., Luray, Va. 22835. Tel: 743-3915

Martinsburg-Berkeley County Chamber of Commerce, 110 West Burke St., Martinsburg, West, Va. 25401. Tel: (304) 267-4841

New Market Chamber of Commerce New Market, Va. 22844. Tel: 422-3212

Roanoke Valley Chamber of Commerce, P.O. Box 20, Roanoke, Va. 24011. Tel: 344-5188

Staunton-Augusta County Chamber of Commerce, 30 N. New St., Staunton, Va. 24401. Tel: 886-2351

Warrenton-Fauquier County Chamber of Commerce, 10 Hotel Street, Warrenton, Va. 22176. Tel: 347-4414

Waynesboro-East Augusta Chamber of Commerce, P.O. Box 459, 144 Church St., Waynesboro, Va. 22980. Tel: 942-8203

Winchester-Frederick County Chamber of Commerce, 29 S. Cameron St., Winchester, Va. 22601. Tel: 662-4418

Woodstock Chamber of Commerce, 134 N. Main St., Woodstock, Va. Tel: 459-2542

Virginia State Travel Service, 911 East Broad St., Richmond, Va. 23219. Tel: (703) 770-2051

906 17th St., N.W., Washington, D. C. 20006. Tel: 293-5350

I-81 (between W.Va. line & Winchester), Clearbrook, Va. 22624. Tel: 667-0758

I-66 (1 mile east of Manassas exit), Manassas, Va. 22110. Tel: 361-2134.

West Virginia Department of Commerce, Travel Division, State Capitol, Charleston, West Va. 25305. Tel: (304) 348-2289

West Virginia Information Center, Harpers Ferry National Historical Park, Harpers Ferry, W. Va. 25425

Superintendent, Blue Ridge Parkway, P.O. Box 1710, Roanoke, Va. 24011. Tel: 343-1581

Shenandoah National Park, Information Office, Luray, Va. 22835. Tel: 599-2241, 599-2242

Virginia Skyland Company, Luray, Va. 22835. Tel: 743-5108

Panorama, Skyline Drive. Tel: 599-2265

Skyland Lodge, Skyline Drive. Tel: 599-2211

Big Meadows, Skyline Drive. Tel: 599-2221

Elkwallow Wayside, Skyline Drive. Tel: 599-2253

Lewis Mountain, Skyline Drive. Tel: 599-2294

WHY YOU SHOULD COME BACK AGAIN

I can think of a baker's dozen good reasons why you should come back to the Blue Ridge and the Shenandoah Valley again and again. For one thing, all of us would enjoy your company. For another, the mountains and the river are ageless. They will always be here, beckoning. But, there is no assurance that the rest of our valley and mountain paradise will be protected from the onslaughts of "progress". We are conveniently close to most of the major urban areas of the mid-Atlantic coast and the inland centers of Cleveland and Pittsburgh. But, with this geographical proximity to large centers of population comes the less-desirable corollary of urban sprawl. Our wilderness and farmland paradise is beginning to be encroached upon.

Time is growing short. Soon there may no longer be the same unspoiled fertile valley to the west of the hazy wooded ramparts of the rolling Blue Ridge. There may no longer be any uncluttered and uncrowded tree-lined river-banks to laze upon or glide by in a kayak or canoe on the softly murmering surface of the ancient river of the Senedoes. No sleepy hamlets will line the old post roads — like delightful Flint Hill, Shepherdstown, and Middletown — dozing away the years in the warm summer sun. So come while you still can. Enjoy this rolling mountain land and lush valley of John Lederer and the galloping Grey Ghost before it is too late. If you have never been here before, come now; come this summer. If you are already an old "valley veteran", come back.

If you are looking for peace and contentment, it is here in abundance: a gentle, easy-going land of mountains, forests, and streams; of horse and cattle farms; of remote towns and roads that have never heard the roar of heavy traffic; a land where, less than forty years ago, the blue curl of smoke from a "moonshiner's" shack still rose into the

241

calm air from many a mountain top. It is still possible to flush a drumming grouse and a corn whiskey "still tender" along the same game trail.

Come see us. And when you do, bring along this history and sightseeing guide to help you ferret out the unusual places. Put on your old pants and favorite walking shoes; wear your wildest sport shirt and that old battered hat with all of the fishing flies tucked along its band. If you have a boat and a dog, bring them too. Then climb in the family car and poke along the back roads, well away from the hectic pace of the city. Live a little! Slip into the past and explore.

If, by chance, you should happen to find something new and wonderful — something I have left out of my story — let me know. There will be a special reward awaiting you: the gift of beauty found, of history discovered, of your own American heritage, understood and savored.

"Oh Shenandoah, I long to hear you . . .
Oh Shenandoah, I'll ne'er forget you . . ."

INDEX